To: Edward

From : Naomi

UNGUARDED

My Forty Years
Surviving in the NBA

Lenny Wilkens
with Terry Pluto

SIMON & SCHUSTER

NEW YORK   LONDON   TORONTO   SYDNEY   SINGAPORE

SIMON & SCHUSTER
Rockefeller Center
1230 Avenue of the Americas
New York, NY 10020

Copyright © 2000 by Lee Le-Ja Inc. and Terry Pluto
All rights reserved,
including the right of reproduction
in whole or in part in any form.
SIMON & SCHUSTER and colophon are
registered trademarks of SIMON & SCHUSTER, Inc.
Designed by Edith Fowler
Manufactured in the United States of America

10 9 8 7 6 5 4 3 2 1

Library of Congress Cataloging-in-Publication Data

Wilkens, Lenny, 1937–
    Unguarded : my forty years surviving in the NBA /
Lenny Wilkens with Terry Pluto.
        p.   cm.
        1. Wilkens, Lenny, 1937–   2. Basketball
coaches—United States—Biography.   3. Basketball
players—United States—Biography.   I. Pluto, Terry,
date.   II. Title.
GV884.W54 A36 2000
796.323'092—dc21
[B]   00-048241
ISBN 0-684-87374-5

Acknowledgments

The authors would like to thank Jeff Neuman, editor at Simon & Schuster, who gave this project a green light. As always, Jeff Neuman is the Red Auerbach of editors. We'd also like to thank Faith Hamlin, our agent on the project, and a word of thanks to Jeff's assistant, Jon Malki, for all his help.

To MARILYN . . .
the love of my life
and
to FATHER THOMAS MANNION . . .
who
has always been there for me.
—LENNY WILKENS

To JOE TAIT . . .
a great broadcaster,
and even better friend.
—TERRY PLUTO

UNGUARDED

CHAPTER ONE

O<small>N MY DESK</small>, there's a picture of my father.

He's a man I never really knew, yet a man who feels very much a part of me today. The man staring at me is always about thirty-five, always in the prime of life, dark-skinned, strong, healthy. He's the father I wished was there when my team in Seattle won the 1979 NBA title, the father I wanted with me when I was inducted in the Basketball Hall of Fame. When I puffed that cigar to celebrate breaking Red Auerbach's record for the most career victories by any NBA coach, I wanted my father there. He's the father I wished could see my children and meet my wife, Marilyn.

He will always be my father, and he will always live in my head because he died when I was only five years old.

His name was Leonard. I'm really Leonard R. Wilkens, Jr. Few people know that about me. Few people know very much about me, even though I've been in the public eye seemingly forever, as an NBA player and/or coach since 1960. That's a long time, forty years in pro basketball. No one has survived the NBA storm longer. No one has appeared in more games when you combine all the years that I've played and coached. And here am I, at the age of sixty-two. I've coached for twenty-seven years, and I still love it. I really do.

I just wish that my father had been there for some of it.

Seeing other kids with fathers made me miss my father. There would be functions at school, and other children would have both parents there. I'd have my mother, assuming she could get off from work. Sometimes, no one was there. Later, as I achieved some things, I wondered what my father would have made of it all: graduating from college. Playing in the NBA. Making All-Star teams. Coaching some wonderful teams, coaching in the 1996 Olympics.

Sometimes I'd ask myself, "What would my father have thought of me? Would he be proud of me?"

There's no real answer to that because he's been gone for so long.

After my father died, my mother spent a lot of time telling all her children how much our father loved us. She wanted us to know that our father didn't want to leave us, that he would have loved to have been with us, but God just called him. I never really understood why he was gone, but I knew it wasn't his fault. He didn't run off; he died.

I missed him then, and I always will.

Those who knew my father say that I'm a lot like him. They say if you look at my hands, you see his hands. That's what I've heard over and over again from those who knew my father—that I have my father's hands, strong, with long, purposeful fingers. I look at my hands and try to imagine my father's hands, then I wonder if he was an athlete. I don't even know if he was a sports fan. Relatives have told me that sometimes I walk like him, or that I gesture like him. I don't know what to say to that, because the more I think about my father, the less I realize I know.

I do have one memory of him: I'm sitting in a high chair at the dinner table. I'm not much more than an infant. My father takes a piece of bacon, ties it to a string from something above my head. That bacon attached to a string hangs down, dangling right in front of me. With my little hands, I bang around the bacon, and that keeps me occupied as my parents eat breakfast.

That was my father, a man who knew how to make a toy for a toddler out of a piece of bacon and a string.

And he baked.

I don't remember seeing him bake, but I remember the smells. Fresh bread. Cakes. The warm aromas filling our brownstone apartment in the Bedford Stuyvesant section of Brooklyn. I can close my eyes and see my sister and myself sitting on a bench. My father is in the kitchen. I don't see him in the kitchen, I just know he's in there, baking.

I can still smell it.

This time, it was a cake. He's baking a white cake with chocolate frosting. With my eyes closed and my memory in high gear, I still don't see him, but I can see the cake. I see my sister Connie and me eating that cake. I know he baked it. But I still don't see him, and I wish I did—just once more, even in my memory. I just know that my father loved to bake: He did all the baking in the house, and forever in my head are the memories of that white cake with the chocolate frosting.

And the bacon on a string.

And the funeral.

My father died of a bleeding ulcer, that much I've been told. He was rushed to a hospital in Brooklyn, which was not far from the brownstone apartment where we lived. The doctors said my father had something called "a locked bowel." They decided the best way to treat him was with an enema.

Actually, it was the one thing they never should have done.

It killed him.

My mother didn't know anything about malpractice. Besides, this was in 1943, a time when you just didn't sue doctors. It was a time when you were glad to have a doctor treat you, a time when doctors seemed like miracle men. And miracle men many of them were—and still are.

But in the case of this doctor and my father, I can't help but think that the man killed my father. I didn't hear this story of my father's death until I was in college. I wanted to do something, but what? Find the doctor? Sue the hospital for something that happened so long ago? Besides, how do you put a price tag on a young family deprived of a father? No amount of money can repay my mother for all the anguish she had to endure as she raised us, a woman alone with four kids all under the age of seven when she lost her husband.

When my father died, they put the casket in the living room. The custom back then was to hold a wake in the home. There was a huge lamp on each side of the casket. Behind the coffin were these black drapes. I can still see the room. It's so dark, it's eerie. The casket is a shiny wooden box, reflecting the light from the two lamps. People are crying. I remember a nun holding me on her lap: She was a friend of my mother's from Holy Rosary Church. My mother's family were staunch Roman Catholics. My father converted to Catholicism to marry my mother. I spent the entire funeral in the arms of that nun. People cried and cried. I clung to that nun.

The casket was open. My father was in there. He wore his best suit and tie. There was no question that it was my father, and no question that he was dead. I just remember that I didn't want to be in that room alone with the casket.

When the wake was over, one of my aunts came up to me. She took me in her arms and said, "Well, you're going to be the man of the family now."

I stared at her. I was five years old. How was I supposed to know what it meant to be the man of the house? But I was the man of that house. I had an older sister, Connie, who was six. My brother, Larry, was three. And there was two-year-old Mary.

Four kids, no father.

I was only five years old, but that aunt's words stuck to me. I was the man of the family. I had no idea what it meant, I just knew that on the day my father died, everything had changed—and more was expected of me. I was his son, and I'll always be his son. That much I know. And his absence had a far more profound impact on me that his presence, because his being gone meant that I had to grow up, and grow up quick. But his being my father also left me a legacy. Because my father was an African-American, so am I. At least that's how the world sees me.

A priest once asked me, "What's it like to have a foot in both worlds?"

He knew I came from a mixed-blood family. My father was African-American, my mother was Irish. But I never hesitated when they asked me to list my race on a form—I'd write I was African-American. There is a racist theory that has always existed in this country, that if you have a drop of black blood in you, then you're an African-American.

One drop of blood is all it takes to define you as black.

Why is that?

If a person is part Irish and part Italian and a little Scottish, we don't say that person is Scottish—to the exclusion of all else—because he has a bit of Scottish blood in him. But if that same person had a drop of black blood? Well, forget about the Italian, the Irish, the Scottish, or any other roots—you're black, period. This was done primarily to keep black people down, to deprive people of opportunity, to keep a bigger slice of the American pie for white people, because for much of our history, being considered black immediately relegated you to second-class status.

The truth is that I'm as much Irish as I'm black, but I've never heard anyone say, "Lenny is Irish." Today, it's illegal to ask for a person's race, but once that was common on most job applications and other forms. If I really wanted to be accurate, I should have listed myself as "African-Irish-American," and then watch what they would have made of that.

Then again, when former NBA coach Cotton Fitzsimmons first met me, he thought I was Puerto Rican!

We used to say America was a melting pot. It was in all my history books, stories of how people came from all over the world to find a home in the United States. I took that literally. They told us that we were all created equal, right?

Then why ask about someone's race?

Why define a person by wanting to know, "Do you have any black blood?"

What is the purpose? Where is the justice?

There have been light-skinned people who have "passed" as white, but I was never into that. I never wanted to put myself in a position of trying to be something I was not. I had a cousin who did, but that was his hangup; I never had a problem with being considered a black man. I am proud of my father, of my African-American roots. I know that when I was in college, some of my professors were shocked when I did well in certain courses. A black person, especially a black athlete, just wasn't expected to achieve in the classroom. Sometimes, I wanted to speak out. I knew what they were thinking, how wrong and racist it was . . . but I just didn't want to give people the idea that I had a chip on my shoulder or that I wasn't proud of being black. Most of the time, I just glared at them. I wanted them to be as uncomfortable as they made me, and for some reason, I just knew that eventually I'd find a way to prove them wrong.

I never heard exactly how my mother and father met. I know that he was a chauffeur, and he often drove around the neighborhood. He got to know a lot of people, and one of them was my mother.

And they were married, which is all I know.

That was in April of 1935, when mixed marriages certainly were rare in most parts of America, but there were more than a few in Brooklyn. The Bedford Stuyvesant of my youth was a true melting pot. On my street was a German deli, a Jewish grocery, an Italian market. Within a few streets were all kinds of people from blacks to Puerto Ricans to Jews to Eastern Europeans. Sure, people were aware of the racial and ethnic differences, but most of us learned to live together and get along. We had no choice, because we saw each other all the time on the streets, on the subways, at stores, and at church. Only later did I come to realize how unique this situation was, and how it affected my life: I never doubted that people from different races could work with each other and be friends, because I saw it every day of my life while growing up.

Granted, there were problems. Some members of my mother's family weren't thrilled about the marriage. My mother had six sisters and two brothers. The brothers were always very consumed with their jobs and families, so they were seldom around. Most of the other members of the family were friendly, but my mother's oldest sister played favorites. She was the oldest and didn't have any children. I felt like this sister and her husband liked my cousins better than us, and my cousins were part-Chinese. My mother's sister had married a Chinese man, and that was OK with some of the family—but my mother was considered an outcast by this sister because she had married a black man. I know this had to be hard on my mother, but she rarely talked about it. Nor do I ever recall her saying anything about what her family thought of her marriage to my father. I imagine there was some initial resistance to an Irish-Catholic woman marrying a black man. I'd hear some comments secondhand, never to our face; I just knew some of the relatives weren't thrilled with our "mixed" family.

You have to understand the times and our family. I was born in 1937, which means I grew up at the end of the Depression, through World War II and then into the Korean War. This was not an era when people had the luxury to become caught up in introspection. Over and over, it was drilled into us, "Don't feel sorry for yourself." We had to work. We were fighting to survive. People knew what it was to be hungry. They still talked about "bread lines" and "going to the poorhouse." They knew what it was to have their husbands and fathers killed on the other side of the world, to see people become instant widows, to see children weeping at a cemetery while clinging to their mother's skirt as their father is buried, to see flags in the windows of apartments and houses of men who had died in the war.

It's not like the affluent times of today, where people look at all the details of their lives, sometimes to the point of distraction. They dig through the fields of their past, turning the same dirt over and over and over, searching for clues to who they are and why they act the way they do. If some of my relatives didn't love us, so what? Shake it off. We were too busy taking care of ourselves, and we didn't really expect anyone to help us. We were taught to be thankful for the people who did care about us, rather than to dwell on those who didn't. Maybe that sounds simplistic, but what other choice did we have? I see too many people today who walk around captives of their past, who have jailed their own hearts with bitterness and regrets about what happened when they grew up, about slights from relatives, parents who somehow failed, money that wasn't there. That can paralyze you.

My mother spent most of her time trying to get us to concentrate on what we did have, not moaning about what was missing. For example, two of my mother's sisters were terrific. They were my favorite aunts because they were so down to earth, they just loved us. Like my mother, they were Irish Catholics, and they quickly embraced her children. It wouldn't have mattered to them if we were purple: We were family to those two aunts. My father's family was also great. He had three sisters, and they accepted us as their own—no questions asked, no hesitation. My father's youngest sister was a loving woman who bought me my first suit when I was in high school. We seemed to spend more time with my father's family. As I mentioned, two of my mother's sisters were outstanding, but all of my father's family was that way; with them, I always felt like "family."

Yes, outside the home, some kids called me "half-breed."

But "half-breed" never bothered me much, because I always had a sense of who I was. Besides, we all were just kids back then, and there weren't the same racial hangups we have today. Kids talked about each other being Jews, Poles, Irish, whatever. It wasn't a putdown, just a statement of fact. Besides, my mother never talked about race. Not at all. She refused to make it an issue.

She would just say, "You can be as good as you want to be."

Or she'd say, "Don't make excuses, you can accomplish whatever you set your mind to, you're just as good as the next person."

I believed her. I didn't let other people define me or limit me. In our immediate family, we didn't worry about race. She was the mother; we were the kids. She refused to feel sorry for herself, and she expected the same from us. But when we went to the store, people would stare at us.

My mother was an Irish woman. My brother and one of my sisters are light-skinned, much as I am. And my sister Connie is a beautiful brown-skinned woman; she favored my father.

Sometimes, people rudely glared. They wondered what that black girl was doing with that white woman, who was obviously her mother. And they stared harder at the rest of the kids. Were we white? Or black? Or what?

My mother would catch them staring and she'd confront them: "Just *what* are you looking at?"

Of course, those people were gutless. They'd never say a word. They'd just look away. Meanwhile, we children were mortified at what my mother would say, how her Irish temper would bubble up, then blow, like a volcano. In these rare instances, she had the vocabulary of a sailor. I couldn't believe my own mother was saying some of those words! When that happened, we kids wanted to disappear. We really didn't know why some people stared at us, we just saw that it upset our mother—and that bothered us.

I still remember a Thanksgiving dinner at one of our aunt's homes. The aunt was married to this white guy who was a grouch most of the time.

As I walked in the door, he growled, "And what do *you* want?"

I said, "I don't want anything."

Then I turned around and walked right out the door. My mother and aunt tried to get me to go back in there, but I refused. I would not go into that place, because I knew that man didn't want me there. I wasn't sure why; I guessed it was because I was black or he was just being a smartass, but I didn't know, I just wanted no part of that man or his Thanksgiving dinner. I was twelve years old at the time. Finally, my mother gave up. I told her that I wanted her to stay and have dinner, that I'd be all right. Then I went home.

Things like that, they really had to hurt my mother. But she never complained about it, at least not that her children heard.

"You're a human being," she'd tell me. "You're accountable for who you are. Be proud of who you are."

Yet there were nights when I heard my mother cry. Things just got to be too much, and she broke down. It wasn't in front of us, but we'd hear her crying. I wanted to do something. I was supposed to be the man of the house. But what could I do? There was nothing I could say, nothing I could do that would bring my father back.

After a while, she'd stop.

Then she'd pray.

No woman ever prayed as much as Henrietta Wilkens. Even before my father died, she prayed: Mass every morning, or at least a Novena. Pray at meals. Pray the rosary at night. I always tell people that I'm living proof that prayer works, because no one ever prayed harder for her children than my mother did. Some people would have pulled away from God after losing a husband as she did, but it just made my mother's faith stronger. And she never cared about me identifying myself as an African-American. She always insisted skin color didn't matter, but your heart and your faith did. To her, what counted was that I had embraced Roman Catholicism. That was the most important thing. Her faith was her lifeblood, her source of hope, her comfort in times of despair. She couldn't imagine living without it, and to her, faith was far more important than race. I think if I had turned my back on the Catholic Church, that would have devastated her. As it was, our life and poverty were piling up on her, the stress taking a toll. She was five-foot-five, but there were days when she just seemed smaller, when her whole body sagged. Everything just wore her down. Before my father died, she was a housewife. She had a good man who provided everything from baked bread to a reliable paycheck. Suddenly, all that was gone.

I know what it means to be on welfare.

I know what it means to have a stranger in the house, snooping around, checking to see if you're hiding something. I know the caseworker was just doing his job, and I know some people did cheat on welfare—but it's still demeaning.

I know what it was like to wait for the welfare check to come so we could buy groceries, or anything else we needed for the house. I know what it's like to be in high school where clothes are important, a mark of status, and to have only one shirt, a shirt I dyed a different color every week to make it seem like I had different shirts.

When I was in elementary school, right before lunchtime they'd sell one-cent candy. Those of us who didn't have a penny would put our heads down on top of our desks while the others bought the candy; no one said a word, but we were embarrassed not to have a penny for candy. I never said a word about it to my mother. Hearing that would have killed her.

And, yes, I know what it's like to work.

After my father's death, my mother took a part-time job at a candy factory. She packed the candies into boxes, which were shipped all over the country. She wore a uniform, an apron, a bonnet. I can close my eyes and see her in the apron, her bonnet holding up her long, fine, light-brown hair. I can see her sitting at the kitchen table, all of the air seemingly wrung out of her. Her body just looks smaller, sagging from sheer exhaustion. She has just come home from the candy factory, and she has to cook for four kids. She has to make sure we do our homework. She has to clean the house, which was a job itself with four kids.

No matter how hard she worked, there was never enough money, enough time, enough energy. After a while, my mother couldn't keep up with the rent on the brownstone apartment on Pacific Street.

That's when I realized we were poor. My mother had to fend for herself; no one on either side of the family had any extra money. I'm sure our relatives helped out a little here and there, maybe with some old clothes or a few extra dollars, but they didn't help us much because they couldn't. We always seemed to be wearing the same clothes longer than the other kids in school. My mother was constantly sewing and patching things together, and the boys had to wait longer for new clothes, because she believed it was more important for the girls to look nice; if the boys were a little ragged, that was OK. That never bothered me. I didn't worry a lot about clothes.

My mother often told us, "God doesn't look at your clothes. He looks at the person inside the clothes." She said that with such conviction that, after a while, I believed it.

But shoes were a different story.

My mother could afford only one new pair of tennis shoes a year for each of us, and I'd wear those out in a month or so playing in the streets and at the playground. Then I'd play baseball and basketball in my dress shoes, which didn't thrill my mother—but she didn't stop me, either.

Then, we started moving.

My mother never explained the moves, we just went from one apartment to another to another. The apartments became smaller, even though her children were growing larger. Our last place was what I'll always remember as our "coldwater flat." There was no heat: You'd light the stove in the kitchen to warm the apartment— well, the kitchen and bedroom next to it anyway. The living room was too far away, so it was freezing in the winter. We'd wrap ourselves up in lots of blankets to keep warm. The worst of that changed during my sophomore year, when it became law that all apartments had to be heated, and the landlord installed steam heat.

What I also remember is cleanliness.

Our place was immaculate. The dishes were done, the clothes were picked up, the furniture dusted, the floors shiny. My mother did much of the work, but we all pitched in. My job was washing and waxing the floors; I also took out the garbage, and I took turns washing and drying the dishes with the other kids. Like my mother, I like a clean house. I can really clean a house. When we were first married, my wife was shocked at how orderly I kept things, and how I could throw myself into a room and scrub and dust it like a pro. In fact, my first job was cleaning a two-story brownstone owned by a lady who was a friend of my cousin's: Every Saturday, I'd start at the top floor and work my way down—washing windows, waxing floors, dusting, picking up trash.

I was nine years old, and that was my job, every Saturday.

Then I went to work at a market where my cousin also had a job. People would order groceries, and I had to deliver them to their houses. The store had a wagon, and they'd really load it up. I'd drag that wagon behind me, struggling with the huge bags and boxes of groceries. At least they seemed enormous to me, because I was only ten.

My pay? Strictly tips.

By the time I was in high school, I worked virtually every day after school at another grocery store; I was a stock boy, a bagger, part of the clean-up crew. Eventually, I was put in charge of the vegetable department, making sure that the food looked nice so people would want to buy it. I loved working at the grocery store, partly because it meant so much to my mother, and partly because we got a discount on the groceries. I gave nearly all the money I made to her, but I was still able to keep a dollar or two for myself—and that was a big deal to me, to actually have some money in my pocket.

I was learning what it really meant to be the man of the house. I never told my brothers and sisters that I gave my mother any-thing—at least not for a long time: I wanted to keep it between us, and I thought my brothers and sisters just didn't need to know. My brother Larry also started working when he was about twelve, delivering newspapers and other odd jobs. All the kids worked at some point to help our mother, although I always felt a little more responsible than the rest of them because I was the oldest son. People sometimes hear these stories and think that I should be angry, that I somehow lost my childhood, but I liked most of my jobs. They made me feel important, and I wanted to help my mother and my family. Besides, I always found time to play ball in the street, or just hang out with friends. Working at a young age gave me confidence; I knew that if I had to take care of myself, I could.

All through high school, I thought little about basketball, and never about pro sports as a career. I didn't follow it closely. It wasn't until my senior year that we convinced our mother to buy a TV set: We found that you could do it on a monthly payment plan, and it didn't take a lot of money to start. It seemed like everyone in the neighborhood had a TV but us, so she gave in and bought one. Turned out that I hardly ever watched it, because I was so busy with school, working, and playing basketball at the Boys Club. Maybe that's why, to this day, I don't watch much TV. I'd rather read.

At an early age, I had learned that the only way most people got anywhere in the world is by making their own way. You had to work. You had to understand there were going to be roadblocks, setbacks, and even heartbreaks. I'm not saying I ever liked any of those things, but I understood that they didn't have to defeat me. Some people act as if responsibility is a dirty word. But it was a big part of my life, and I grew to like it. I enjoyed the independence and satisfaction that came from earning money to buy my own basketball shoes, which is virtually unheard of today when young players just expect their coaches, schools, and summer teams to supply several pairs of $150 shoes for free. I appreciated my new shoes, because I'd *earned* them. What's wrong with asking young people to work for things, to contribute to the family's budget, especially if the family is poor? I grew up without a father, as a member of a minority, in a family that was sometimes on welfare. Some people might say those circumstances doomed me to failure; others act as if being poor entitles you to special privileges. You can either allow your circumstances to be a trap and ensnare you for the rest of your life, or you can use them to learn what it takes to succeed in a world where things won't always go your way. I had a friend who ended up in jail; he came to us and wanted us to help him break into a candy store, and a few of us refused. We knew it was wrong, and maybe we were more afraid of our parents than any peer pressure he could apply. We didn't think that being poor gave us the right to steal from someone else, so we didn't.

It almost seemed like all the adults in the neighborhood tried to help us stay straight. If you were in a fight with another kid and you saw an adult walking by, the fight would just *stop*. The kids would stand straight, look at the adult as if nothing was happening and say, "Nice to see you, Mrs. Smith." Priests, policemen, teachers, parents—almost any adult demanded and received your respect.

Today, there isn't the same sense of community: Ask yourself how many of your neighbors do you even know, I mean where you know their first and last names and the names of all their kids? Families are often scattered across the country: How many of your aunts, uncles, cousins, parents, or grandparents live in your immediate neighborhood? Probably not many. But I had a lot of relatives very close by as a kid in Brooklyn. You had the feeling that either someone from your family or someone from church was watching you. I remember once sneaking onto a trolley car for a free ride; I was sure no one saw me, until I got home—where my mother was waiting, fuming. My uncle had spotted me and told her. My mother didn't spank me often, but she did that day. There was no debate. I was guilty until proven innocent, and I was given no chance to present any sort of defense. And I didn't have any. I think it's good that she held me accountable for my actions.

In today's society with so many broken families, and so many families where both parents work long hours and their kids are in daycare or left alone after school, it's no surprise that kids get into more trouble than we did. Who's watching? Who holds them accountable? When both parents are working and are dedicated more to their jobs than their families, they often feel guilty about not watching their kids as they should—so they spoil their children and excuse behavior that ought to be punished. I see the same thing with some single mothers who feel completely overwhelmed: They simply don't have the energy to discipline and demand excellence from their children.

In our home, that was never a problem. My mother got tired, sure, but she had the help and support of an extended family, a community, and most important, the church—especially one young priest who played a big part in shaping my future.

CHAPTER TWO

HE WAS A BIG MAN in an enormous black robe. He wore a white collar. He had reddish-brown hair and penetrating blue eyes. They were the kind of eyes that bored deep into your soul, eyes that demanded you stand a little straighter—and no matter what, those eyes insisted that you tell the truth.

His name was Father Thomas Mannion.

I know now that he was only five-foot-eight with an average build, but he seemed much larger then. Maybe it was because he walked with such purpose, that long black robe trailing behind him. Or maybe it was his handshake: The man seemed to have hands of steel. Or maybe it's that he came along at a time in my life when I needed a father. He arrived at Holy Rosary, our home parish, when I was in the fourth grade. As Father Mannion once said, "The first time I saw Lenny, he was no bigger than a basketball." Because of my mother's devotion to the Catholic Church, I already had tremendous respect for priests and nuns. She wouldn't have it any other way. But Father Mannion was unique. He was special because he made me feel special by keeping an eye on me. I later learned that my mother had asked him to do just that.

I was an altar boy. I loved the Mass, the Catholic church service. The Mass back then was said in Latin. I learned the Latin; I took comfort in the words, which sounded strange to most Americans. I took it as a challenge to master something different, to be able to do more than just mumble the words of those Latin prayers. I loved putting on the black cassock and the white surplice, hanging it just right. The pleats in my outfit were just perfect; it was starched just right, thanks to my mother. I loved to wear that cassock and kneel at the side of the altar as Father Mannion said the Mass. I loved ringing the bells when the Host was raised during the consecration. I loved the smell of incense that filled the air during the High Mass. Holy Rosary was a relatively small church, but it seemed huge to me. The altar. The stained-glass windows. The crucifix. The statues of the Blessed Virgin Mary. It may as well have been the Vatican to me, or at least St. Patrick's Cathedral. I loved the ceremony, the quiet contemplation, the public prayers. Nothing was better than being an altar boy when Father Mannion said the Mass. He seemed like a spiritual giant, a true man of God.

For an Irish-Catholic woman, there could be no greater blessing than for one of her sons to become a priest. My mother never told me that directly, but she'd say that Father Mannion was a great guy, and she'd talk about "the wonderful life" of the priests because "they help so many people." The priests impressed me, too. I used to pretend to say Mass in our apartment. We'd set up a little altar on the sofa, and we had cups and saucers and water and a little bread to serve as the Communion. I said the Mass in Latin. I thought it was really neat.

There was a 7:00 A.M. Mass in the convent for the nuns, and I was the most requested altar boy for that service. Some of the nuns knew my mother, so they were happy to have me around. They also said I did a good job as the altar boy. Before I served Mass, my mother always made sure that my fingernails were clean. To her, it was a mortal sin to be an altar boy with dirty fingernails, especially in the convent where all the nuns would see me. But what I liked best was that after the Mass I could stay and eat breakfast with them. It might be anything from bacon and eggs to pancakes or waffles or all kinds of things I never had at home. I liked being an altar boy, and I felt special to be near the priest as the Mass was said—and those breakfasts were a real bonus. It was a welcome change from the oatmeal we had for breakfast every day at home.

Oatmeal. Oatmeal. And more oatmeal.

After a while, I hated oatmeal, and when I grew up, I didn't eat oatmeal for nearly forty years. It was a reminder of how we had nothing else for breakfast, how oatmeal was all we could afford.

In Brooklyn of the 1940s, you identified your neighborhood by the nearest Catholic Church. You could tell someone, "I live by Holy Rosary . . . I live by St. Paul's," and people would know exactly where you meant. A church was more than a church; it was the center of the neighborhood for both blacks and whites, as about 30 percent of our parish was minority. This was before most homes had TVs, before computers, before most people had cars, and before anyone had ever heard of a shopping mall. It was a time when a bingo game or a fair with small games of chance and lots of baked treats were a real blessing. Pot luck dinners were common. So were dances for teenagers and basketball games in the gym. Father Mannion ran the gym and the dances. Today, he'd probably be said to be in charge of the youth ministry; back then, he was just a young priest who decided to work with the kids. No one assigned him the job, he just did it.

Because my mother went to Mass almost every day and because I attended Holy Rosary School, the church was a second home to us. It was where we found friends, where my mother felt secure because her children were being taught and cared for by nuns and priests. I know that some people hated going to Catholic schools, and claim to be still scarred by some of the nuns who taught them—but I firmly believe in Catholic education. Sure, some of the nuns would grab you by the ear and seem about ready to tear it off—but most of the time we deserved it. OK, once a nun jerked me so hard by the ear I swore I felt blood, and all because I had tried to sneak in front of another kid in line. I thought that was a little extreme, but I sure wasn't going to say anything to her—or to my mother, who would just support the nun, and the nun would have given me worse punishment for mouthing off. So you kept quiet and took it and were grateful that your parents never found out about what happened. I remember sitting at my desk and turning around, talking to a kid behind me—and *whap!*—the nun cracked me across the hand with a ruler. I was whacked on the butt for talking in line. It really wasn't a big deal. We all knew that the nuns usually liked the girls best; some of them were quick to spot us boys messing around, and then come roaring down the aisle of little wooden desks. They looked like enraged penguins. They'd tell us to stick out our hands and—*whap! whap! whap!*—you'd get up to five *whaps* across your hands with that ruler. And these were nuns from an order called Sisters of Mercy! But I liked most of the nuns back then, and I still have some nuns who are among my best friends today.

At Holy Rosary, we had to wear a uniform to school. That was fine with me, especially since we had so little money for clothes anyway. I had nothing against having to wear blue pants and a blue or white shirt to school every day. It sure beats the chaos we see in some schools today, where some kids are so fashion-conscious that they steal and even kill each other for jackets and shoes.

The Catholic Church was the answer to my mother's prayers. It was a place where her children could receive extra discipline, a place where there were strong male role models—critical for kids being raised without a father. When I was about twelve, Father Mannion pulled me aside, putting what felt like an iron fist around my puny bicep. I thought he was going to squeeze all the blood right out of my arm. Usually, Father Mannion greeted me with a smile that made me feel like I was one of the most special people in the world. Not this time. He had a stern look, his eyes hard, prying. He said only that he wanted to talk to me in private, in his office. He sat behind his desk in that black robe, that white collar, that air of holy authority about him, and I feared the wrath of God was about to fall down on me.

"I don't like some of the kids you're hanging out with," he said.

I said nothing.

He mentioned a few names. He told me that those kids were headed for trouble, and I'd be doing the same if I stayed with them.

I was shocked. I couldn't figure out how he knew so much about me and my friends. Later, I learned that my mother had told him, and basically, this was an inside job designed to set me straight—which it did.

As I think back, I don't remember Father Mannion telling me, "Don't be friends with those kids any more."

He didn't have to. I knew what was on his mind. The meeting could not have lasted more than a minute, but I knew what had to be done.

I changed my friends.

It's funny how these same themes are there for young people today. Bad company does corrupt good character, and as a coach, I've had this same discussion with players about their friends more than a few times, how they had to be careful whom they allow to get close to them. The last was with J. R. Rider in my final year as the coach of the Atlanta Hawks. Of course, that was only one of several problems we had with Rider. But some young NBA players worry more about looking like phonies or sellouts in front of their friends, and they don't realize how easily they can end up in the wrong place at the wrong time doing the wrong thing—just as Father Manion warned me. That's happened to a lot of athletes over the years. Just look at the football player Ray Lewis, who ended up involved in a murder trial because of the alleged actions of some of his friends. When I coached in Cleveland, we traded Ron Harper because ownership was worried about his friends. I talked to Harper about it several times, and he slowly was coming around, but teams sometimes fear that a player will be dragged down by his friends.

Among young people, you hear the phrase "Keep it real." Of course you don't just cut off everyone whom you grew up with, but you also don't allow them to dictate your life. Is it phony to want to better yourself, not just financially, but in terms of your own character? Some people think it is. But to me, that's the essence of life: making new friends, learning new things. It's not disloyal to cut off someone who is constantly in trouble and doesn't care if he gets you in trouble, too. That's just common sense. When Father Mannion first had that discussion with me, I wasn't happy about it. No one likes to be told what to do. But I also respected Father Mannion. I believed that he wasn't just exercising his authority for the sake of it, he really cared about what happened to me. I listened to him because I was sure he had my best interest at heart

The word "respect" is tossed around a lot, but it's not really understood. Some young people demand respect, even though they

have no idea how to give it to anyone else—nor have they done anything to deserve it. They just believe that, somehow, they're entitled
to it. And when they run into any sort of authority, they rebel—be
it against a teacher, a coach, or a policeman. A big reason for this is
that so many young men have no older males in their lives who are
worthy of respect. And they don't have a Father Mannion, because
churches have lost their importance in many families. Too often, the
drug dealer or the gang leader seems like the only male who has any
success or sense of himself, and these criminal types are romanti-
cized in the music and movies that are so popular with young people. They've made going to prison or being gunned down in the
street look like a noble cause, instead of a waste of a human life. This
isn't going to change until more adults get involved with kids, until
children are active in churches and community centers where they
can see the right kind of adult males who care about them. Would I
have gotten in real trouble if there was no Father Mannion in my
life? It's hard to say. But I do know that I owe a lot of my success and
my knowledge of what it takes to be a man to him.

In the Holy Rosary gym, we played a lot of basketball games.
There was a CYO league, the Catholic Youth Organization, and the
PAL, the Police Athletic League, and of course there were pickup
games. On Sunday night there were two games, followed by a dance
for teenagers. Father Mannion ran it and he loomed over it. A lot of
kids came to those dances who didn't belong to our parish, kids who
would be considered gang members today. They liked to fight, liked
to drink, and maybe tried drugs. But when they were at Holy
Rosary, there was none of that: Father Mannion made sure of it. He
demanded it. And he had such respect in the neighborhood, even
from the kids who didn't belong to the church, that they were afraid
to test him—at least after they saw him grab a couple of kids by
their jacket collars and drag them right out the gym door. Word
spread: You didn't mess with the young priest at Holy Rosary.

Those dances brought together kids from the parish, kids who
were considered hoods, and kids we called "400s." I don't know why
they were called 400s, but they'd be considered preppies today. They
had nicer clothes than we did. Some of them drove cars. A lot of
them were pretty smug, as if they thought they were better than us.

Today, I fully appreciate what a presence Father Mannion was in that gym to create an atmosphere where kids from so many different backgrounds could gather.

When it came time to go to high school, I attended Boys High, which was a public school in Brooklyn. But Holy Rosary remained a big part of my life. In addition to Mass on Sunday, I attended the classes they had for religious instruction, classes designed for kids who attended public schools. After those classes, we'd go roller skating.

The church was a sanctuary. The streets were a different story.

When I was about twelve, I saw a policeman shoot a man. The guy was drunk and was playfully chasing us. The policeman stopped him, and the guy shoved the officer. The next thing I knew, the officer shot the man right in the chest. Blood splattered everywhere. The man lay on the street, twitching. He was dead before the ambulance arrived. I was surprised by what happened, but I wasn't shocked. It wasn't like people were killed every day in the streets of my neighborhood, but it did happen, and we all were aware of it.

On another occasion, I was playing a pickup basketball game at PS-35, Public School 35. Suddenly, the basketball court was surrounded by a bunch of guys, I mean guys with bicycle chains, sticks, and knives. They started shaking all of us down, taking our money. There was nothing we could do: There were more of them, and they had weapons. When they came to me, a guy shoved his hand in my pocket and pulled out a couple of Catholic rosaries, which I carried around with me. That stopped them for a moment, as they stared at the rosaries. Then one of the guys recognized me as "Myer's cousin."

It turned out that I had a cousin who was in that gang, and another cousin who was in a gang that was considered friendly. These guys began asking me about relatives and friends we had in common—then they gave me the money back, so I could return it to the kids who were playing with me.

While all this was going on, a girl spotted the gang moving in on us. She ran and told my mother, who called the police. Rumors flew that I had been stabbed. When I came home, my mother and aunt kept asking if I was OK. I told them that I was fine. They didn't believe me, and they made me take off my shirt so they could check for knife wounds.

I was lucky because I had cousins in the gangs, and they made sure I was left alone. Or as Father Mannion said, "Lenny was smart enough to know how to stay just friendly enough with the gangs so he wouldn't get his head knocked off."

Some people say that I've spent much of my life walking between two worlds, between black and white, between the streets and the church. But I knew who and what I was—an African-American Roman Catholic. I knew I wanted something more than the streets, and I knew that hard work was the only way to get it.

That also was true of basketball.

My older cousins used to play pickup basketball at the Holy Rosary gym. They usually wouldn't let me in their games—and when they did, I shot the ball every time. They started calling me "The Heaver." I wasn't a good player. No one would pick me to play on their team. So I had to call "Next," and sometimes wait a couple of hours for a chance to play with four other guys who thought I stunk and didn't want to play with me. When I did get on the court, they didn't want to pass me the ball, because they figured I'd just mess up.

When I somehow did end up with the ball, the last thing I intended to do was to pass it to them! So I shot it, no matter how ridiculous the situation. I didn't care where I was on the court, I was going to get off a shot. Naturally, my team lost. I would get angry because nothing was working out, and I really hated it when they started yelling "Heaver" at me, because I knew it made all the kids laugh at me.

Father Mannion didn't have to be Red Auerbach to notice I wasn't exactly on my way to an NBA career. In fact, he saw that I had no clue when it came to the fundamentals of basketball. I didn't even own a basketball. I had only one pair of basketball shoes for each year: I'd wear a hole in them, then cut out a piece of linoleum to cover it. Father Mannion gave me a basketball, then he took me into the gym when he knew it would be empty. We brought ten chairs onto the court and he lined them up.

"What you need to do is dribble around the chairs," he said. I stared at him.

"You dribble around the chairs, switching hands," he said. "You're small. You're going to have to be a guard, so you need to be able to handle the ball, to dribble the ball with both hands."

I spent hours dribbling around those chairs. Left hand, right hand. Back and forth, from one end of the gym to the other. It was boring, but I kept at it, day after day. I liked the routine, the practicing alone in the gym. Left hand, right hand. Back and forth, over and over. Then came shooting: ten layups from the right side of the rim, ten from the left. I practiced jump shot after jump shot after jump shot. I shot until I developed a knack for getting the ball on my fingertips, then releasing it with a flip of the wrist, the ball rotating nicely in the air until it gently dropped through the rim. I loved to watch the ball swish through the net. In the same way that I was attracted to the ritual of serving Mass, I came to enjoy these solitary workouts. The drills, the chairs, the sweat, the echo of the ball bouncing in an empty gym—that became part of my life.

I suppose I also was so dedicated because Father Mannion was the one who taught me the drills. Here was an older man, an important man, paying attention to me. I was a kid without a father, a kid looking for a male influence. If he wanted me to dribble around chairs, I'd dribble around chairs. If he wanted me to shoot one hundred jumpers, I shot one hundred jumpers. I wanted to please him because I knew that he cared about me. I knew it not just because he took the time to talk with me, but because he did things like buy ice cream for a bunch of us. He didn't have much money, but he knew that we usually didn't have any. I wanted to be a good altar boy for him, and later, a good basketball player for him.

I was lefthanded, which was pretty unusual back then. I remember my third-grade teacher making me print with my right hand because she thought being lefthanded was strange, and no one should write with his left hand. The nun who taught my fourth-grade class was lefthanded, so I was saved—and not surprisingly, my penmanship really improved. This was a time when adults—especially teachers—represented authority. If a teacher said, "Print with your right hand," you printed with your right hand. It didn't matter if you were lefthanded—and your parents were going to back the teacher, not make a case that their son's creativity was being stifled by writing with the wrong hand, and this would psychologically scar him for life. Parents would say, "You do what the teacher says, and you better not let me hear another word about it."

While NBA guys who played against me said I "always went left," that wasn't true. I went left a lot, but I could drive right—and they knew that, which set up my lefthanded moves. I could dribble equally well with either hand, and I have Father Mannion and those chairs to thank for that. I smile as I think about those chairs, and I think about all the formal ballhandling drills the kids are doing today. They work fine, but no better than those chairs set up by Father Mannion. When I coached the Cavs and Steve Kerr wanted to improve his ballhandling skills over the summer, that's what we did—we set up chairs for him to dribble around. Michael Jordan said he did the same thing after his rookie year: He knew he needed work on his dribbling, so he set up chairs in a gym—and went through the drills, alone.

I played on the eighth-grade team at Holy Rosary. Our coach had never coached basketball before. We wore black cloth Converse shoes, which was a real upgrade from the Keds we used to buy at a neighborhood store known as Cheap Charlie's. The name fit the place, and the prices were the only ones that could squeeze into my mother's tight budget.

Holy Rosary's gym would look tiny to me today. At one end of the court was a basket with a balcony above it. At the other end was another basket—with a stage directly behind it. I remember taking the basketball, running off that stage, and jumping and dunking the ball. That was my first dunk, off that stage. The backboards were big wooden squares. There were only a few rows of wooden bleachers, and they crowded the floor.

Basketball was hardly an obsession for me. I played a lot of sports, especially baseball, stickball, and softball with Tommy Davis, a good friend who later went on to be a fine hitter with the Los Angeles Dodgers and other teams. If you were a good athlete, it was expected that you'd play several sports. Wilt Chamberlain was a track star in high school, as was Bill Russell. Gene Conley, Ron Reed, and Dave DeBusschere played both big league baseball and NBA basketball. Willis Reed played flanker as a high-school football player, and also threw the shotput in track. John Havlicek played football, baseball, and basketball in high school. Pat Riley was a star high-school quarterback in addition to playing basketball. Not only was Phil Jackson a center on his high-school basketball team, he also played center in football! Coaches didn't push you to specialize at an early age, to quit playing everything but the one sport where you supposedly showed the most ability. That's very common today, especially when so many parents are obsessed with turning their children into pro athletes. They all want to stand on stage when junior is taken in the NBA draft—on national TV, naturally. There are a lot of problems with that approach. It leads to kids burning out on their sport, because they not only play and practice it during the season, they attend off-season camps, off-season conditioning, everything you can imagine, all aimed at excelling in that one sport. They almost turn these kids into twelve-year-old pros. I'm not saying every coach does it, but too many fall into that trap. And these kids are twelve, fourteen, and sixteen years old. They're still kids. And a young man or woman might show a lot of talent in one sport at thirteen, then suddenly grow and be better at another sport at sixteen. Or he or she might stop growing at thirteen, and maybe would be better off playing a different sport. That's why I encourage young people to play as many sports as they want, as long as they keep their grades up.

I'm a Hall of Fame point guard, but I never played high-school basketball until my senior year.

After eight years at Holy Rosary, I moved on to Boys High in Brooklyn. A mob of kids went out for the freshman team. I was nothing but skin and bones: all elbows and knees. The coach was Mickey Fisher, and he cut the team down to fifteen. I was on the list—the last name on the list, and that was no accident. Coach Fisher made it clear that he planned to play only eight kids per game. I could tell from the practices that I was the fifteenth kid out of the fifteen players. I was so far down at the end of the bench, the coach probably couldn't find me even if he wanted to put me in the game.

My mother was still struggling to pay the bills, so I couldn't justify sitting on the bench of the freshman team instead of working to help support the family. In the back of my mind, I never forgot that I was the "man of the family." I may have only been fourteen, a freshman in high school, but I had to act as much like a man as I could, and I knew a man didn't waste time sitting on the bench. That not only wasn't any fun, it didn't help my mother. So I quit the team and took that job at the grocery store instead, giving most of the money to my mother. The pay was a dollar an hour, which was very good for the time, and the discount was a big help.

I played a lot of pickup basketball in my spare time. I still remember winter days when the Holy Rosary gym was locked, and I'd shovel snow by the outdoor hoop just so I could play—often practicing by myself. I played in some amateur leagues. The more I played basketball, the more I liked it, especially as I sensed I was really learning how to play the game.

In my sophomore year at Boys High, I had a geometry teacher whom I really didn't like. I started to cut the class, then I was tossed out of the class for missing it too many times. I was really discouraged with everything, and at sixteen, I figured I was a man.

"I'm going to join the Marines," I told Father Mannion.

This led to a long talk with Father Mannion about life and school and my future.

"Just go back to the geometry teacher, apologize, and then stay in there and lick the class," he said. "No reason you can't do it."

When Father Mannion told me to go back to geometry class, keep my mouth shut, and study hard, I did. I think I got a B in the course. Father Mannion also put me in charge of working with the girls basketball team at Holy Rosary. This was my first coaching job, and I took it as a test: Father Mannion wanted to see if I was grown up enough to coach some girls, most of whom had a limited idea of how to play. I didn't know much about coaching, but I had them shoot layups, I called timeouts, made substitutions, and acted as much like a coach as I could at that age. I took it seriously because I didn't want to let Father Mannion down. He gave me a job, and I did it. I think he also knew that I'd respond to the challenge, that I welcomed responsibility.

I've always been like that.

I still played a lot of pickup basketball, especially at lunchtime against the kids who were on the varsity team. At this point, I was able to play as well as most of them. Tommy Davis was on the basketball team, and he kept saying I should go out for the varsity. Tommy Davis later became a good major league baseball player.

During the summer, I sometimes had Saturday off at the grocery store. I used to play pickup games at the park with some of the local high-school players. One day, a college kid named Vinny Cohen showed up: He was a star at Syracuse, about six-foot-two and built like a rock, a very muscular guy—or at least he was compared to me, because I was only five-foot-ten and 140 pounds.

I was matched up with Cohen, and guarding him very close. I stole his dribble, made it hard for him to catch passes and get off his shot. I was much quicker, and I used my speed to frustrate him, to keep the ball out of his hands. Some people were watching the game, and they started to get on him: "Hey, All-American . . . you ain't showing me much." That kind of thing. Making it worse, he was being shut down by a kid who wasn't even on his high-school team. Finally, he just blasted me with a forearm to the chest and began to shove me around. I played him a little softer, because I didn't want to get into a fight.

But after that game, several guys told me that I had really improved, and maybe I should try out for the high-school team. Understand that the New York playground games of my era were much different from the playground games of today. The accent was on teamwork, on passing, on setting picks and working for a good shot. The idea was to win the game, especially since the winners stayed on the court. Older guys taught younger players the value of moving without the ball, of always keeping your eyes open for a pass. The pick-and-roll play, which remains one of the keys to scoring in the NBA, was considered an art form on the New York playgrounds of my youth. Now, you're more likely to see a dinosaur wander across midcourt than to see kids use the pick-and-roll. So much of the playground game has disintegrated into one-on-one, guys trying to dunk in a guy's face, or blocking his shot. The individual now rules where the team once did. TV has a lot to do with it, as many kids seem to be constantly auditioning for ESPN's Sports-center, and they act like one in-your-face, rim-rattling dunk is worth ten layups off a finely executed pick-and-roll play. Today, playground ball can ruin good players; in my era, it made me a great player because it translated perfectly into organized basketball, although I wasn't aware of that until much later.

Tommy Davis kept after me about playing for Boys High. I still wasn't sure. The job at the grocery store was important to my family. Basketball was fun, but it wasn't as if I saw it taking me anywhere after high school. I found out later that Tommy talked to Father Mannion, so the priest came to me one day and said, "Why don't you go out for the high-school team?"

That was the last shove I needed to take the plunge. If Father Mannion thought I should do it, why not?

Father Mannion also talked to me about going to college, which sounded about as realistic as going to the moon. We didn't have the money. No one in my family had gone to college. What I needed to do was get my high-school diploma, then get a full-time job.

"You never know," Father Mannion said. "Sometimes, things work out. Just get good grades, so you'll be qualified if you get a chance."

I thought, OK, maybe he means I can work in the daytime and go to night school. That's a possibility.

I played very well for Boys High, but I graduated in January. I had done so well in school that I skipped a semester and graduated early. I couldn't play with the team after January, and I thought that was it for my basketball career. I'd started and had some excellent games; I scored 35 points against Jefferson High and a kid named Tony Jackson, who went on to play at St. John's. I averaged about 20 points, and I sort of surprised myself with how well I played. But I still didn't think about playing college basketball. I had a full-time job at Montgomery Ward. They did a lot of mail-order business, and I filled the orders from the warehouse, packing clothes into boxes. My dream was to save enough money from January to September so that I could go to City College of New York in the fall, and keep working part-time.

To me, high-school basketball was what it should be to 99 percent of the kids playing today: It was fun. It was a way to learn about teamwork, to burn off energy, to make some good friends. It was about hard work, character, and all those other values that are almost dismissed today. It was not about a college scholarship, the NBA lottery, or thinking that the world owes me a living and a college education because I could throw a basketball through a hoop. In a sense, I was blessed to grow up in an era when pro sports didn't rule the consciousness of most high-school athletes. Even college sports seemed out of reach to most of us. The temptation to not study in high school because you thought basketball was all you needed for a meal ticket . . . well, that mentality just didn't exist. I wish it were possible to instill our way of thinking in kids today who sell their souls and their futures for a shot at the NBA. They have a better chance to be struck by lightning or win a state lottery than to be picked in the first round of the NBA draft.

CHAPTER THREE

IN 1956, IT REALLY DID SEEM EASIER to jump to the moon than to go to college, especially for kids from my economic and social background—and especially when you're talking about a private school such as Providence College. Today, a chance at college is a given for many kids. It's expected because their parents often went to college, their friends attended college, and college is a part of life for many Americans as we head into the next century.

I didn't receive a single recruiting letter from a college. Not even a form letter. Not one telephone call from a coach.

Nothing.

After I graduated from Boys High, Father Mannion wrote to Father Bagley, the athletic director at Providence College, recommending me for a basketball scholarship. The letter was passed on to coach Joe Mullaney, and the amazing thing is that he actually read it and eventually checked it out. Father Mannion was not a former player at Providence, not a basketball star anywhere: He was just a priest writing a letter to a Catholic college about a kid he liked. I did have some good games before I graduated, but when I graduated in January it was like I disappeared, dropped off the radar of the college coaches. In 1956, recruiting was not the full-time obsession that it is today at every major basketball program. There were no summer showcase camps, no recruiting magazines touting the top high-school players to college coaches; for the most part, it was done by checking the newspaper stories and word of mouth. Most colleges were lucky to have one full-time assistant coach, not the army with three-piece suits and clipboards that you see today.

I didn't even play basketball in my first three years of high school, then I played only half a season as a senior, so why would any college coach know about me?

Coach Mullaney came to New York to see the Public School Athletic League high-school championship game at Madison Square Garden. Boys High was in the game, so I went to the game to support my ex-teammates. I was introduced to Coach Mullaney, who was very polite: He told me about Providence, and he gave me a school catalogue and an application form. He then invited me to an informal tryout at Chaminade High, which was way out on Long Island. Today, that would never happen: The NCAA prohibits college coaches from having open tryouts with high-school players. I arrived at the gym and saw about two hundred kids. I was shocked, angry, and intimidated—partly because I didn't know a soul. When I finally did get into a game, I was out there with a bunch of guys who should have been named "Heaver." It really was every man for himself. Whoever got the ball, shot it. It wasn't a great situation for a point guard to show what he could do, and I know I didn't play very well.

I did fill out the application to Providence and mailed it in, but I never heard a word. I had given up hope of getting a basketball scholarship.

Meanwhile, I still liked to play. In the spring there were some postseason tournaments for high-school players, and I was eligible. The best was the Flushing YMCA Tournament, and two teams loaded themselves with the best high-school players from New York. Tommy Davis convinced the coach of a team called the Gems that I'd help them, but they decided they had too many guards and cut me.

No one else wanted me. That infuriated me, because I knew I could play with the guys on those teams. I had played against most of them in the summers. But they had played high-school basketball longer than I had, and they had bigger reputations.

One of my old Boys High teammates, Eddie Simmons, also was cut by the Gems, so we decided to form our own team and enter the tournament. We convinced some of our friends from Brooklyn to join us. We won the tournament, beating Dan Palmer's All-Stars, who had defeated the Gems earlier. I scored 32 points and was voted the tournament MVP. We had the worst uniforms in the tournament, some ratty green shirts with holes in them. Joe Mullaney's father was watching that final game, and he sent the small newspaper write-up to his son, along with a note saying that he liked how I played and adding, "This can't be the same kid that Father Mannion wrote about."

Joe Mullaney remembered me from Father Mannion's letter, and also from meeting me at Madison Square Garden. After months of not hearing a word from Providence College, I was accepted in a matter of days and given a full basketball scholarship.

The way it happened still amazes me.

I received a scholarship because Father Mannion cared enough about me to write Joe Mullaney . . . because Joe Mullaney bothered to read the letter . . . because I got mad when the Gems cut me and started my own team . . . because Joe Mullaney's father happened to be in the stands on the day of the championship game, when I happened to play one of the best games of my life.

All of that had to happen for me to end up at Providence College.

And the welfare department had to help, too.

During my senior year in high school, my mother was receiving Aid to Dependent Children. The welfare department had a rule that after a boy passed his seventeenth birthday and graduated from high school, he had to go to work to help support his family or the welfare benefits would be cut off. I didn't find this out until after I received the scholarship from Providence, and suddenly I saw everything crumbling. I couldn't go to college: I was the man of the house, and the law was that the man had to support his family, even if the "man" was only seventeen.

Father Mannion stepped in again. He pleaded for me with the caseworker, telling him that I was a good student, that I had earned a college scholarship, and what that meant to my family. To me, the caseworkers were the people who stopped by our house and made us feel like criminals: They were always checking to make sure we weren't hiding money, or that we didn't have a luxury such as a telephone.

I admit, I was angry with the whole situation. We didn't want to be on welfare. My dad had died. My mother worked. I worked. But we just couldn't earn enough money, and it wasn't like my mother was having kids out of wedlock. But they made us feel as if we were cheating the government.

Father Mannion talked to a caseworker who understood the opportunity presented to me. I just remember him being called "Mr. Walker," and he came to our house to meet with my mother and me. "Lenny," he said, "I'm going to stick my neck out for you. The only sensible thing is for you to attend college so that you can do something positive for your future and your family. You go to college and we'll see to it that your family continues to receive its benefits."

In my first day at Providence College, they brought all the freshmen together in a big hall. One of the speakers told us to look to our right, then look to our left. "Odds are you won't see at least one of those people on campus at the end of the year," he said. "So you better keep your grade averages up."

The message was scary, and it was supposed to be. At Providence, they wanted you to know they were serious about academics. It wasn't like some schools where athletes were assigned cupcake classes designed to keep them eligible; all freshmen took the same basic core courses. That really didn't bother me. I expected to do well in school. I expected to study, and yes, I expected it to be hard. I didn't come to college just to play basketball, and I didn't entertain thoughts of an NBA career for even a second. Freshmen weren't even allowed to play varsity basketball, and that was fine with me: School came first, and basketball was just a way for me to pay for it. I'd make it work. I went to college with that attitude: I would not fail.

I told myself that when I looked around that assembly hall and began counting the black faces. I didn't need many fingers to do it: just seven.

Seven black kids in the entire school. I had attended a grade school that was about 33 percent black. Boys High was about 50 percent black. And now, I was one of seven blacks in four grades of college? A thought struck me: "I've never seen so many white people in my life!"

In my church and neighborhood, there were a lot of white people, but it wasn't like this. I mean, this was a sea of white people. This was nothing but white people. And they were from all over the East Coast. For me, a big trip was to go from Brooklyn to Manhattan. I'd left the New York area only once, and that was to go with some friends to Philadelphia for the Penn Relays during my senior year. Oh, I did go to Providence for a visit before I received my scholarship, but that was it.

So I wasn't exactly a young man of the world. But I was comfortable with the Catholic Church and the priests. Because of Father Mannion, I believed the priests cared about everyone, not just the white students. And because Father Mannion and my mother continually told me that I could make it as a college student, I believed it.

Never underestimate the impact of teachers and other role models. As a senior in high school, I had a history teacher by the name of Mr. Schuler. He was one of those guys who, when he talked to the class, you swore was talking to you and no one else. He made you feel important, because he seemed to be interested not just in his own subject, but in making sure you were fascinated by it, too. He smoked a pipe and wore a sports jacket with patches on the elbows. We thought he was very cool. He often said, "Are you going to settle for what everyone says you can be, or will you go for something more? Will you strive for what you want?"

That meant a lot to me, because again I sensed that Mr. Schuler was speaking right to me and no one else. I know that wasn't the case, but it was how he made me feel. Besides, I knew he liked me, and when a student senses the teacher likes him, the student really responds. It's a natural thing.

If I have any advice for a teacher or coach, it's this: Make your students or players feel special, not by coddling them, but by taking an interest in them, by pushing them the right way, by being demanding without being demeaning.

That was Mr. Schuler, and that was every good teacher and coach I ever had.

So I went to Providence with a lot of confidence.

But I also had a choice.

When you're a minority, you can either spend your time with your guard up, ready to be insulted and prepared to use that as an excuse to fail, or you can be determined to show people you're as good as anyone else. It's really that simple: You prepare yourself for failure or for success.

I was not about to fail.

What I remember most from my first day of school was logic class. The teacher was Father Heath, a gruff-looking Dominican priest who immediately wanted us to know he was in charge of the class, and he was not about to tolerate anyone who felt like playing the part of a fool.

He passed out cards and had us fill out our names and some other information. He collected the cards and said he'd use them to learn our names.

He stood in front of the class, shuffling through the cards. It was so quiet, you could hear his fingers going through the cards.

"Mr. Wilkens!" he roared.

Maybe he didn't yell, but it seemed like it to me. He had a gravel voice. He was a hulking six-foot-four. You had a feeling that if he ever smiled, his face would crack. And the last thing I expected was for him to call my name. I stood up, and I tried to keep my heart from pounding its way through my chest. I felt like my knees were shaking. My throat was dry. I looked around and saw all these white faces staring at me.

I was the only black in the class.

Then Father Heath called out another name: "Mr. Whalen!"

Dick Whalen stood up, no more happy about it than I.

"Now listen to me," he said. "Mr. Wilkens and Mr. Whalen, you are basketball players. I do not like athletes in general, and basketball players in particular. I just want you to understand that. So don't you cut my class. Don't even dare to think about cutting my class. Do you gentlemen understand that?"

We both nodded.

"Good. You may sit down," he said.

You can tell these were the old days, before athletic departments were manned by an army of tutors who helped the athletes with their schedules and steered them away from teachers such as Father Heath who may have had a problem with athletes. And Father Heath was aware of who the athletes were in class because Providence was a relatively small school, and it was no secret who the new basketball recruits were, because basketball was the most popular sport on campus.

As it turned out, Father Heath had no problem with me. I made it simple. I went to class, I handed in my work. I got a B.

Dick Whalen cut a couple of classes. He flunked and had to take the course again in summer school.

But it really came down to a matter of choices. I could have decided that Father Heath was picking on me because I was a black athlete, or at least because I was an athlete—since Dick Whalen also was singled out, and he was white. I could have decided, "This guy will never give me a break, he's gunning for me."

Instead, I was going to show him that I could do the work, that I wasn't in school just to play basketball. That's something else missing with a lot of athletes today. Instead of viewing the scholarship as a ticket to a free education, it's supposed to be a free ride to the NBA. Classes are just something they have to do in order to stay eligible, not to earn a degree and plan a career. When I enrolled at Providence, I had no hoop dreams. I had never even seen an NBA game. Honest! Not one! There were few NBA games on TV in the 1950s and I never went to a Knicks game. I loved basketball, but I never imagined that it would become my life. The NBA wasn't something my teammates talked about. It may seem outrageous in today's culture, but we were all there to get an education. You hear people say, "I never got a chance," and in some cases, it's true. But often, they don't recognize their chance when it comes along. I could have rejected Father Mannion's guidance. I wasn't the only kid he advised, and not all of them listened to him. I could have said, "He's just a priest, what does he know?" We can always find a reason not to do something that's good for us. If we continually battle authority, we often don't see the doors that open for us—because we don't take the time to listen to those who want to lead us in the right direction. I made it a habit to listen to what most adults had to say, and then at least think about it.

Another temptation would have been to approach college with the idea of just doing enough to walk away with some sort of degree, not really challenging myself in the classroom because it would take away from my basketball. Instead, I decided to major in economics.

That was fine with my mother, because it sounded like a course of study that would lead to a good job in business. But my mother really wanted me to be a priest. Even though I admired Father Mannion, I didn't want to spend my life working in a parish. I loved the church, but thought I could serve it in another way. Eventually, I wanted to get married and have a family.

I thought about being a doctor, which my mother also would have loved, but I wasn't passionate about it. And, I admit, this is where I ran into a conflict with basketball. In the premed courses, there were a lot of laboratories in the afternoon, which would conflict with basketball practice. More and more I leaned to economics. I had worked most of my life, and I knew what it was like not to have any money. I wanted to make a decent living, and I wanted to know how to handle money. Economics seemed like the perfect major. In my first economics class, I had a priest named Father Quirk as a teacher. He would call on most of the kids, but kept skipping a few of us. He never called on a kid named Ray Weber or myself, and we were both basketball players. He didn't call on Ray Labie, a hockey player. I began to see the pattern: Because we were athletes, he didn't think we knew the answer. That really upset me, so I raised my hand.

"Yes, Mr. Wilkens," he said.

"How come you skipped me?" I demanded. "I know the answer."

He laughed. Then the class laughed. Then I started to laugh.

"OK," he said. "What's the answer?"

I gave him the answer.

After that, he treated me like any other student, and I really

wanted to be a part of that class because economics was my major. I
didn't want to just sit in the back, vegetate, and get a passing grade.

The next year, I was on the varsity basketball team. We had a
road game, and when I got back, I had a theology test. The teacher
wanted to give me an extra day to study.

"No," I said. "I'll take the test with everyone else. I prepared
for it. I took my books and I studied on the road. I'm ready."

The teacher couldn't believe it, but I didn't want any special attention. I didn't want to be treated like an athlete. I wanted to show
I could compete with every kid in that college; all I needed was a fair
opportunity. I was going to be the first member of my family to earn
a degree, and I wanted a degree that would lead to a good job so I
could take care of my family. I was driven by that. Never again
would there be a day when I opened the icebox, and it was empty—
as was the case more than once in my youth.

Once when I was still in high school, Father Mannion took me
to dinner at a place called the St. George Hotel. I had been sick and
lost some weight, and Father Mannion wanted me to have a really
good meal at a place where I'd never been. This was a special restaurant, white linen tablecloths, silverware all polished and glittering
in the lights from the elaborate glass chandeliers. There were hard
rolls, which I had never tasted before; salad forks, which I had never
seen before. Because we were poor, we never went to a restaurant, at
least not like this. I felt like I was in a Cary Grant movie. Father
Mannion wanted me to see the place, to see how other people lived.
I was a little intimidated, but I also liked it. I wanted a life where I
could afford to eat at places like the St. George Hotel, and I knew
college could get me there. Not basketball—college. A degree.

At Providence, they posted everyone's grades by the Dean's
Office. Good or bad, your name and your grade point average were
up there. My goal was to stay in the top third of my class, because
that was the Dean's List. I wanted everyone to see my name up
there high, and I usually made it.

As I mentioned, Providence was a very white school.

In the freshman class of about three hundred young men, the
only blacks were a kid named John Woods and myself. We were

roommates, and John has gone on to become an executive with a major corporation.

John and I went to a dance with two other white guys. There was a black girl there. John danced with her, then I danced with her. Soon, I was dancing with other girls—white girls. I didn't think twice about it because it wasn't uncommon for me to dance with white girls in high school. Anyway, some of the other white guys at the party started giving me looks and whispering things. This had never happened to me before. I was so naive, I had no idea what was going on.

One of the white guys with us, Jack Bagshaw, confronted some of the bigots. I still didn't have a clue what was happening, until he shoved one of them. I walked over, and everything just stopped. I mean, it died. No one said a word until later, and that upset me— although I really appreciated Jack Bagshaw standing up for me, and we're still close friends today.

A lot of the students went home on weekends, but I didn't have any money, so I stayed. It could be pretty lonely. I rarely called any-one because I didn't have the money for that, either. I was a minor-ity within a minority: Not only was I black, I was poor in a school where the vast majority of the students were at least middle class, if not wealthier. I worked in the cafeteria, which was really a dining hall with the meals served family style. I waited tables. Some people would have gotten hung up on that, feeling like a servant at their own college; to me, it was just another job, a way to pay my college expenses.

I made friends with a priest named Father St. George, who taught French and was head of the Glee Club. When no one was around, he'd shoot baskets with me. He also loved to eat out, and Fa-ther St. George took me to some really nice restaurants. From him, I figured out some of the things I liked to eat and how to conduct myself in that kind of setting. He also had a taste for opera: He loved Maria Callas, and to this day, when I hear her voice, I think of Father St. George.

At Providence College, I had very few racial problems. I was ac-cepted, even voted senior class treasurer. Once I got used to being in such a small minority, I didn't think about the racial composition of the school very often. The teachers and students also were very accepting of me, because I did my work and I didn't complain. I wasn't trying to prove any point about race; I was just doing what I was taught. I knew that if I produced, race wouldn't be the kind of roadblock that could stop me.

But I remember little things, like once going off campus to church with a teammate. We were in a small Massachusetts town. During the Mass, the guy passing around the collection plate skipped right over me. Was it because I was black, and he figured I didn't have any money? Or wasn't my money good enough? Was my money black? A lot of things like that ran through my head. But I tried not to dwell on it, or it would eat me up.

I dated this Italian girl. Her father was a huge Providence basketball fan, and he really liked how I played the game. Then he found out that his daughter was dating me. Instead of coming to me, he went to one of the Dominican fathers. The priest called me in, and the conversation is something that bothers me to this day.

The priest started telling me about this man being a friend of his, and how he had a daughter . . . and how he heard I was dating the daughter . . . and how, maybe, I should . . . you know, kind of think about it, about her being Italian and me being . . . you know, what I was.

I was stunned.

This was a priest, a man of God. He was supposed to know better, to judge all men as Jesus would judge them, that all men are equal before the eyes of God.

"Father," I said. "How can you say that? Does God see the color of a person's skin? You teach God's word, right?"

The priest retreated. He said I didn't quite understand. But of course I understood. I was black. The girl was Italian. Her father was the priest's friend. This was the late 1950s, and blacks weren't supposed to date Italians—not even if I was a good student and a star basketball player. On a spiritual level, it was hard for me to accept this. That's why what the priest said hurt. Of all people, a priest should know better. But a priest is also a human being, and human beings sometimes don't see the world as they should, even if they are priests. That's not a reflection on God; it's just that they are people who are flawed in some areas.

Eventually, I broke off the relationship with the girl. I liked her, but I knew that we didn't have the kind of love that would lead to marriage. Her father tried to make her stop dating me, and I'm sure she received pressure from other people, but she was willing to hang in there. I decided it was best for us to stop going out. Why put her through all that? I didn't look at it as giving in to her father, but rather sparing her from problems—and doing that out of respect for her.

I found that the vast majority of people at Providence were very accepting and wanted to help me reach my goals, in the classroom and on the court. I played well on the freshman basketball team, averaging about 20 points. So did the other guard, and I remember that this kid was a lot more interested in basketball than school. His English professor told me, "Tell your All-American buddy that if he doesn't start showing up for class, he'll be bounced right out of here."

The kid still cut classes, and he left school in the middle of his sophomore year—so they did take academics seriously at Providence, because that kid was a good player.

After my freshman year, I worked for the Domino Sugar Company on the docks in Brooklyn. My job was to load sixty-pound and hundred-pound bags of sugar onto railroad cars and trucks. It was grueling, and I weighed only 160 pounds myself at the time. One summer of that was enough. The rest of the time I was at Providence, my summer job was at a knitting mill loading boxes of sweaters, which also wasn't easy—unless you compared it to bags of sugar.

I realize now how different my college experience was from that of the kids who now play major college basketball. Granted, some of them are after an education, and some of them work very hard—but those kids have become the exception, while I was the norm for those of us who went to school in the 1950s and early 1960s. We spent our college years preparing for a whole life, not for a game that, if we were incredibly lucky, we'd only get to play for a little while.

CHAPTER FOUR

By THE END OF MY PLAYING DAYS at Providence, I thought that I was going to be an economics professor. Don't misunderstand: I was a good player and I knew it. I loved basketball, especially when my team won. I loved having the ball in my hands during a big game when the crowd was screaming, the score was close, and the clock was ticking down. I took just as much satisfaction from setting up one of my teammates for a winning basket as I did from scoring it myself.

I wasn't obsessed with being a pro basketball player, but the game was important to me, especially when the game was played right. I played four years of basketball at Providence, and I never dunked. Not even once. Not even in practice. You just didn't dunk at Providence in the late 1950s. Our coach, Joe Mullaney, considered it a hot-dog play. So did most other coaches.

Even though I was only five-foot-eleven when I enrolled at Providence, I could dunk a basketball. I had done it in high school: not in a game—that was considered showing up the other team— but I did it before practice, when some of us were messing around in the gym. I didn't think my hands were big enough to cup the basketball and jam it through the rim, but after a couple of tries, it happened. I jumped as high as I could, my hands soaring above the rim, and suddenly, I just threw the ball down.

Just like that, a dunk. It was fun. Some guys whistled and shouted and we all had a great time. But I never considered dunking an important part of the game. In the late 1950s, the accent was on outside shooting, on passing, on moving without the ball, catching the defense napping, then breaking to the rim just in time to catch a pass and gently lay the ball off the backboard and into the net.

Two beautiful points.

I fell in love with basketball as if it were ballet. I loved the smooth movements of all the players, and I was fascinated by how it all came together. The passing. The ball moving from one player's hands to the next. The player moving from one spot on the court to another, setting a pick to free a teammate for an open shot.

Then the pass.

That was my favorite part of basketball, throwing the perfect pass that led to two points for someone else. Sure, there were games where they needed me to score, especially in important games against good teams; on those nights, I went for 20 or 25 points, especially against a guy who was considered better or had a bigger reputation. I had to relish that. Part of what drove me to excel on the court at Providence is that I really came to that school with no reputation and few expectations, yet I started every game.

When I was at Providence, freshmen were not allowed to play varsity basketball. It was a good rule then, and it would be a good rule now. It enabled an eighteen-year-old to concentrate on his studies, to adjust to campus life and actually spend some time in the library, without being under the pressure to produce immediately on the court at the varsity level. Today such a rule would eliminate a lot of traveling (and missed classes) that come with playing big-time college basketball, where holiday tournaments are held everywhere from Alaska to Hawaii to New York. Making freshmen ineligible for varsity basketball wouldn't hurt their development as players: They'd still be practicing, and they could even practice against the varsity. We did that at Providence, until our freshman team began to beat them in a scrimmage. Suddenly, the coach thought that wasn't good for the varsity's confidence, and the scrimmages stopped.

But a freshman basketball player can practice, lift weights, condition, play in games against freshmen teams from other schools. He just doesn't have to do it at the varsity level. He can learn from his mistakes without those blunders being seen on national TV. He can learn a little humility from having to sit and watch the varsity play. He can learn that the earth and sun and planets don't revolve around him.

Most of our gifted young athletes know very little about patience. They're constantly made to feel as if they're a member of a privileged class, royalty in Nikes. Adults want to give them things, to curry their favor. And the kids want what they want when they want it—and they want it yesterday. Immediate gratification isn't fast enough. I'm speaking in generalities of course; a number of young men have solid values and don't fall into this trap, but it's a snare that grabs many kids—and their parents. When I was fourteen years old I was dribbling around those chairs in the Holy Rosary gym, and I was coaching the girls team. Today, fourteen-year-old basketball players are already being recruited. Some are receiving letters from colleges. Think about that, about being a freshman in high school and finding a letter from a school such as UCLA, Ohio State, or St. John's in your mailbox. What would that do to your head? Imagine being the high-school coach trying to discipline this young man.

At fourteen, the top amateur players these days compete on summer teams that travel all over the country for tournaments in places such as Las Vegas, Chicago, and New York. They're recruited to play at different summer basketball camps run by the top shoe companies—and that leads to more travel around the country. They're often recruited by different high-school coaches, although the high-school coaches deny this. Many of our current NBA players attended more than one high school or college. They didn't have money, but they had beepers, cell phones, and jewelry. Where did that come from? Some of the summer teams in New York and other big cities are sponsored by agents. Some of these kids come from messed-up home situations, and they end up on the street with the wrong people because those people are willing to slip them money in exchange for hanging around with a kid who may be a star one day. They may not be giving the kids drugs, but they're exposing them to a lifestyle these kids aren't ready to handle. The player's entire focus is on a pro contract. I'm not knocking the kids, I'm just saying they're products of a system that often corrupts them, especially if they don't have strong parents or some other relatives in the picture.

So here is the situation: The best high-school players are constantly being recruited by summer league coaches, by high-school coaches, by college coaches, by summer camps, and by renegade adults who want to be their agents. None of this is healthy psychologically, nor does it lead to making the kids better players. Too often, they aren't coached in the fundamentals of the game, because no one wants to get in their faces and tell them what they can't do. They worship at the shrine of the dunk, which is a symbol of how the game has changed. At Providence, Joe Mullaney hated the dunk because he thought it took away from team play, put too much emphasis on the individual. There are times when a dunk is a good play, a strong, powerful statement when it occurs as a player is trying to score inside while an opponent attempts to block the shot. In that situation, the dunk may even be the best possible play. But we have guys who seem to be auditioning for the Slam Dunk Contest on breakaway layups, twirling and spinning and making their bid to appear on ESPN Sportscenter. The kids see this, and they imitate it. I modeled my game after the older, team-oriented athletes whom I played against on the New York asphalt, and so it's natural that the kids of today would take after what they see on TV, especially ESPN. But the game isn't highlights, and a brief clip rarely shows team basketball. It usually features players doing something like a dunk to draw attention to themselves. And some coaches of high-school and college players don't want to demand too much because the player might quit and take his talent elsewhere. This is especially true if the coach is inexperienced, or at a school that hasn't had a winning reputation.

I think about a player like J. R. Rider, whom I had in my last year with the Atlanta Hawks. He is a wonderfully talented but confused young man. He attended two junior colleges and Nevada–Las Vegas. That's three colleges in four years. He played in the NBA for three years in Minnesota, three in Portland, then got cut near the end of his first season with Atlanta. He was virtually uncoachable. He felt no connection to his team or his teammates. He wanted to do things his way, because he had always been allowed to do so. Fines meant nothing; he just wrote the checks. He figured some team, some coach, would always want a guy who could score 20 points a game, even if that player didn't feel like showing up on time or passing the ball. The keys in my life were hard work, discipline, a strong spiritual life, and an accent on academics. For me, basketball was a way to a free college education, which was enough of a winning lottery ticket for me and my family. The bouncing ball was not my heartbeat; if I'd had to, I could have lived without it. Rider and many young players of today would have no idea what I'm talking about when I say I had no problem playing on the freshman team, even though I knew I was good enough to start for the varsity.

Too many kids pick their college with one thing in mind: How quickly can that school get me to the NBA? What they need is to wait a little bit, to let their minds and their maturity level catch up with their basketball skills. Too many kids enroll in a college, don't get as much playing time as they think they should as a freshman— and they transfer. Sometimes they attend two or three different schools, becoming basketball gypsies. They play for too many different coaches. They don't develop an identity with a school, any real sense of being part of a team. All that switching around reinforces their "Me First" mentality, which is not good in basketball or life. Furthermore, kids lose credits when they transfer, so they often leave school without a degree. And how many young men actually have a significant NBA career? Not more than twenty-five each year, and that's probably being very generous.

If these young people had a year of freshman ball that virtually guaranteed them plenty of minutes in a less-pressured setting where they could work on their basketball and their schoolwork at the same time, it wouldn't end all the corruption that comes from the summer leagues and some high-school situations, but making freshmen ineligible for the varsity would cut down on the number of kids transferring, help academics, and slow the frenzy about a career in the NBA.

I say all this as someone who averaged 21 points as a freshman while our team had a 23–0 record. We were good enough to beat the varsity, but I didn't feel cheated being on the freshman team. I waited, and in my first varsity game, I scored 18 as we beat Fairfield, 80–63.

The story in the Providence newspaper read, "Wilkens starred defensively throughout the fray, constantly harassing the Bridgeport Jesuit school's guards and tying up their offense."

You can say they don't write sports like that anymore, and we're all probably better off for it. As a sophomore, I led our team in scoring, and I was the only sophomore selected to the Eastern Conference Athletic Conference (ECAC) All-Conference team.

In our junior year, we added a player named Johnny Egan, who was a High-School All-American, highly recruited, and the first guy I heard talk about the NBA. Supposedly, the Celtics wanted him. I was established as the star of the team when Johnny joined it, yet he received far more publicity. If I wanted to, I could have let that become a problem between us. Instead, I kept an open mind when it came to Johnny. I found that I liked him personally, that he wanted to win as much as I did. We formed a terrific backcourt. I didn't worry that Johnny would get more shots or more hype; I didn't worry about having to share some of the limelight, or share the ball. I wanted our team to receive a bid to the National Invitational Tournament, which was bigger than the NCAA tournament back then since every game was in New York. This was an era when teams didn't travel coast-to-coast as often as they do today; The Garden was still considered a basketball mecca, and it was where every college basketball player wanted to play at least once in his life. Furthermore, the New York media dominated the country even more than they do today, so the NIT was a great place to get "discovered."

I really wanted to play in front of the fans from my hometown. When we made the tournament, we beat Manhattan College in our first game, then followed it up with a double-overtime victory over St. Louis. The New York media found me in that game.

Louis Effrat wrote in *The New York Times:* "Pandemonium followed the buzzer that ended the marathon. Those Providence players who were not lifted on shoulders were knocked down by numerous fans. Hats, eyeglasses and St. Patrick's Day flowers were flying all over the Garden, and the special police and ushers had no chance to check the rush. . . . The most credit for cutting the Missouri Valley team down to size must go to Leonard Wilkens, a 6-foot-1 junior from Brooklyn Boys High. Aside from his 30 points, Wilkens' alertness, his ballhandling and his steadying influence paid off in the end."

Gene Roswell wrote in the *New York Post:* "Len Wilkens, a defensive genius, has a simple basketball philosophy, 'Never let the other fellow's right hand know what your left hand is doing.' By actual count, Wilkens made 15 steals and so many deflections the Providence statistician stopped recording after he passed 18 in the first half."

St. Louis was the top seed in the tournament, which is why that victory was so impressive to the New York media. When I fouled out of the game with 1:05 left in the second overtime, I received a thunderous standing ovation, which meant a lot to me because it was in New York and my family and Father Mannion were at the game. We didn't win the NIT, but I had been noticed in the media capital of the world. Providence also received a tremendous amount of publicity from the NIT. Over seven thousand of our fans had followed us to New York. When we bused back to Providence, fans started cheering and waving at us from the Rhode Island state line all the way to the campus. We received an escort from the Rhode Island state police. It was a wonderful experience, and it let us know that something very special had happened with our basketball team.

Yet I still wasn't thinking about the NBA.

In my senior year, we lost only four games. I was being called a defensive specialist. One of my best games saw me hold a guy named Al Butler to 11 points; Butler was the leading scorer in the country at the time. We returned to the NIT, but we lost in the finals to Bradley, which had a great forward named Chet Walker who later became a star with the Chicago Bulls. Even though we lost, I was voted the tournament MVP. In the regular season, I averaged about 14 points. In the NIT, that went up to about 25 per game.

When my college career was over, I was the second-highest scorer in school history. But I was known more for my defense, my rebounding, and my ballhandling. I had grown to be six-foot-one and 180 pounds. In some ways, I felt I was underrated. I played for Joe Mullaney, an interesting guy who could balance three broomsticks—one on each hand, and one on his nose!—and could juggle three basketballs at once. During games he would pace back and forth, howling at the moon (or at least the officials), and seemed ready to pull out his hair. He was an entertaining guy to be around. I knew he appreciated me, but I was like most players—I thought I was a little better than the coach did, or at least better than I thought the coach considered me. Maybe I was just being too sensitive because I wasn't recruited out of high school, and then saw other guys come to Providence with a lot more hype and a lot less talent than I had. If nothing else, that kept me from getting a swelled head, and I learned a lot of basketball from Joe Mullaney. He was far ahead of some of my first NBA coaches. Coach Mullaney emphasized double-teaming and trapping defenses, something seldom seen in the NBA of the early 1960s. He had far more complex offensive schemes than the pros. And he even used a blackboard for his Xs and Os! You'll find this hard to believe, but I don't remember a single time in my early NBA years when a coach wrote on a blackboard: We just scrimmaged, or practiced shooting on our own. Defense was strictly man-to-man, with little help coming from a teammate. Coach Mullaney gave us a graduate course in basketball, and in some ways, going to the NBA felt like I had returned to elementary school, at least in terms of strategy.

After the season, I was invited to play in the East/West All-Star Game, which was a big deal. All of the best college seniors were invited, and they all accepted the invitation because they knew all the pro teams scouted the All-Star game very seriously. Today, most of the top college players turn down a chance to play in the various All-Star games, believing it will do nothing but hurt their stock in the NBA draft. But in 1960, scouting was so primitive that you could have a good career at a school in the Midwest or on the West Coast and maybe never be scouted, or just be seen once. Very few games were on TV, so there was little film on players—just the opposite of today. A kid who plays at a top program such as Duke has virtually every game on some cable or network channel, and NBA teams hire video coordinators who do nothing but put together tapes of the top players. Teams will have tapes of some kids playing in as many as twenty-five games, in addition to all the scouts who've seen them play live. That's why a top pick today can say, "I don't need to play in an All-Star game, you've seen me enough already."

In 1960, every top college player wanted exposure. At the East/West games, I was transferred into another world. These guys were talking about NBA careers, and a few were every bit as obsessed with it as the kids are today. They constantly talked about what teams might draft them, who coached those teams, who played on those teams, and how they'd fit into those teams. I also was careful not to say anything because I didn't want the other players to realize how little I knew about the NBA. I played on the same team with Jerry West, who had been a star at West Virginia. The word was that West would play for the Lakers, who had just hired his college coach, Fred Schaus, as their new coach. West and I were named co-MVPs of the game, which meant a lot since Oscar Robertson was on the other team and Oscar was one of the greatest players—ever.

What I really wanted out of that game was an invitation to travel to Denver for the tryouts for the 1960 Olympic team. There were twenty-four players going to Denver for the Olympic trials, and the Olympic people were going to base their decision for some of the spots on who played well in the game. Since I was co-MVP with Jerry West, I assumed I would be on my way to the tryouts: Our team had won, 67–66, and as I recall, I scored my team's final eight points. I had 18 points, West had 23.

West went, I didn't.

I found out that they were taking publicity pictures of the players whom the Olympic Committee wanted on the team the day before the game. The committee had a much stronger say over the composition of the roster than coach Pete Newell, as I later learned. They had already made up their minds before the game and had lied to us. I had received a letter saying the game would have a tremendous bearing upon the makeup of the Olympic team, so this wasn't just something from my imagination. I had outplayed three or four guys in that game who were picked over me—and I knew I was a better player than they were. To me, the Olympics were huge. I wanted to represent my country. I had taken part in the ROTC program in college. During my senior year, my basketball goal wasn't the NBA, it was the Olympics.

That's why I was so upset when the final decision was made. It was a scam, and it was hard for me not to believe race played a part in it. I know several blacks were selected—Oscar Robertson, Bob Boozer, and Walt Bellamy—but I also think they were worried about the black/white ratio on the team. One kid was invited to Denver who scored something like four points in the East/West game. How could they explain that? He came from a smaller basketball school, he didn't play nearly as well as I did, yet he made it, and I didn't. He was white, I'm black. There are very few things in this life that I *really* wanted, at least when it came to basketball, but the Olympics was one of those. Pete Newell coached the team, and later he told me that he wanted me on the roster. I believe him. I was an unselfish point guard who made his reputation as a defensive player; I would have been a perfect fit for a team full of high-scoring stars. Pete Newell knew that, and I have a newspaper clipping from 1960 where Newell said, "Wilkens is terrific, I don't know why he wasn't named to the team."

Down deep, I knew, and it was like a dagger to my heart. There was a lot of politics involved, and the Olympic coach really had little say in picking his own team. I think they were worried that there would be too many black players on the Olympic team, too many blacks on the world stage, so they enforced an unofficial quota, and I was one of the victims. There also was a bias toward players from the Industrial Leagues, most of whom were white and seemed to be assured of spots on the team.

I was named an alternate for the team. While Pete Newell had Oscar Robertson and Jerry West, he wanted me to be the point guard because both West and Robertson had played a lot of forward in college. I tried not to believe that race was behind the decision, but there was no other explanation; when I looked at some of the other guys on that team—Jay Arnett, Adrian Smith, Les Lane, and

Allen Kelley, all white players—I could come to no other conclusion.

This was the first time in my life that I believed I had been held back because of the color of my skin. They still could have invited me to the trials. *The New York Times* wrote a scathing story on the slight by the Olympic team, and coaches such as Joe Lapchick (St. John's), Gene Smith (Cincinnati), Ned Irish, and Frank McGuire (North Carolina) endorsed me, yet nothing happened. Eleven players from the East/West game were invited to the trials, but the co-MVP was not. So I stayed home, and I couldn't even think about the Olympics without having a sick feeling for some thirty-two years, not until the 1992 dream team.

On the day of the 1960 NBA draft, I was in class.

I wasn't in New York at an NBA draft party that would be carried on TV. I wasn't in a fancy hotel suite with an agent. I hadn't just spent months trying to figure out what team would draft me, nor had I been traveling cross-country, meeting with one group of NBA executives after another, being interviewed and working out so they could get to know me and decide if I was right for their team.

I didn't have an agent. This was 1960, and no one had an agent. The NBA of 1960 wasn't considered the meal ticket for an entire family. It was the best basketball league in the world, but few people knew it. The Boston Celtics had one of the greatest teams the world had ever seen, yet they didn't sell out Boston Garden. Few NBA teams sold out.

The games weren't played in luxurious arenas with corporate boxes with wine and cheese and caviar served to the prime customers. They were often found in something called an "armory," an old barn of a building that smelled of stale cigar smoke, spilled beer, and hot dogs on the grill. Those places were dark, and felt like a great place for a boxing match, which often was the big moneymaker for those old buildings. The NBA of 1960 wasn't the big business that it is today. In most cities, it was number three in the minds of sports fans—behind baseball and football. In some cases it was fourth, as a lot of people also loved and followed boxing. The game was great, but the money was small, the exposure minimal, and there was no reason to believe that was going to change.

I had returned to school after the East/West game and graduated in June 1960 with a B average and a degree in economics. I was treasurer of the senior class, a perfect job for an economics major. I was vice-president of the Cadet Officers Honor Corps, which was an elite branch of the ROTC. I was also on the honor roll and was listed among Who's Who for college seniors that year. Father Charles Quick was the head of the Economics Department, and he said he could get me an assistantship at Boston College, where I could earn my Master's in economics and teach undergraduate courses to help pay for my tuition. His grand plan was for me to return to Providence as an economics professor. My specialty was money and banking. I read *The Wall Street Journal* every day. I wanted to know how money was made, how corporations worked, and why some businesses were successful while others failed. I loved economics, and the thought of teaching it was enticing.

Then I was drafted by the St. Louis Hawks.

As I think back, I remember meeting a guy named Marty Blake during the NIT in New York. I talked to him in a hotel lobby for maybe five minutes. There were a bunch of people around, and frankly, I didn't catch his name or what position he held. Later, I'd learn he was a scout for the Hawks.

My only other NBA contact came from Carl Braun, who was with the New York Knicks. He called a few days before the draft to say that the Knicks liked me, but not enough to take me in the first round. If I was still available, New York would make me its second-round choice, because they were going to take Darrall Imhoff with their first pick. I didn't even know who Imhoff was, so that conversation meant little to me.

All I know is that on the day of the draft, I was sitting in a class when I received word to report to the Athletic Department. On my way to the gym, a couple of students said, "Congratulations," but I didn't know what for. I had forgotten that this was the day of the NBA draft.

Can you imagine a top college senior player saying that today?

When I arrived at the gym, Joe Mullaney and Father Begley

(the athletic director) told me that I was the first pick of the St. Louis Hawks. They said a couple of local newspaper reporters wanted to interview me. I don't recall what I said, because the NBA still wasn't in my plans; I was pretty bitter about basketball after the Olympic fiasco, and I knew absolutely nothing about the St. Louis Hawks. I couldn't name their coach or a single player. People don't believe me, but at this point in my life, I had yet to even watch an NBA game.

I realize this sounds very strange today. Even after I was drafted, I still wasn't thinking about the NBA. The Hawks invited me to visit them in St. Louis during my spring break, but I turned them down because one of my Providence teammates was getting married, and I was his best man. That wedding was more important to me than whatever the Hawks had to say.

I was still planning to teach economics.

Today's NBA draft is like the Academy Awards for these kids. They dress up in a new suit. They have family, friends, agents, and other members of their "entourage" at their side. Their names are called. They come to the front of the stage. People cheer. They are given a cap with the name of the team that drafted them. Their mothers and sisters are crying. Their agents are rubbing their hands, their eyes flashing dollar signs. It's what a college commencement ceremony should be like, or maybe the Nobel Prize luncheon. But really, what have they done? They have yet to play a pro game.

It's totally overblown, and it leads some young players to having a wildly inflated view of themselves once they come to the NBA. They have the contract, the millions in bonus money, the cars, the house, the agent—and they've yet to play a pro game! It takes an exceptional individual to keep his hunger and his willingness to be coached after all that. The great ones can do that; they refuse to let the money and the other off-court trappings corrupt their games and their desire. But many kids just don't have the strength of character to handle all the temptations, to realize that because they've suddenly become millionaires, they still have much to learn. If you don't think so, then why do some rookies report to training camp so out of shape? Would they do that if their contracts weren't guaranteed? I doubt it. Hey, it's hard to keep working when you're handed a million bucks at the age of twenty-one, and the contract says the millions are guaranteed to keep coming over the next three years.

Not long after I was drafted by the Hawks, I was approached by Technical Tape, a company in New York that made tape, but that also had a basketball team in the Industrial League. This was a relatively big deal back in 1960, as companies such as Goodyear, Phillips 66, and others sponsored basketball teams. They signed top college players to work in their public-relations departments and play for their teams.

In 1960, there were only eight NBA teams, so there were plenty of talented players available and a number of sizable cities without pro basketball. That was where the Industrial League came into play. Technical Tape had a couple of players from my old Brooklyn neighborhood, including a kid named Jim Daniels whom I knew. The coach of the Technical Tape Corporation, which was known as the Tech Y Tapers, visited me in Providence. His name was Stan Stutz, and he wanted me to play for him. He asked me to go to dinner with him. Since I didn't know Stan, I asked a Providence teammate of mine to come along, sort of to help me feel at ease. The teammate said he'd come if we could get tickets to the Celtics game. I mentioned this, and Stutz secured the tickets. It turned out that the game at Boston Garden was against St. Louis in the NBA Finals. It was the first time I ever saw NBA players. I had a chance to watch St. Louis, especially the Hawks guards. They had Slater Martin, a great player who was getting ready to retire. The other guards were people such as Si Green, Johnny McCarthy, and Al Ferrari.

I was watching that game and thinking, "I'm at least as good as those guys, probably better. They don't shoot real well. They're not real quick. They don't run a team well at all."

As the game went on, I started to think that maybe I should give the NBA a try. That was on my mind when Stan Stutz talked to me after the game, telling me about Technical Tape and how he could offer me something like $9,500 to work and play ball for them.

I still had no real interest in Technical Tape, but seeing that game had opened my eyes to the NBA.

A few days after, I received a call from Ed Macauley, who was the general manager of the Hawks. He said he'd be in Providence the next day, and wanted to meet with me at the downtown Biltmore Hotel. He offered me $7,000 to sign. Then it was $7,500. I was twenty-one years old, I didn't have an agent, and I didn't have a father. My coach said he didn't know much about the NBA, so if I was interested in the NBA, I'd have to handle the contract talks myself.

I didn't know the market value, but I thought $7,000 and then $7,500 was low—and I told them so. Then I said, $8,000—and they agreed.

I thought about the $8,000, and I thought about the St. Louis guards. I knew that the Hawks needed me, because they were so weak in the backcourt. My economist-trained mind also said:

1. Most accountants start at $6,600 a year.
2. Most economists start at $6,000.
3. I was being offered $8,000 to play basketball, which was something I really enjoyed doing. The Hawks had a couple of great forwards in Bob Pettit and Cliff Hagan, and I'd play with them. I decided to sign with the Hawks, but I wanted a better deal. I asked for a $1,500 signing bonus in addition to the $8,000 salary. I told the Hawks that I had been offered $9,500 by Technical Tape.

They agreed to the bonus.

Then I said, "I want a no-cut contract."

They said, "You want what? We never heard of such a thing."

I said, "A no-cut contract. Even if you cut me, I still get paid."

I was surprised, but Ed Macauley also agreed to that. I later realized Macauley couldn't wait to get my signature on that contract, because I had sold myself short: Most first-rounders were getting $10,000 to $12,000, and Oscar Robertson supposedly signed for $15,000. I knew very little about the NBA. St. Louis had won four Western Division titles without me. I worried that if I asked for too much, they'd decide they didn't need me—and suddenly, what I wanted to do more than anything else was play pro ball. But I also had some doubts. Maybe I wasn't as good as I thought. Put yourself in my position: I was making the first business deal of my life. I was totally overmatched. Later, Ed Macauley would admit that I was one of the easiest players he ever signed.

But at the time, I didn't know that. I took my $1,500 bonus check and put it in the bank. A few months later, I used some of the money to buy a car—my first real car. It was hardly like the Mercedeses and Corvettes driven by rookies today. It was a 1959 Chevy Impala convertible with a white body and a black roof. I got it cut-rate from a dealer in Providence who was a big fan of our team. I had been driving—get this!—a 1939 green Plymouth. The thing was nearly twenty years old, and I poured oil in it about every time I put in gas. I bought it for $100 so I had something to drive while in college.

Now I could afford a car that would get me all the way to St. Louis. If I'd had any inkling of what I'd find when I got there, the car would have been the least of my concerns.

CHAPTER FIVE

IT WASN'T UNTIL I BECAME A PRO basketball player that I really felt the true slap of discrimination right across my face.

In my rookie year with the St. Louis Hawks, there was only one other black veteran on the team, a guard named Sihugo Green. There were a few other black rookies in training camp. Green wasn't with us on this day when we walked into a greasy spoon for lunch. The place was a dive; they should have been glad to see anyone come through the door, regardless of color, as long as their money was green.

A white player named Rolland Todd was with us. We sat down in a booth and waited for service.

And waited.

And waited.

The place was nearly empty, yet no one was paying any attention to us.

We waited some more.

Finally, the waitress asked to speak to Rolland Todd for a moment, and she told him that they couldn't serve us.

"Why not?" asked Todd.

"You know," she said.

"Know what?" he asked.

"They're, well, black," she said.

That was the reason, and the waitress made no pretense about it. This was St. Louis in 1960, and there were places in St. Louis in 1960 where a black person would not be served, period. It didn't matter if the black person in question was a pro basketball player, the top draft choice of the local team. Nor did it matter that the person in question had just graduated from Providence College with a degree in economics, or that he had done nothing in his life but work hard, play by the rules, and attend church on Sunday.

Only the color of my skin mattered, and the skin of the other blacks with me.

I was confused. I was angry. I was embarrassed.

Nothing had prepared me for this. Growing up in New York and attending college in Rhode Island, I had seen and experienced racism, but it was a subtler kind, such as the slight by the Olympic Committee or the harsh stares of some white guys when I danced with a white girl. I had never heard anyone say, "You're not good enough to be served a greasy burger"—in a joint that probably should have been condemned.

It's hard to explain to people who have never been in this situation how degraded it makes you feel, how you just seethe inside. I grew up without the advantages of most people, yet I'd made something of myself. I'd beaten the odds. I deserved some respect for that, not to be told, "Hey, you're not the kind of person we want to have eat at our crummy diner."

Who was that waitress to judge me? How could anyone make a decision like that, without even knowing me? This was America, the land of the free. I believed it, and I tried to live it. I was in the ROTC. I was determined that no one would hold me down, that I was entitled to the same opportunities as every other American, and I planned to capitalize on those opportunities. Which I had by becoming a member of the St. Louis Hawks. Which I had by performing so well in the classroom that I had a chance to pursue a Master's degree in economics at Boston College. Which I had by staying out of trouble and working one back-breaking job after another to help support my mother.

Yet none of that mattered.

All of this went through my mind when that woman only saw my black skin and decided that was all she needed to know about me.

People say, "Shake it off, it was just a stupid woman in a lousy diner."

That's true on the surface, but it was also something deeper, something that really opened my eyes to a world that was very new to me. I remember walking out of that diner feeling utterly humiliated. What did I do wrong? Why couldn't I order a meal anywhere I wanted in St. Louis, assuming I could pay for it? What kind of life had I just entered?

I don't know exactly what I expected from pro basketball, but it sure wasn't what I found. Much like that day in the diner, I found myself surprised, and sometimes ambushed, by what happened to me.

After I signed with the Hawks, I stayed in New England and worked for the Gilbane Construction Company, pouring concrete. Can you imagine a number-one NBA draft choice doing that today? Probably if he wanted to, the team that signed him wouldn't allow it, worrying that he'd get hurt building and tearing down concrete forms, which was another part of my job. I just figured it was a good way to make some decent money while getting physically stronger for the NBA. No one told me otherwise.

The Hawks had a summer camp at Kutsher's Country Club, which was in the Catskill Mountains of upstate New York. The team's key veterans were there, guys such as Bob Pettit, Cliff Hagan, and Clyde Lovellette. For them, this was mostly a vacation. I was one of several rookies brought in. We scrimmaged with the veterans, and the games meant a lot to us.

Just to show you what life was like in 1960, I'd never taped an ankle before I played. Never even thought about it. It's commonplace today to tape a player before a game, and it has been for years. The first day, I sprained my ankle. I tried to keep playing, but it was obvious that I wasn't myself. Part of my game was based on my quickness, jumping ability, and defense, but I could barely move. Yet no one said a word about my ankle. They had to know I was hurt, yet no one asked if I was all right.

In fact, most of the veterans didn't even say a single word to me. Not even a hello. Not a handshake. Nothing. Sihugo Green had gone to my old high school, but he was only slightly congenial. Even the rookies barely spoke to each other. I understood that, because we were all terrified that we wouldn't play well and would get cut. Even though I had signed my "no-cut contract," I still worried that the Hawks would let me go.

So I played on a bum ankle, and the Hawks probably thought I played like some bum off the street. Not that I knew, since hardly anyone spoke to me.

Paul Seymour was the new Hawks coach. He had been a hard-nosed guard in the NBA during the 1950s, a tough guy who liked to leave you bruised and limping after a game.

He greeted me by saying, "Hello . . . Rook."

That was it. I lost my name, and gained a new one—Rook. Just like all the other rookies. All of us felt nameless, faceless, scared. Because this was pro basketball, I expected some serious coaching. I thought each practice would be critiqued, and I wanted to know what I did right and wrong so I could improve.

Instead, I heard nothing.

We really didn't practice, we just played pick-up games.

I left that summer camp knowing that the Hawks had to be disappointed in how I'd played. But Seymour didn't say anything other than to tell me when I was to report to veterans camp.

I didn't realize that the NBA of the 1950s and early 1960s had so little hands-on coaching, at least on some teams. Often, the best player would retire, and he'd be named coach. His approach was usually to roll out the balls in practice and have the guys scrimmage to stay in shape. There was little individual instruction, little scouting, little of anything that would help a rookie adapt to the NBA.

In fact, most veterans either hated rookies or just acted like it. The rookie was there to take their jobs, to steal the food right off their table. The veterans seemed to have their own clique, and the rookies were the outsiders, the ones who weren't in on the jokes, who weren't sure what (if anything) to say or where to go. We trained at a place called Concordia Seminary, where there were two locker rooms. All the veterans were in one room, the rookies and free agents (guys not under contract) in the other. The practices could be brutal. I remember one scrimmage where every time I tried to cut through the lane, a guy gave me a forearm to the chest, or to the gut—a sledgehammer-like forearm to some spot of my body. The coach had to see what was happening, but he said nothing. I assumed he wanted to see how I'd react. Finally, I caught the ball, and the guy moved in on me, ready to deliver another forearm—only this time I whacked him in the face with the ball. Then we squared off, ready to fight, when other players stepped in and broke it up. Within a few minutes, we were playing again—and the forearms stopped.

Marty Blake was the Hawks' new general manager, and he'd sit at some evening practices with airline tickets in his hand. He'd watch practice, slapping those tickets against his knee. The players knew Blake was the general manager, they knew those tickets had someone's name on them, and that after practice, Blake was going to go up to someone and hand him a plane ticket home. You were cut, just like that. Here's your ticket, pack your bag, and don't let the gym door hit you in the rear end on the way out.

Blake seemed to take delight in sitting there, tapping those tickets against his knee, knowing that he was tormenting us, turning up the heat as if we weren't already under enough pressure.

It was a cold, heartless business.

That's a huge change from the modern NBA, where most veterans will welcome a rookie and try to help him, especially if they see the young man has a good attitude, works hard, and has the talent to help the team win. Most teams have a few veterans who'll go out of their way to introduce themselves to some of the rookies, to teach the young players the offensive and defensive schemes. When I coached the Cleveland Cavaliers, Larry Nance was an All-Star forward but he loved to take the rookies out for dinner, or even to his house where he had a small fishing lake. He wanted to put them at ease.

That just didn't happen when I was breaking into the NBA. With the St. Louis Hawks, I was just Rook.

I remembered having watched the Hawks in that Finals game at Boston Garden, and how the Celtics just dared the St. Louis guards to shoot the ball. I remembered how slow those guards were, how they made so little impact on the game. In today's NBA, I would have been greeted warmly by a team such as the Hawks, who were desperate for guards. The pressure would have been for the team to play me, because I was the first-round pick at a position where they were weak. But in 1960, it was just the opposite: The coach wanted to keep the veterans on his side, so he was reluctant to play a rookie, any rookie.

A few days into training camp, I received a strange phone call from Joe Mullaney, my old coach at Providence.

"Lenny, I heard a rumor and wanted to know if it's true," he said.

"What rumor?" I asked.

"I was talking to [Lakers coach] Fred Schaus, and he said you've been put on waivers by the Hawks," Mullaney told me.

I was dumbfounded. I hadn't heard a word about being waived, cut, or anything else.

"That's news to me," I said. "But I can tell you that I really haven't had much chance to prove myself here."

Mullaney said Schaus would love to have me on the Lakers. Just imagine if that had happened and I'd ended up in the same backcourt as Jerry West. Wouldn't that have been something?

I never did hear anything else about the rumor, so I don't know if the Hawks put me on waivers—and some other team claimed me, and St. Louis decided to keep me after all. Or maybe it was just a baseless rumor—but I did know that it was yet another indication that the Hawks didn't like how I was playing.

I just wished they had told me so to my face, and then told me what I needed to do to get better. The situation was so frustrating: hearing nothing . . . seeing the questioning stares . . . feeling like I was on some kind of basketball island . . . then being told by my old coach that he heard my team didn't want me.

When the season began, I was on the roster.

I was the fourth guard, behind three veterans, none of them stars. I didn't expect to walk in and start, but I was playing only one minute here, thirty seconds there. Even in the exhibition season, I started only once—and scored 12 points before I fouled out. I didn't seem to be in their plans, whatever those plans happened to be. The worst thing was the silence, so those plans were a mystery to me.

Early in the season, I ended up on the floor at the end of a close game. We were ahead by one point with twenty-two seconds left. I had the ball, and a clear lane to the basket. So I drove in for what should have been a layup.

This was before the 3-point shot, so a 3-point lead would have been very significant.

Anyway, I laid the ball on the backboard, and a player from the other team just took it off the board. It was a clear goaltending violation, but there was no whistle from the officials. The other team scored, and we lost by a point.

In the dressing room, none of the players spoke to me. Several of the veterans just looked at me as if I were the dumbest man on the face of the earth, but they said nothing.

Then Paul Seymour came up to me and said, "Well, Rook, did you learn anything?"

I said, "Yes."

I thought we were going to talk about it, how I should have dribbled out the clock, or what other options I had.

Instead, he just walked away.

Not another word, just walked away.

And really, how did he know if I had learned the right thing? He didn't ask, and I found myself buried deep on the bench for several weeks after that. I sat on the bench knowing I had blown that game, that I should have just hung on to the ball until the clock expired. I took a bad gamble, and it cost us a victory. I now know that I was a rookie, feeling insecure, just wanting to make a big play; instead, it backfired. After that, I played very sporadically and briefly. Whenever I was on the court and made a mistake, I was yanked out of the game.

One day, we had a game in Madison Square Garden. During warmups, I was making shot after shot.

Seymour said to me, "Hey, Rook, how come you don't shoot like that during the game?"

I said, "How would you know? You never play me."

A little later, he came up to me and said, "OK, Rook, what's on your mind?"

"You have all these veteran guards who've been in the league for a long time," I said. "I see them throw away four or five passes, and you leave them in the game. I get in there, throw away the ball once, and I'm out of the game. I've been sitting here for half the season, watching these veterans make the same mistakes they made back in training camp. Why don't you pull them out?"

"I want you to learn," he said.

"Just how much can I learn on the bench?" I yelled.

For a long time, he said nothing—he was just staring at me, trying to size me up.

"Rook," he said. "You may have something there."

Then he just got up and left. I had no idea what that meant, but I spoke out because I had nothing left to lose. I was already nailed to the bench.

The next night, we played the Knicks. Our guards were struggling. Early in the game, I was totally shocked when Seymour called me off the bench. The first time I touched the ball, I had Bob Pettit open down court for a fast break basket—and I threw the ball over his head. I glanced over at the bench, expecting Seymour to take me out. Instead, he looked the other way and stuck with me for the rest of the game. I scored 14 points, had 8 assists, and played decently.

That was the turning point.

The next night, I was in the starting lineup—and stayed there for the rest of the year.

When it came time to find a place to live in St. Louis, my options were limited. Just as I couldn't eat in some places, there were neighborhoods and landlords who made no secret of the fact that I wasn't welcome.

Sihugo Green set me up in an apartment in a mostly black neighborhood. Really, it was the upstairs of a house, owned by an Italian couple. They were concerned with one color—green. They worried only that I could pay the rent, not about the color of my skin. So that was a break. The place had hardwood floors and little rugs. You'd pick up a rug and on the floor was a sign reading, RUG GOES HERE.

I made friends with a black guy who owned a grocery store in the neighborhood. He told me where it was OK for a black man to go, and where the danger zones were. I ate dinner at his house a few times. I was learning what it meant to be black in the South, even though some people were surprised to find Jim Crow alive and well in St. Louis.

As my rookie season went on, the veterans began to accept me for one basic reason: I got them the ball. When I joined the Hawks, they didn't have a play for the point guard to shoot: You were there to pass the ball to the forwards, Cliff Hagan and Bob Pettit. That made some sense, because Hagan and Pettit were All-Stars who later became Hall of Famers. They were the reason the Hawks consistently were Western Conference champions in the late 1950s.

But a guard has to take a shot when he's left open, or the defense will sag back and cover the players under the basket. In other words, if I didn't take—and make—a few outside shots, it would be more difficult for Hagan and Pettit to score.

To his credit, Paul Seymour understood this. He encouraged me to take those open fifteen-footers. He saw that the other teams were very worried about my quickness driving to the basket, so they backed off me, daring me to shoot. And Seymour gave me the confidence to shoot. As the season progressed, I found that you could talk to Seymour, that he was a pretty good guy, he was just a product of his age. We developed a mutual respect. But on the court, there were times when I was still just a rookie. I remember the first time I guarded Bob Cousy. I cleanly stole the ball from him, just took away his dribble. But the official blew the whistle.

"How can you call a foul on a play like that?" I demanded.

"Because it was a foul," he said.

"Come on, you know better than that," I said.

He stared at me and said with a straight face, "You can't take the ball away from Bob."

"Hey," I said. "If I were a star, you wouldn't have made a call like that."

"Well," he said. "You'll never have to worry about that."

The official laughed, and I smiled.

The NBA of the 1950s and 1960s was different in lots of other ways.

I often hear how the players of today are quicker and more athletic than those of my era. All of that is true. People's bodies have changed over the last forty years; life is physically easier because there are fewer debilitating diseases, partly because nutrition and medical care are better. On most of my teams in the 1960s, only a few guys consistently played over the rim. Today, virtually every player does that.

Look at the pictures of today's stars compared to those from the early 1960s. The current athletes are wider: They have wider shoulders, wider arms, wider legs. More muscle. Bigger bones. That's a result of weight training and nutrition. In addition to a trainer, every NBA team now has a strength coach and a state-of-the-art weight room. These guys work out far more often than the players of my era, many of whom grew up being told they had better not lift weights, because that would make you muscle-bound and ruin the soft touch on your jump shot. Now, even the smallest point guard lifts weights. Every player wants to get stronger, and every player knows that unless you turn yourself into a WWF wrestler, weight training won't hinder your movement or your ability to shoot. We were so far in the dark that we didn't even know smoking was bad for you, that it robbed you of endurance because it had a negative impact on your breathing. We didn't know what was good to eat, what was the best way to train, or even that it was a good idea to stretch your legs. We just played the game.

That said, Elgin Baylor would have been a great player in any era. People talk about the amazing things Julius Erving and Michael Jordan did athletically, but I saw Baylor do many of the same things—only this was in the early 1960s. He had the spin moves, the dunks, the head-above-the-rim attacks on the basket. He played way above the pack.

Bill Russell remains the greatest shot blocker I've ever seen, because he'd come up with the block in critical situations of the game—and he'd make sure that his team kept possession of the ball. He'd just tip the ball to a teammate, or to himself. Today, too many players want to hammer the ball into the seats; they block shots like a tennis player trying to ace a serve, hitting the ball as hard as possible so no one can touch it. That looks great on TV, very macho. But it's not nearly as effective as Russell's technique of almost gently guiding the ball to someone such as Bob Cousy, who'd start a fast break in the other direction. Compare that to the guy who blocks the shot and screams as it rockets into the crowd: For all the theatrics, the shot blocker's team still doesn't gain possession of the ball; it returns to the team that shot it.

One of the most underrated players in basketball history is Bob Pettit, partly because he played in St. Louis. He had long arms that made him seem even taller than his six-foot-nine frame. Pettit averaged 26 points and 16 rebounds for a career that went from 1954–65, and most of the time, he played under the rim. But he blocked out. By that, I'm talking about the art of a big man putting his body between the basket and the player guarding him. The idea is to create room to rebound. If a player is on your back—or blocked out—it's nearly impossible for him to jump over your back and grab a rebound without fouling. The best rebounders of today still do that. At the end of his career, Dennis Rodman had lost much of his leaping ability, but he still was a monster on the boards. Why? He blocked out. Charles Oakley never was a guy with pogo sticks for legs, but he blocked out. Bill Laimbeer couldn't jump at all, yet he continually was near the league lead in rebounds. He blocked out. All over the NBA, coaches scream, "Block out," at their players, and most of the time, the players ignore them. That's because most of today's players are so athletically gifted, they never learned to block out when they were young. They just went after the ball, figuring they could outleap anyone else on the court. Today's players jump higher, but the players of my era were generally better rebounders for the simple reason that they worked harder at it, practicing basic fundamentals such as blocking out, creating space near the basket to rebound.

Wilt Chamberlain was the strongest man in the NBA during his era, and I'm convinced he'd be that today if he were still in his prime. Wilt was different from many NBA players. He believed in weight training and didn't care what some of the other coaches and players said. He was listed at seven-foot-one, 275 pounds, but he always seemed even bigger to me. He just towered over everyone on the court, not only because of his height, but also his strength. You had a feeling Wilt could score any time he wanted, as long as he wasn't at the foul line. Wilt averaged 50 points in one season. He scored 100 points in a game. He averaged 30 points and 22 rebounds a game for his career. He averaged 46 minutes a game. No one knows how many shots he or Russell blocked, because no one kept track back then.

Imagine how dominating Pettit, Chamberlain, Baylor, Russell, or Jerry West would be if they grew up in this era of basketball camps, intense coaching, weight training, and nutrition. You can't compare players from one era to another without taking into consideration these environmental factors. Wayne Embry is one of my favorite people because he is such a gentleman. I enjoyed coaching under him when he was general manager in Cleveland. Wayne also was a six-foot-eight, 280-pound center. Wayne "The Wall" was his nickname, and he'd be a wall even by today's standards. But just imagine how wide Wayne Embry would be today if he had been on a serious weight-training program, instead of just adding muscles by working on his father's farm in rural Ohio. Oscar Robertson would dominate in any era. So much is made of a triple/double, a player getting at least 10 points, 10 rebounds, and 10 assists in a game. Well, Robertson *averaged* 31 points, 12.5 rebounds, and 11.4 assists for the 1961–62 season! No one knows how many triple-doubles he had, because no one bothered to keep track back then. I remember when Embry and Robertson played together, and I'd try to guard Oscar. He'd run me right into one of those Embry-picks, and I'd get lost in Wayne's wide body. Do that just once, and you knew why he was called Wayne The Wall. Your jaw ached, your fillings came loose. You never defended Oscar again without keeping one eye open for Embry, just as the players of today will tell you that you never guard John Stockton without being aware that Karl Malone will show up and flatten you with a bone-rattling pick.

When you compare players from the fifties and sixties to today's, you have to remember that we were the best athletes of our time, and we'd presumably benefit from the same advantages today's players have if we were somehow transported forward in time. I know that I would have been as good a player today as I was back in my era, and I believe that would be true of the best of our players from those years. It's almost comical to think about how little we did to take care of ourselves back then. For example, a lot of players smoked. At halftime of the games, some guys would sit there, sweat pouring off them, and light up a cigarette right there in the dressing room, waiting for the game to resume. Of course, this was before anyone knew the full dangers of smoking, but I was really surprised when I first saw it happen, and suddenly I knew I wasn't playing college basketball any more.

One night, some of the veterans took me out to a bar, and then pointed to an empty table. "See that?" said one of the players. "We're gonna drink beers until we fill that table with empty bottles."

That was a real culture shock to me, and I knew I couldn't drink with those guys and then be able to play the next day. I was surprised to learn how many players drank—and I mean, they drank a lot.

As star center Johnny Kerr once said, "Back then, we did everything wrong. We smoked. We drank. We ate red meat and all the foods that are supposed to bad for you. But Lord, did we ever have a great time."

I didn't smoke. I seldom had more than one beer. I watched what I ate, so I was an exception. But I also was very serious about basketball and conditioning. A lot of it was just common sense. How were you supposed to play well when you'd been out drinking all night? Some guys, you could smell the beer as they sweated it out in practice the next day. I just thought that wasn't a professional approach to the game, and I wanted to be a very good pro.

So if I had to fetch the veterans hamburgers, I did just that. I was the rookie, and rookies were supposed to get the veterans food or soft drinks if they told you to do it. Rookies were supposed to haul around these huge twenty-four-second clocks to practice, much larger than the twenty-four-second clocks you see today. Back then, they sat on the floor and probably weighed twenty-five pounds. No one wanted to carry those clocks, so the job fell to the rookies—and I was a rookie. I did it without complaint.

But by the end of my rookie year, I was playing more like a veteran. I started the last thirty games, averaging 17 points. I set a team record for the highest shooting percentage by a guard.

More and more, I heard veterans say, "Nice game."

Not much more than that, but those two words—"Nice game"—meant a lot to me, the Rook.

The clearest sign of acceptance came when Cliff Hagan invited me to his house for dinner. Hagan was a product of Kentucky, a courtly southerner, so it wasn't every day that he had a black man in his house. But he opened his door to me, and I'll always remember and appreciate that. Hagan had huge hands; the ball looked like a grapefruit when he held it. He had a wonderful running hook shot and averaged 18 points while playing ten years for the Hawks. So when he broke the ice by bringing me to his home, it was a signal to the rest of the team that I belonged.

I wish they hadn't needed that kind of signal, but it felt awfully good when it finally did come.

CHAPTER SIX

IT WAS NOT LOVE AT FIRST SIGHT.

I was the athlete, she was the friend of a friend. She thought I was trying to take my friend away from her friend, trying to take my buddy to a party with me where there would be other girls, instead of allowing him to go out with his regular girlfriend, who was also her girlfriend.

Complicated?

When people see Marilyn and me, they assume we have been together forever: that I saw her, she saw me . . . bells rang . . . fireworks exploded . . . and we lived happily ever after.

There's a lot of truth to that, because we've been married since 1962. But the first time Marilyn met me, she thought I was a jerk. And I barely paid any attention to her at all.

I was a junior at Providence College. My friend was John Woods, and we had just played a game at St. Francis College in Brooklyn. I asked if John wanted to go to a party with me.

"OK," he said, indicating he didn't have much else to do.

"There are some people waiting for me after the game," I said. "Some girls I know are having a party."

That sounded good to John.

After the game, we headed out of the dressing room. Waiting for him was a girl named Althea, who I later learned was John's girlfriend. And with Althea were Marilyn and Marilyn's sister.

This created a problem for John.

"You can go with them," I said. "Or you can go to the party with me. What do you want to do?"

After some hesitation, he came with me.

I later learned that Marilyn was outraged that I'd asked John to go to the party with me. I didn't know that John and Althea were that serious, and John sure hadn't told me. Later, John and Althea got married, and I was his best man. But back then, I had no clue about their relationship.

As for Marilyn, I barely noticed her, and I didn't think twice about her. She had no idea whom she'd marry back then, but the one person she was sure it wouldn't be was me.

A year later, I saw Marilyn again.

She was dating a guy named Dennis Gurmores, who also played basketball for Providence College. He was a year behind me, and we were pretty good friends. Marilyn was at the school for the junior prom, and I met them at a party. That was the first time I really remember seeing her, and I thought she was attractive—but I also knew she was with someone else. I had no idea she was the same girl who was with Althea after that St. Francis game.

I didn't think a lot about Marilyn because she was dating someone else.

She told friends that I was "stuck up" and "aloof," and "I walked around with my head stuck up in the air."

Other than that, she liked me a lot.

The next time I saw Marilyn was after I had just completed my rookie year with the St. Louis Hawks. I'd been in the ROTC program at Providence, and I had some active military duty coming up. I was supposed to report on May 25.

Along about the end of April, I got into another one of those convoluted dating stories.

A friend of mine wanted to date a girl named Lori.

He didn't have a car.

I had a car.

He wanted me to go with him on a double-date, especially since Lori had a friend and she wanted to fix her up with someone.

I had no date for that night.

And Marilyn was the girl.

I found this out before I met her, from talking to Lori about her friend. I didn't think the double-date was such a good idea, because I remembered Marilyn from that party at Providence, and I knew that I wasn't her dream date. I called Marilyn on the phone to explain—exactly what, I wasn't sure—but I thought I owed her a phone call, because Lori had set up this date and Marilyn did know me from before. I realize this may not sound logical or mature, but I was only twenty-two, and dating often isn't rational at any age.

Marilyn was very nice and polite on the phone. We talked a little, and I just liked how she sounded. She was attending Hunter College in Manhattan. I still lived with my family in Brooklyn, and she lived in the Bronx. We had most of New York City covered.

Anyway, I mentioned that I was going to be in Manhattan the next day; I was going to lunch with Larry Fleischer, who was the head of the NBA Players Association. I asked Marilyn if she wanted to meet me after her classes for a cup of coffee, and I'd give her a ride home to the Bronx. Having a car was a real advantage, because most New Yorkers travel by subway. I don't know if Marilyn had changed her mind about me, based on that one phone conversation. I suspect she mostly wanted to avoid that subway ride home to the Bronx.

I don't remember much about that first get-together other than Marilyn just was very different than I had remembered. People who know her now have a hard time believing that Marilyn was quiet, a great listener, and almost shy. Today, Marilyn says exactly what's on her mind and really doesn't care what anyone thinks. I love the Marilyn of today as much as I appreciated the reserved Marilyn whom I really met for the first time in that coffee shop. She told me that in addition to attending Hunter College, she was going to night school at Mandell Medical Center, studying to become a lab technician. I appreciated the fact that she was hard-working and ambitious. I knew she was surprised that I was different from the Lenny Wilkens whom she'd first met, that I wasn't just some jock looking for the next party.

Soon we were going out several nights a week. I was so taken with Marilyn that I sort of forgot that I was due to report for military duty on May 25, 1961, in Fort Lee, Virginia. On that same May 25, I had a date with Marilyn to go to dinner and a Broadway show. We were in Times Square when I remembered I was supposed to be in Fort Lee. I noticed a Western Union office, and I thought I'd send a telegram to the base, saying I was sick and needed a few more days of rest before I reported.

The Western Union lady understood my situation.

"What rank are you?" she asked.

"Lieutenant," I said. I had that rank from being in the ROTC.

"I wouldn't say I was sick if I were you, sir," she said. "You being an officer, they'd send an ambulance for you. I would suggest that you ask for a delay due to car trouble."

It sounded as if this lady knew more about it than I did, so I went with the car-trouble story. We sent the telegram off, and within a half-hour, had a reply granting a three-day extension before I had to report. Marilyn always says it was that day when she knew she had me, that day in the Western Union office where I was trying to figure out how to stall the military so I could be with her.

At Fort Lee, I was placed in an eight-week Basic Officers Orientation Course. Once in a while, I had a free weekend. I immediately drove to New York to see Marilyn, even though I wasn't supposed to drive any farther north than Washington, D.C. They didn't want me having car trouble or being delayed coming back for any other reason. I didn't tell them about New York, I just went; I had to see Marilyn.

Her father was a cab driver in New York. If you can imagine a blustering New York cabby who liked to talk, had plenty of opinions, and wasn't afraid to give them to you—in depth!—that was Ashley Reed, Marilyn's dad, who drove a cab for over twenty years, an incredible guy who could talk to anyone about anything. He's one of my favorite people. And today, Marilyn is just like her father.

Back then, she was more like her mother, who was a quiet, thoughtful woman who also worked as a registered nurse. Her father worked a night shift, so I saw more of her mother. Both parents were very nice, very receptive to me.

When it became obvious that Marilyn and I were getting serious about each other, her father asked, "What does he do again?"

He knew I was in the military, but he also knew that was a temporary situation.

"Oh, he's a basketball player," Marilyn's sister said.

"Great," said her father. "When is he gonna get a real job?"

He loved baseball, but he didn't follow pro basketball. Marilyn and her sister explained that I really did get paid to play basketball, and was paid pretty well. He liked me, so he accepted that.

I loved her family because they were very close; there were always brothers, aunts, and sisters around. Marilyn's mother is from St. Croix in the Virgin Islands, her father is a black man from Kentucky. They considered themselves African-Americans and never said anything about my race, or me not being "black enough" for their daughter. They appreciated who I was, and there was no debate about race. My family situation, the strain of losing my father so young, and the division that my parents' interracial marriage had caused with some members of our family only made me love Marilyn and her family even more. It was the kind of family where I saw I'd be accepted and loved, and that meant a lot to me.

It was an eight-hour drive from the base in Virginia to New York. I spent Friday night driving, Saturday and part of Sunday with Marilyn, then Sunday night driving back to the base. I was supposed be back by midnight, and sometimes I was a little late, but I had a friend who made sure that he signed me in on time.

One spring weekend, Marilyn was able to go to Washington, D.C., to visit some relatives and also make it easier for me to see her. I drove to D.C., picked her up at her aunt's home, and took her to the base. We had lunch with some officer friends of mine, some of whom were married. That night we drove back to Washington and went to a show. Then we went for a walk along the Potomac River. I can still see the light on the cherry blossoms, the moon reflecting off the Potomac. At that moment, Marilyn was the most gorgeous woman I'd ever seen. I couldn't imagine her being anything but my wife. We walked past the different monuments, and we came to a place near the river where there was a big spotlight on the Potomac.

I had been nervous all day, knowing that I wanted to ask her to marry me, but not sure if I should. Or when I should. Or how I should do it. I thought she'd say yes, but there was a little doubt. I was just nervous about the whole thing, and I had been waiting for the right time that entire day.

Finally, by the Potomac River, I just asked, "Would you marry me?"

She said yes.

We kissed.

And that was it, we were engaged. I didn't have a ring yet, so we didn't make it formal until Christmas.

On Christmas Day, I gave her a big box. I could tell she was disappointed. She was looking for a little box, a ring box.

"It was delayed," I said. "It's going to be another two or three weeks."

She wasn't really happy as she opened that big box.

And found a smaller box inside . . .

And she opened that box . . .

And found a smaller box . . .

And inside that box was an even smaller box . . .

Finally, after opening five boxes, there was a little box, a ring box.

And inside was her engagement ring.

All the while we were dating, even after we were engaged, I had to have Marilyn home by midnight. We didn't think twice about it. They were in charge, they meaning Marilyn's parents. They wanted Marilyn home by midnight, so we made sure Marilyn was home by midnight. The U.S. Army I could finesse; with Marilyn's parents I wouldn't dare.

When it came time for us to get married, there was a problem, since I was a Roman Catholic, and Marilyn was an Episcopalian.

Our wedding date was July 28, 1962, fourteen months after we started dating. But in 1962, the Roman Catholic Church was not as open to its members marrying someone from another denomination as it is today.

When we decided to get married, I wanted it to be at Holy

Rosary Church, my home parish in Brooklyn. Father Mannion had been transferred to a different parish, but he was coming back to do the service.

Well, the Catholic Church had a lot of red tape about marriage in 1962. Marilyn was supposed to take "instruction" at the church. She also had to sign a document saying her children would be brought up as Roman Catholics, or we couldn't be married in the church. She lived in the Bronx and was still attending college in Manhattan, so it was a long trip to Brooklyn for these "instruction" classes. Futhermore, I was still in the military in Virginia, so I couldn't drive her there because they were held at night during the week. Marilyn went once or twice, but that was enough for her.

My mother was a little cool to our wedding plans—not because she had anything against Marilyn personally, but because Marilyn wasn't Catholic. She wasn't about to say anything, but my mother wasn't quite her warm and friendly self when Marilyn was around, and I knew why; back then, to marry a non-Catholic wasn't exactly a sin, but it was close. A good Catholic just didn't do it.

At the time, I wished I had the presence of mind to tell my mother, "Listen, when you married my father, he wasn't Catholic." (My father had later converted.) Instead, I just let it go, hoping my mother would come around. She did, but it took her a couple of years.

I didn't worry about Marilyn's religion. She was a good person, and I knew she'd be a good wife, a wonderful mother. I had matured in my faith to the extent that I knew that God would judge us on who we are and what we do, not on our race or religion. If God is who He says He is, then He isn't going to hold Marilyn's not being a Catholic against her or our marriage.

So the wedding plans moved on. I had saved up some leave so we could be married and have a honeymoon. I stopped by Holy Rosary to make sure everything was in place for the ceremony.

Then a priest said, "You can't marry Marilyn."

"Why not?" I demanded.

"She didn't complete her instruction. You don't have a dispensation," he said, meaning I didn't have permission from the Church to marry a non-Catholic.

I looked the guy dead in the eye and said, "Either we get married here, or it will be downtown at City Hall."

We were supposed to be married the next day, and I was not going to let this guy and his petty rules disrupt our wedding.

Immediately, his demeanor changed. He called the bishop, and the bishop knew who I was. The bishop told the priest, "Give Lenny my congratulations, tell him that I'm happy for him."

That changed this priest's whole approach. Suddenly, everything began to fall into place.

But still it was 1962, and the Roman Catholic Church had its rules: We could be married in the church, but not at the altar. Go figure that. I had Father Mannion doing the service, I had the blessing of the bishop, I had six Dominican priests who were friends of mine attending the wedding—but we had to be married outside the altar rail. It was completely ridiculous, but those were the rules. I wanted to be married in the Catholic Church and at Holy Rosary because that was important to me. Even though I didn't like some of the rules that the men of the Church had made, I never let that interfere with my feelings toward God; I knew He was right, even if what men did in His name was sometimes wrong.

Not long after I was married, my mother came to visit us in St. Louis. Marilyn and I were squabbling about something, and my mother immediately rushed to my defense. At that point, I should have said, "Mom, keep out of this, it's between my wife and me." But I didn't say anything. Marilyn got upset and ran into the bedroom, slamming the door behind her. It was Sunday morning, and we were supposed to go to church. So my mother and I went to church. I knew what was happening: My mother was still not thrilled that I had married Marilyn. Because my father had died so young and I was the oldest boy, I had been the man of the house, and when I got married she felt more like she'd lost me than that she'd gained a daughter. That was especially true because Marilyn wasn't Catholic. If you don't become a priest, then every Catholic mother at least wants her son to marry "a good Catholic girl." My mother was fighting all of that, and I suddenly realized it after Marilyn stormed out of the room.

As we drove to church, I told my mother, "I love you very much, but you have to understand that Marilyn and I are married. Nothing will ever change that. She is my wife. I love her with all my heart. She is number one in my life. I will always love you, but I can't put anyone in front of Marilyn."

My mother didn't say anything for a while, and I could tell that she was thinking about what I'd said. In her heart, she knew I was right. After that, things became much better between Marilyn and my mother. Eventually, she realized that we're all family.

I tried to prepare Marilyn for St. Louis. She had never been in the South before. I was starting my third season with the St. Louis Hawks, and I knew it was going to be a big culture shock for her.

The first time I saw the South was in my sophomore year at Providence. We played in a tournament in Virginia, and I saw bathrooms with signs reading COLORED on the doors. I had heard about Jim Crow; I had read about separate washrooms and swimming pools and drinking fountains, but it was never real to me until I saw it. That was when I realized that certain places divided everything into WHITE or COLORED. I had this terrible feeling in the pit of my stomach that something was radically wrong with us as a people when you saw that. We were playing that basketball tournament on a military base where the facilities were open to everyone, but when you stepped outside the base it was another world, an ugly, prejudiced world. I thought about the guys on the base who were black, guys who were willing to die for our country if there was a war—and black men had died in World War II, Korea, and all the other wars—and how they couldn't eat in some restaurants, or even use the same bathroom as a white man.

It got crazy sometimes. Once I was driving alone through Petersburg, Virginia, and I stopped at a small restaurant for a cup of tea. It was just a little place, nothing special. When I sat down, the waitress looked at me, then quickly went into the kitchen. I saw this black head peek out the kitchen door, then go back in. The guy and the lady looked at each other, then the waitress came out, took my order, and served me the tea. Back then, I wasn't sure what was happening. Now, I know that the lady was asking the black cook if I was a black man. She couldn't tell from looking at me. He must have said I looked white, because she served me.

You never get used to this. Never. You deal with it, you try to control your anger, but you never get used to it, and deep down it gnaws away at you. Not all the time—you can suppress it—but then something else happens and it comes out.

In St. Louis, there was a cafeteria-style restaurant that had pictures of several Hawks players in the window, including me. Everyone knew the restaurant only served whites, but there was my picture. They thought I was good enough to be in their window and maybe help bring in business, but I wasn't supposed to eat there. The hypocrisy galled me. I decided to go in there and dare them not to serve me. I got in line, and they put the food on my plate. Hardly anyone said a word to me. Everyone was staring, but no one had the guts to challenge me. I took some solace from that, because I was ready to tell them about the picture in the window, and ask how dare they not serve me? But I ended up eating in silence, then I left.

At first, I thought that I had made a point. But later, I thought that maybe they weren't sure if I was black or white. Sometimes, people would just ask, "What's your racial background, your heritage?"

If that's not an insulting question, then what is? People asked that question more often back then—not just about race, but ethnic background. It was more of a concern than it is today.

I always told them that I was black—or now, I say I'm African-American.

I know that there have been times when even black people have stared at my light skin and wondered, "What is he? What is he mixed with?"

This made me resent people's attitudes, but never made me feel uncomfortable or ashamed about who I am. My attitude is that I'm just as good as you, period—and I don't care who you are, or what color you are, or even who you think you are—and I was never afraid to tell people that even if it made them uncomfortable.

When all this was going on in St. Louis, America was often referred to as a "melting pot." That's what they wrote in the history books, about how people came from everywhere—all countries—to America, where we all were supposed to be treated as equals. And God said we all were equal in His sight, and we were supposed to be One Nation Under God, right? Then why would anyone care about my racial background? And where was the church in all this, especially my Catholic Church? That really angered me, because the priests had to know better, but so many of them were silent for so long. This still didn't shake my faith in God; as with the silly rules that prevented Marilyn and me from exchanging our vows in front of the altar, that was man, not God. I would never indict God for the failings of men.

It was into this setting that Marilyn came to live with me. We first stayed at the Plaza Square Apartments, but we were shopping for a house, and found one in the St. Louis suburb of Moline Acres. It had been repossessed by the bank. It was a great buy, but it needed some work inside. A friend and I would go there to sand and buff the beautiful wooden floors, paint the walls, spruce the place up. The neighbors saw us, but I later figured that they probably assumed we were just two black guys who had been hired to do the work. The house had been vacant for a while, so no one knew who bought it.

Until we moved in.

Then the FOR SALE signs popped up, one after another after another. No one came to the house to meet us. No one knew, or cared, that I played for the St. Louis Hawks. It didn't matter that we'd put a lot of work into the house and had it in better shape than it had been for years. Or that I had an economics degree from Providence. Or that Marilyn was college educated. Or that we were a young couple with solid values who just wanted a nice, safe place to live and we could afford to buy the house.

Nothing mattered at all except that we were black.

Our next-door neighbor was amazing. We had carports, which are like garages, only there's a roof but the sides are open. They were right next to each other. Sometimes we both were out there at the same moment, but this guy not only refused to even say hello, he'd also make sure that he got out of his car with his back to me, and would walk into the house that way, even if it meant he had to go the long way around his car. He'd do anything just so he wouldn't have to look at or talk to me.

It was comical . . . almost.

I didn't want anything from the guy. But he was so filled with venom and prejudice he refused to even acknowledge that we lived next door. It was just pathetic.

We had a collie puppy named Duchess. After a while, the FOR SALE signs weren't enough, the cold shoulders and stony silence from the neighbors weren't enough, the ugly glances when they saw us outside weren't enough.

They had to poison our little dog.

At least *someone* did. How low could they go, to kill a little dog? It was about as cruel an act as I could imagine, and making it even worse, there was no way to find out who had done it. Marilyn was shattered when our dog was poisoned. Part of you wonders, "What will they do next?" But my wife is a very strong-willed person, as those who know her now will be quick to tell you. She never said, "Maybe this isn't a good idea. Maybe we should move." She was mad and wanted to find out who killed our dog. If anything, that made her more determined to stay. No one was going to scare us, to run us off. We had as much right to live on that street as anyone.

We stayed at Moline Acres for three years, then realized we needed a bigger home. Marilyn found a home she really liked in a neighborhood she really liked. I was on the road with the Hawks, so the plan was that when I came home, I'd visit the house, and if I liked it we'd buy it. The real-estate agent was anxious to sell to us. She knew we had the money to buy. By the time I returned home, the agent had called us and was crushed: She explained that the house was no longer on the market, at least not to us. It was in an area called DeFere, and the neighbors had pressured the owner of the home not to sell to us. They heard we were black and they didn't want us on their street. Not long after that, I was invited to speak to the DeFere Chamber of Commerce. I was still hurt, and I just turned them down. Now, I'd have gone and told them at the meeting, "You think I'm good enough to come here and talk to you now, but I'm not good enough to live in your neighborhood."

We later found a home in a neighborhood called Town &

Country. It was a nicer place than the home we first wanted to buy, and the neighbors were very open and several became good friends of ours. So in that respect, it worked out.

Nonetheless, all of us are shaped by prejudices either for us or against us. I've always taken it as a challenge to show you that I'm as good as you, that all I need is an opportunity to show that I'm a good neighbor, a person you'd want to know. But these things tend to linger. They do affect you. And they pop up everywhere. A few years later, I was in church in Ohio, and the Catholic Church has a thing called the Sign Of Peace, where you shake the hand of the person next to you and say, "Peace be with you." The man next to me—a white man—refused to shake my hand. Here he was in church, claiming to believe in God, and he wouldn't shake the hand of the guy next to him in a pew. He was a hypocrite, and I told him so to his face when we walked out the door. He was just stunned, and I think he then felt bad and wanted to sort of melt, just disappear. He wasn't sure what I was going to do next, but I just walked away without another word. What else would I want to say to that man?

I try to keep race out of things, but it's hard not to think about it when you've experienced your share of prejudice. And I also know that what I've endured is nothing compared to what so many people in this country have faced. But suppose you are a black man and you walk into a restaurant at about the same time as a white guy. Maybe you were there just a minute before, but they wait on him first. You tell yourself that maybe they didn't see you get there first, but part of you wonders: Did they wait on him first because he's white? You can't deny the thoughts that cross your mind, but you also can't let them make you bitter, or they'll destroy you—and I was determined not to let that happen.

CHAPTER SEVEN

THE LIFE WE LIVED as pro basketball players in the 1960s would be unimaginable to the players of today. There is much they are able to take for granted—and I'm not saying that's a bad thing. But I wonder how well they'd function under the conditions that prevailed when I first broke into the NBA.

I ask myself that question as we travel on our chartered jet, with every seat first class, every aisle wide, every player well fed. We even have a video system so we can watch tapes of the games. All of this on a jet, our own jet, where we don't need a ticket, we don't even have to walk through an airport: The bus just drives us onto the runway and right up to the door of the plane. Takeoff is whenever we're ready. That's how virtually every NBA team now travels from city to city.

Then there are the hotels: Ritz Carltons, Four Seasons, Hyatts, Westins, and Marriotts. All first class. All with a staff that wants to make our stay "enjoyable," as they like to say in the advertisements. Suppose you're playing Monday in Cleveland, and you have a game the next night in Boston. Here is what you do: Late Monday afternoon, you pack your bags at the downtown Cleveland Marriott, and you call the bellman, who takes the bag. You never see that bag again until you arrive at the Westin in Boston.

In the meantime, a bus takes you from the Cleveland Marriott to Gund Arena, where you play the Cavaliers. After the game, a bus takes you from Gund Arena to Cleveland Hopkins Airport, where your jet is on the runway, waiting for you. You fly for a few hours, eat a first-class meal, then arrive in Boston. There, a bus is waiting for you and takes you from Logan Airport to the Westin in downtown Boston. There, your bags are delivered to your rooms.

For many NBA players, this is the only way they know. It's how the NBA has traveled since the early 1990s, when most teams switched from flying on commercial planes to chartered jets or their own private jets. Given the demands of an eighty-two-game schedule that carries you from one end of the country to the next over a six-month period, this type of travel makes sense. It helps avoid fatigue, and it keeps the players as rested as possible. I still marvel at how far we've come in the NBA, in everything from salaries to arenas to travel. There are a few things about the old NBA that I liked, such as the closeness of the players and fewer distractions because the money wasn't as big. But no one in the league now would want to travel or play in the places we did during my early days in the NBA.

One of my very first road trips as a pro was to Detroit, where the Pistons played in a place called Olympic Stadium. They led us to what was supposed to be a locker room, only a locker room is supposed to have lockers, right? This joint had nails in the wall. That was where you hung your clothes—or you could spread them on a folding chair. Olympic Stadium was built for hockey, and the place felt like a refrigerator. It was so cold sitting on the benches, they had heat lamps installed to keep the players from icing over.

That was my first look at the NBA.

Detroit was bad, but places such as Boston Garden weren't much better. Most of the arenas were dark, smoky, gritty, and more than a little depressing. It's strange to see pictures of those crowds from the early 1960s. Most of the men are in suits, ties, and formal hats. The women are in dresses. A lot of people smoked right there in the arenas, and the smoke hovered over us. You could see it every time you looked up at the lights.

In the dressing room, your last name was written on a piece of white tape, which was stuck right next to your personal "nail" in the wall of the dressing room at Boston Garden. Then Red Auerbach— or someone—made sure that the temperature was either ninety degrees or fifty degrees in there. Always too hot or too cold. And the same was true with the water in the showers. The Celtics blamed it on the problems with the old building. Maybe they were right, but we always had our suspicions. Either by design or because of incompetence, Boston Garden was no bargain for a visiting team, and not just because the Celtics had such great players. In my early NBA days, I was shocked that so many of the places we played were worse than the arenas and dressing rooms I saw in college. I mean, every locker room I had in college at least had lockers.

From 1961 to 1966, the NBA had only nine teams. Usually, there were only ten active players on the roster. Each team usually had a player on the injured list, but that meant there were only one hundred professional basketball players. In this era, pro basketball was a distant third in the pecking order of most sports fans, well behind major league baseball and pro football. In some areas, it also was dwarfed by major college sports. The games were carried on TV only once a week—yes, one game a week, and it usually featured Bill Russell's Celtics against whatever team had Wilt Chamberlain at center.

We flew in the early jets, the kind that had to stop in places like Des Moines or Rapid City to refuel if we were flying cross country. We were like any other passengers; we waited in line for tickets, and we sat where we were told. We usually flew at the crack of dawn, because we had a game that night and didn't want to risk missing it by taking a late-morning flight, then running into weather or scheduling problems. When I was with the Players Association, one of our victories was to convince the league to order the teams to give us three-for-two airline seating. That meant that the team had to pay for the three seats across the row, but only two players could sit in them; the seat in the middle was open between the two guys, so we had a little room to spread out.

Commercial airplanes are built for the average guy, who is about five-foot-nine. NBA players run at least a foot taller, and those big men ended up flying with their knees nearly jammed under their chins. Sometimes we could get into the first-class cabin, but that depended upon availability, and most first-class cabins back then didn't have enough seats for a full NBA team. That created another problem: Suppose only six first-class seats were open. Who sits there? Do all six seats go to the players, or does the coach sit there? The players never wanted the coach up there, which confused me at first; the coach is the boss, so he should be up there. Of course, that was exactly the reason they didn't want the coach up there: In first class, the drinks were free, and they wanted the coach in the back of the plane so he wouldn't know what, or how much, the players were drinking. Generally, the seating got assigned on seniority, although some of the taller young guys felt they should sit up front, because they needed the extra leg room. This was yet another problem the coach had to sort out.

Today you'd play that night game in Cleveland, then fly immediately afterward to Boston. In my era as a player, we'd play that game in Cleveland, go back to the hotel, and wake up at 5:00 A.M. to be at the airport in time for a 6:30 A.M. flight to Boston. That meant we hardly slept at all: Who can go directly from playing a game right to bed? Few people in any job go right from work to bed. Most people want to at least eat something. Usually, it seemed like we had just dropped off to sleep when the phone would scream in our ears with the wakeup call. You'd see teams trudging through the early-morning airports as if they were the walking dead, which was exactly how we felt. Say you had four games in five days in four different cities—which happened several times a year. By that fourth game, you had no idea where you were, your legs were lead, your head had a dull ache, you'd been eating lousy airplane food that felt like a roll of socks sitting in your gut, and you felt as if you hadn't slept for a week. Even into the 1980s, we still flew commercial flights. Some of my players would stagger bleary-eyed into the airport at 6:00 A.M. and head to the snack bar for something—anything—to eat. I can still see big Melvin Turpin, who played center for me in my first year coaching the Cavs, ordering a couple of those hot dogs from the snack bar, the kind that had been rolling over and over and over on those grills for hours and hours, maybe even days and days. Turpin wasn't the only one chowing down those things at 7:00 A.M. Guys guzzled gallons of coffee, shoved down stale jelly doughnuts, and called it breakfast. It was amazing we all didn't suffer from severe stomach cramps when it came time to play. That was part of the reason NBA teams often won 70 percent of their home games in the old days: The visitors simply were in no shape to perform.

Most athletes work what amounts to a night shift. For games, they get to the arena around 5:00 P.M. and they leave around midnight. That's why it makes sense to fly immediately after games whenever possible. So what if you don't get to your room in Boston until 2:00 A.M.? You can sleep until ten in the morning and catch up. Your sleeping schedule is almost the same as it is at home. The improvement in travel, especially private or chartered planes for teams, is the biggest reason NBA teams have better road records than they did twenty years ago. It's still hard to win on the road, where the crowd is against you, the floor is foreign, and the other team is in its comfort zone. Let's face it, when you were a kid and in a pickup game, you'd rather play on the hoop in your driveway or at your favorite playground than at your buddy's house. But just imagine having to go to your friend's place and play a big game when you haven't slept for more than three hours a night for the last four days: That was what it was like to play on the road in the old NBA.

In my early years in the league, there just wasn't a lot of glamour to pro basketball. We felt more like third-rate traveling salesmen than the men who supposedly were "the greatest athletes in the world," according to the NBA publicity machine. I roomed with Zelmo Beaty—yes, we all had roommates back then, not like today where most players have their own rooms. And tall guys like the six-nine Zelmo slept in normal beds, which meant their feet hung over the end. There weren't the king-sized beds like today's, which are standard in every player's room as requested by the team.

In those early years, our meal money was $8 a day. We used to look for places like Tad's Steakhouse, where they sold you a steak for $1.50. It wasn't a great steak, but it was a steak and it was only $1.50. Once, a few us went out to a place called Al Cooper's Steakhouse in New York. The steak was great. This was no Tad's. But neither was the price. It was $25, which meant we spent three days of meal money for one steak dinner. Today, the NBA meal money is $84 a day. You can eat very well on that, and sometimes you don't even have to pay for any food since those wonderful meals on the plane are free.

When we had back-to-back games on the road, the team didn't even provide a simple service like washing our uniforms. I'd take the uniform with me right into the shower after the game and wash the stupid thing by hand. I'd roll it up in a towel, take it back with me to the hotel, wring the soggy thing out in the sink, then spread it on the radiator to dry. That's right, a radiator, which was how most hotels were heated back in the 1960s, or at least the hotels where we stayed. I had to wash my underwear in the hotel sink and hang that on the radiator, too. In the morning, the clothes on the radiator would be dry, but a little stiff—but then again, so were we when it came time to play.

In the early 1960s, the best thing about basketball was playing the game. That sounds obvious, but I wonder if you'd get the same answer today. A lot of players say the best thing about being in the NBA is the money, the first-class travel and hotels, the attention from the public, the parties, limos, women, and other perks. Yes, they like the game, but they love what the game brings them.

I love the game. Always did, always will.

Even as a coach in the year 2000, my favorite thing about the NBA is the games. The winning and losing. The action. The feeling that comes when the lights are on, the music is turned up, and the game is ready to begin. As a player, I loved being across from the other guy, looking into his eyes as he was trying to guard me, and knowing I could beat him to the basket and make something good happen for my team. I just knew it. He may have thought he could guard me. He may have thought that I always dribbled to the left, and all he had to do was "sit on his left hand," as they tell a defender of a player who is lefthanded. I didn't care who was guarding me, I knew I could penetrate to the basket. I could force someone else to leave his man and try to stop me, then I could find an open teammate for a pass. Or I could throw in a little lefthanded hook from seven feet away, doing it while moving directly off the dribble. Or perhaps I could get all the way to the basket and flip in a nice finger-roll layup. And what I was absolutely, positively sure about was this: Not only could I beat you off the dribble, I'd keep myself under control. I would never be moving so fast that I ended up forcing a bad shot at the basket, or a wild pass to my teammate. I don't think about my playing days very often, usually only when someone asks me about it or when I happen to see an old tape of a game I played in. Then I remember the feeling I had, where the ball felt like it was part of my hand. I knew that the whole offense started with me, and that I could set up my teammates so they could take shots from the spots on the floor where they were the most comfortable.

When I came into the NBA, I had to be the dumbest guy in the league when it came to knowing the other players, the history of the teams, the basics of pro basketball. I'd hear my teammates talk about great players of the past, and the names meant nothing to me because I'd never followed the game. I was too embarrassed to say, "Hey, I never heard of that guy." I just kept my mouth shut and listened. If you're quiet and listen, you learn, which is what I did. Then I was blessed to play against greats such as Bill Russell, Wilt Chamberlain, Oscar Robertson, Jerry West, Bob Cousy, and Elgin Baylor. I came into the NBA in 1960, the same year as West and Robertson. My St. Louis Hawks teams had two of the best forwards in NBA history, Bob Pettit and Cliff Hagan. They also were two of the first players to accept me, for the obvious reason that I could get them the ball. They were scorers. I was a point guard who looked first to pass. I could score, and I averaged 20 points in some of my seasons later in my career, but in my first years with the Hawks I scored about 12 a game. I sacrificed my offense, and the players respected that—and they respected me for it.

In the early 1960s, the NBA was not as quick, or as integrated, as it is today. A lot of teams ran set plays to get their stars shots. When I joined the Hawks, we must have had twenty plays to get the ball to Pettit and Hagan. As I played, I short-cutted those plays. In other words, I saved us a pass or two and found a way to get the ball directly to Hagan and Pettit, exactly where they wanted it. Together, we improvised; rather than pass the ball left, run right and set a pick, then run back and catch another pass and throw it to Hagan . . . well, I'd just beat my man off the dribble, head to the spot to create the proper passing angle, then throw the ball to Hagan. This saved time on the shot clock, and created fewer chances for turnovers because the ball didn't go through as many hands.

During the 1960s, the game became faster. There were more guys dribbling behind their back, more guys dunking, more guys making flashy passes. It was still a big deal to be on TV. I think it was in 1964, and we were playing the Cincinnati Royals on TV. There was a loose ball, and I dove for it along with a Cincinnati player named Arlen Bockhorn. In fact, Bockhorn sort of tackled me as the ball went out of bounds. They called a foul on him, and he smiled and told me, "Bet that looked great on TV!" Now, virtually every game is televised somewhere. Most of the players have been performing on TV since college, some even in high school, as cable TV now carries all kinds of games. But back then, it was special to play in a game your family and friends might see on TV.

Our games were pretty physical. Guys handchecked, meaning they'd put their hands on your back and try to push you a bit, knock you off balance as you dribbled the ball and keep you from going where you wanted to on the court. But that never bothered me, because of my quickness: If a guy was close enough to put his hand on my back, then I could just drive past him. He was too close to keep up with me.

There were a lot of fights in those games, primarily because there were only eight or nine teams. With an eighty-two-game schedule, that meant you played most teams about ten times each year. That created rivalries, and it also caused players to build up grudges. A guy stuck you in the gut with an elbow then shoved you to the floor last week, and a week later you'd play him again. You were just waiting for something, anything, to happen; he'd just stare at you the wrong way, and bam, there'd be a fight. I rarely got into fights, but the bigger players did because there was so much contact under the basket. We had excellent officials back then, men such as Earl Strom and Mendy Rudolph, and they knew the players and their personalities. They knew if they let some guys just fight for a few minutes and get it out of their systems, there'd be no more trouble for the rest of the game. With other players, they knew to step in quick, or these guys were really going to hurt each other.

Now, if a player throws a punch, it's an automatic ejection, a big fine, and probably a suspension. Back then, they might throw you out—or not—depending upon how the officials felt about you. The officials would ask themselves, "Is this guy going to give me any more trouble, or is he just blowing off steam?" If they thought you'd calmed down, they'd call a technical foul on you but let you stay in the game. Rarely was a player ejected for fighting, and we had some real brawls back then.

The NBA was a smaller place, a community of one hundred athletes and nine teams during some of those years. That made it easier for the officials to know us, and for us to learn to trust them. There was a sense that we were all in this together, all trying to make sure that the league survived. Because the money wasn't that big and there was no such thing as free agency, players stayed with teams longer. The stars of the team didn't seem that much different from the guys on the bench, at least in the dressing room and when we traveled. Most of us even had summer jobs, because we needed the money. In my early years with the Hawks, I earned between $15,000 and $20,000. My final season in St. Louis was 1967–68; I was a five-time All-Star, and I was making only $35,000.

When I came into the NBA, we didn't have a pension plan. Bob Cousy was the president of the Players Association, which was our fledgling union. Bob Pettit and Bill Russell were vice-presidents. In my third year in the NBA, I made the All-Star team. Pettit and I flew from St. Louis to Los Angeles for the game. As we walked into the hotel lobby, we saw Tom Heinsohn, Russell, and a guy in a suit who I knew was an attorney named Larry Fleischer. They stopped Pettit and said, "We're starting a meeting right now. It's about our pension plan. They won't give us one, and we have to do something!"

The pension plan was crucial; with salaries so low, it was easy for ex-players to wind up destitute. I don't think anybody could have ever imagined a world of free agency or million-dollar contracts. But we knew that the baseball players had fought for a pretty good pension plan, funded in part by proceeds from their All-Star game. So our All-Star game seemed like a good place to make a stand.

I went along with Pettit up to the suite where NBA Commissioner Walter Kennedy was staying. The 1963 All-Star game was going to be the first carried under the new TV contract signed by the league. I never said a word, but I watched as our union told Kennedy that if we didn't receive some sort of pension plan, we were going to strike and not play the All-Star game. Kennedy was shocked. Heck, I was shocked. Here I was in my first All-Star game, and I was supposed to strike?

Kennedy looks right at me, the youngest guy in the room and the one who he sensed was the most likely to buckle under pressure.

"Lenny," he said. "You mean to tell me that you're really going to strike this game?"

I gave a little nod and my voice was barely above a whisper, but I managed to say, "Yeah."

Kennedy shook his head again and said he'd take our demand to the owners' committee.

That night, we all got ready for the game and waited to hear something from the league. There was no word. At 8:00 P.M., ABC-TV went on with its pregame show. The game was supposed to start at 8:30. We said we weren't going to play. At 8:15, ABC told the league that if the players weren't out there at 8:30 for the game, they were going to cancel the TV contract for the entire season. In the meantime, Lakers owner Bob Short sent a message to the dressing room that Elgin Baylor and Jerry West would never play in L.A. again if they boycotted the game. Other threats were made. But about ten minutes before the game, Kennedy came into the room and said we'd have a pension plan in place by June 1. So we went out and played.

Players now can't believe how little we made, or how we had to work in the summers. They're surprised to hear that we had to worry about a pension plan at all. But that was all a part of the almost blue-collar world of the NBA back then.

☐

When I say most of us worked in the off-season, I mean a job, not working out with a personal trainer, as players do today. We sure weren't hanging out in L.A. and singing on someone's rap video, or appearing in a movie. I worked just as a teacher or anyone else would who had the summer off and needed to pick up some extra cash.

My first few summers in St. Louis, I worked for the Jewish Employment and Vocational Services. The organization had a government grant to work with high-school dropouts. My job was to interview the kids, give them a test, and try to determine where they fit into the world of work. We offered courses in such areas as electronic assembly, nursing, and clerical work.

A man named Dr. Wolf started the program. He approached me because I was a pro athlete with a college degree, and he thought the kids would relate to me. In essence, I was a counselor. I'd meet with some of the kids who were already in the program, and I'd listen to their problems and try to keep them from getting sidetracked. Many of them were like the kids I grew up with in Brooklyn. They had messy family situations, they came from poverty, and they had few skills and little hope, because no one in their family had an idea what it took to succeed in the world. I grew up without a father, and so did a lot of these kids; I could understand what they were feeling, and I also could speak to them from my own experience. Yes, I'm a pro basketball player, but my father died when I was five, and I'd worked at menial jobs for much of my childhood and adolescence. I told them that how you looked and how you spoke were very important in finding and keeping a job. I taught them the basics of grooming, of manners, how to fill out employment applications, what to wear to a job interview. There was one young woman whom we worked with who was a natural typist. She just breezed through our clerical training program, but still had trouble getting a job. She had no clue how to dress, so we went back to the basics. We got her hair cut and styled so that it looked nice but nonthreatening to the middle-aged people who were doing the hiring. We helped her pick out the right kind of dress, showed her how to do the little things that tell an employer you know how to function in the working world. The day she got a job remains one of the best days of my life, and she did extremely well, moving up in that company. I learned that even a little success goes a long way toward helping people believe in themselves and change their lives.

I spent three years at this summer job working with people who were at the bottom of the social and economic scale back in the early 1960s, most of whom were black. I'd like to think a program like this could do as much good today, but the truth is that there's a huge difference between people's desire to remake themselves now compared to back then. In the early 1960s, there wasn't as much despair and hopelessness. Drugs just weren't the plague they are today. A "bad" kid back then smoked cigarettes, stole hubcaps, and maybe carried a knife. He didn't like authority, but he wouldn't shoot you down in cold blood because he thought you'd looked at him the wrong way. And to be honest, people had lower expectations; they just wanted a decent job, an apartment, and a car that would get them around town. Naturally, I'm speaking in generalities, but these were my impressions. Today, those same people tend to come in with massive drug and family problems. There have always been gangs, but the gangs of forty years ago were nothing more than social clubs compared to the drug-lord gangs you see today. We have an insane society where a thirteen-year-old kid can make $1,000 a week working for a drug lord. How can you tell this kid, "What you really need to do is clean up, get some manners, learn how to read and write, and then you can get a job at McDonald's or a factory." The kid couldn't care less.

The influence of TV on society is enormous. Most of the kids I worked with at the Jewish Employment Services didn't have a TV in their homes. Their expectations weren't that high, because what they saw was what was around them in their own neighborhoods. TV today makes everybody believe they're entitled to nice cars, big houses, and all kinds of other things, and that's had a devastating effect on society. We're told of all the things we deserve to have—and that we should have them *right now!* In that environment, it is much harder for someone working in a program like I did to convince people to wait their turn, work hard, pay their dues, and that in the end it will pay off. I have a lot of respect for those who work in social services and try to help the poor because I remember how difficult it was when I did it—and it's far more demanding today.

My other summer job while I was in St. Louis was with the Monsanto Corporation. A Providence College graduate headed the packaging division, and he offered me a chance to work in their marketing and sales department. They made packages for many products, such as Tide detergent and Dove soap. Most people remember Monsanto as a chemical company, the inventors of Astroturf. Their organic division made the pills for Excedrin, and our packaging division made the bottle and the box for the product. They were such a huge corporation back in the 1960s that they built a plant in Cincinnati right next to a Procter & Gamble plant, just so they could service P&G's packaging needs. They also did all the packaging for Avon products.

I went through their sales training program, then went out with some salesmen to learn the trade from guys on the front lines. We'd call on companies that didn't use Monsanto for its packaging, or we'd go to companies that were clients and make sure they were happy with our service and to see if they wanted to change or expand their packaging. I learned a lot. For example, for a while we tried to sell a clear plastic tray for meat packaging, but if the meat bled a little and the temperature wasn't just right, condensation would form, and suddenly you couldn't even see the meat. That was a fiasco. The best packaging for meat is a white styrofoam tray, because the color of the meat stands out.

None of this may sound particularly exciting compared to basketball, but I enjoyed working for that company. I had a degree in economics, and it was a great experience for me to see how a major corporation operated. I didn't mind the selling because we had a good product with excellent service. Maybe because I knew it wasn't my full-time job, I never had bad vibes about selling. I didn't take rejection personally. I guess it comes from sports, from winning and losing. You know you don't win every game. And you soon learn you don't make every sale. To me, it was a challenge. I prepared to go out and sell those products just as I would prepare to face an opponent today while coaching in the NBA. I studied the scouting reports. I considered the strengths and weaknesses. I put together a game plan. The details were different, but the approach was the same.

I felt very comfortable with Monsanto. In fact, when the team moved from St. Louis to Atlanta, they offered me a full-time job. For a moment I considered it, because my final season with the Hawks was probably my hardest in all of pro basketball.

CHAPTER EIGHT

BIG PROBLEMS START WITH LITTLE THINGS. They happen when feelings are hurt, when basic communication breaks down.

That's how I came to be a malcontent.

It was 1967–68, my last year in St. Louis. I had been with the Hawks for seven years, an All-Star four times. I was captain of the team, popular with the fans. I had fought with the front office for more money, but virtually every good player in the 1960s found himself doing that. That wasn't the problem.

Then came The Tour, which shouldn't have been a big deal, either.

At the end of the 1966–67 season, the U.S. State Department was putting together a group of NBA athletes to play and tour in South America. My coach, Richie Guerin, was in charge of the team and he picked the players. I just assumed I'd be invited. Not only was Richie my coach, we had played together in the same backcourt for three years. But Richie invited forward Bill Bridges and backup big man Gene Tormohlen. I admit, my feelings were hurt. I had seniority, and I was a better player than either of them. I had been an officer in the Army; this was a government-sponsored tour, and I wanted to go—or at least, I wanted to be told why someone else was invited over me. But I didn't find out what had happened until after the players were picked for The Tour.

And even that was awkward, because Bridges told me, "I'm not supposed to say anything, but Tormohlen and I are going to South America."

Why wasn't he supposed to say anything?

"Richie told me not to," he said.

Of course, Bridges did say something. That's invariably what happens when you tell someone, "Don't tell So-And-So about this." The first thing they do is tell So-And-So.

I knew Bridges was one of Guerin's pet players. Richie was a knowledgeable coach, but he clearly played favorites. He liked Bridges. He liked Tormohlen, who was a role player at this stage of his career. He liked me as his point guard, but obviously I wasn't one of his friends.

So, his friends went . . . and I stayed home.

And Guerin never did tell me why the decision was made. He could have called me in and said he was taking Bridges and Tormohlen. I wouldn't have been happy about it, but I'd have accepted it; it was his team, his decision. But it seemed as if he was sneaking behind my back, as if everyone knew some secret except me. Even the wives of Bridges and Tormohlen were told not to say anything. The issue was like a pot left on the stove all day with a little flame on the burner; after a while, it simmers. Then it boils over.

When training camp opened the next season, Bridges showed up completely out of shape. He was dragging up and down the court, messing around, and not approaching practice seriously. I was a veteran, the team captain, and the point guard—and I told him to bear down.

"Well, you're not passing the ball to me," he said.

"If I wasn't a team player, you'd never get the ball from me," I said. "So pipe down and do your job."

He got upset, but he didn't say anything else. Then the whispers started, claiming that I'd yelled at Bridges because I was jealous of him, angry that he went on The Tour and I'd stayed home.

I didn't ask Guerin about The Tour because I knew he'd picked his friends. That was obvious. It also was clear to me that as team captain, I should have been invited. A captain is an extension of the coach on the floor, or he should be. I took the role very seriously, so I wasn't afraid to tell my teammates things they needed to hear. That was why I said something to Bridges, not any silly reason like an off-season junket.

That's when Hawks owner Ben Kerner called me in.

"What's on your mind?" he asked.

"Nothing is on my mind," I said.

"If it's about The Tour, I'll send you on a tour next year," he said.

"You don't understand," I said. "It was how it was handled. I'm not hung up on this thing, but you people ought to be more careful how you make decisions. I'll do the best job I can for you, but I just wanted you to know the whole thing was handled badly."

Kerner didn't say much else.

As training camp continued, we went into a losing streak, about five games in a row. But this was training camp! These were exhibition games, but people were panicking. Then Bridges told me that I was putting a strain on his relationship with Guerin. In essence, he said he couldn't be friends with me and the coach.

Doesn't this sound stupid?

Well, it was. But it's also what happens when things are allowed to fester, when everyone would rather talk behind each other's back than bring it out into the open. And it continued when Guerin called me in and said, "You're not going to be team captain any more."

I asked why.

"Because you're jealous of Bridges," he said.

"I'm not jealous of Bridges," I said. "The only reason I said something to him was because he was out of shape and not working hard."

"No, it was because of The Tour," he said.

The Tour was getting to be like something in your eye. What do you do when that happens? You rub it. And what happens then? It gets worse, and it seems as if it will never go away.

No one thought I was jealous of Bridges—until The Tour. No one thought I was unfit to be captain—until The Tour. No one thought I was unhappy—until The Tour.

Then it got worse.

Guerin had decided not to play that season, to be a full-time coach. He had Joe Caldwell set to take his spot in the backcourt with me.

"I think you're jealous of Joe," he said. "I heard a story that you supposedly were afraid Joe would make the All-Star team."

The implication was I worried Caldwell would be an All-Star instead of me, that I felt threatened by Caldwell's talent.

"Listen, if Joe makes the team, I'll be the happiest guy in the world," I said. "I'm the point guard. My job is to get the best out of everyone on the team."

Guerin and I left the room not thrilled with each other. I was no longer captain. He thought I was so insecure that I wasn't going to pass the ball to Caldwell? The more I thought about it, the more it hurt. Rubbing an eye for too long can lead to an infection, right?

Now, I can see it was ridiculous.

Back then, I believed my reputation was at stake, so I called a team meeting. I told the players what Richie had said about me being envious of Caldwell.

"Richie said someone on the team told him that," I said. "I want to know who it was, so we can have it out. Stand up right now, so I can call you a liar to your face."

Of course, no one did.

"The only way I know how to play is to make sure everyone gets the ball," I said. "I want Joe Caldwell to make the All-Star team. I want everyone to be a star. That means we'll have a great team."

A few weeks later, Guerin told me that I was captain again, which was after we had just won four exhibition games.

I just nodded.

We had a truce. It was shaky and delicate, but it was a truce.

We opened the regular season on the West Coast and won three games. While we were gone, the wives had a get-together at the Guerins' house. You have to understand that things are often a bit touchy between the wives of players. Little slights become gaping wounds. Suspicions surface, grudges become entrenched.

And sure enough, at the little party, The Tour came up. Tempers flared. Charges were made, fingers pointed. Just when the subject was dying down in the dressing room, it became a roaring fire in the homes of the players. At the next game, some of the wives discovered their seats had been changed. This can be a real minefield. Most wives sit in the same section, so they can sit together if they wish—or put a few rows between them to keep the peace, but they still sit in the same area. For this game, Zelmo Beaty's wife, Paul Silas's wife, and my wife found themselves sitting in three different corners of the arena. They weren't near each other, or any of the other wives. The wives of Guerin, Bridges, Tormohlen, and the rest sat together, as they always had.

The Tour wouldn't go away.

Bridges and Tormohlen went on The Tour, and their wives sat together in their regular seats. Everybody noticed the three women who had been scattered to the far corners of the arena. Zelmo Beaty was our center, a six-foot-nine, 240-pound man who could take Richie Guerin and squeeze him into a box of cornflakes, which was about what Beaty wanted to do. You can insult a player, but don't hurt the feelings of his wife. I told Beaty that I'd talk to Richie about the tickets. The amazing thing is that we still started the season at 4–0, with all this bickering and back-biting happening behind the scene.

I told Guerin, "We've got a problem with the wives' tickets. I know some of the wives are unhappy, but you can't go spreading them all over the building. You can have your wife sit somewhere else, but a lot of the other wives want to sit together."

"I was just looking out for the best interests of the club," he said, indicating that he thought the wives sitting and talking with one another during games just made emotions run higher. He thought separating them would cool things down.

"But you made a bad situation worse," I said.

Wives are very sensitive to status. Some are hung up on clothes, wanting to dress as well as the wives of the stars. Others are angry because their husband doesn't make as much money as the husband of a teammate, when they just know their husband is the better player. And most wives aren't thrilled with the coach, because they want their husband to play more, shoot more, get more of the best things.

Under the best circumstances, a few wives always feel left out or angry about something. But this ticket mess was turning that speck in the eye into a cancer on the team. The Band-Aid they tried to put on it was to have the wives of Paul Silas, Zelmo Beaty, and myself sit together—because they were friends. At this point, nothing could repair the damage.

Through all this, somehow, we kept winning. We had run our record up to 16–1 when Guerin decided to call me in for a meeting. He showed me some shot charts, which keep track of which players shoot the ball and from where on the court.

"Our forwards aren't getting enough shots," he said.

The implication was that the guards—specifically, myself—were shooting too much.

"Richie, we're 16–1, we must be doing something right," I said.

The numbers showed that Zelmo Beaty and I were each averaging about 23 points. Joe Caldwell was scoring 21 a game. Our forwards were Paul Silas and Bridges, both of whom were known more for their rebounding and defense. Neither was a strong outside shooter. It made no sense for them to shoot the ball more, especially with us winning.

Then it dawned on me: *The Tour. Bridges.* He thought I still didn't like Bridges because of The Tour and the flare-up in training camp, so that's why he didn't get more shots. It was my fault, I wouldn't give him the ball. Bridges was shooting maybe six times a game. I don't believe Bridges complained to Guerin, but Guerin was just suspicious of me.

"If a guy plays forty minutes a night, he should shoot more than that," he said.

"Richie, our team has changed over the years," I said. "We run the ball more than when we had Cliff Hagan and Bob Pettit. Silas and Bridges get the ball off the boards, throw it out, and start our fast break. We're 16–1. It's your job to tell Bridges what he's doing and why we're winning."

"Don't tell me how to do my job," he screamed.

"Fine," I said. "We'll get him the ball more."

I said that just to get out of there, to bring an end to another conversation that never should have happened in the first place.

At this point, we were winning but not drawing very well. For the first time in the history of St. Louis basketball, we were consistently starting five black players—Bridges, Beaty, Silas, Caldwell, and myself. No one ever said anything, but suddenly we traded for Don Ohl, a good white guard who was at the end of his career. I mention his race only because I believe that was the reason the deal was made—to get a white player in the lineup. The thinking was that maybe more white fans would come out if there were white players on the court for the home team. No one said it, but I sensed it. Ohl moved into the lineup, and Caldwell went to the bench. Caldwell was scoring 20 points a game, so he couldn't figure out what he'd done wrong. At this point in their careers, Caldwell was the better player, yet Ohl was starting. And Ohl was white.

And suddenly, the race issue was tossed into the simmering pot and threatened to blow the lid right off the team.

Then there was another problem with the wives.

Because the crowds were small in St. Louis, some of the wives would invite friends who were originally sitting in other parts of the arena to come and sit with them. Who cared? The seats were empty, anyway, and the people had bought tickets to get into the building. Well, the ushers began checking tickets, telling the friends they couldn't sit with my wife and some of the other wives. They even checked the tickets of our wives, although they knew the women were the wives of the players. It only happened to some of the wives, not all. Naturally, my wife and a few others thought they had been singled out for this petty harassment by the front office, and we husbands weren't happy about it, either.

There had been yet another stupid incident in the previous season. Guerin called the team together and talked about the Rookie of the Year race, which was between Lou Hudson, who played for us, and Dave Bing of the Detroit Pistons. Back then, the players voted on the award, but you couldn't vote for anyone on your team. Guerin said that we could help Hudson to win the award by voting for anyone except Dave Bing. I realize that's part of how politics works, but it bothered me. I had nothing against Lou Hudson; I liked Lou Hudson. But I also thought a vote said something about you as a person, about your integrity.

I stood up and said, "I don't think that's right."

Guerin stared hard at me.

"You should vote your conscience," I said. "We should vote for the rookie we think is the best."

No one said anything, but I could tell that Guerin was steaming. He took it as an insult, that I was questioning his authority. To me, it had nothing to do with Guerin; I don't care who suggested it, I thought it was wrong. And as team captain, I felt obligated to say so. But I'm sure Guerin took this as another example of me being a troublemaker.

We should have had a tremendous team in 1967–68. We won fifty-six games, best in the Western Conference. But we were upset by the San Francisco (now Golden State) Warriors in the first round. We lost our cohesiveness as a team, and after the playoffs I was mentioned as the scapegoat despite averaging 20 points and 8.3 assists. Strangely, for a supposedly selfish player, I had a career high in assists; only Wilt Chamberlain had more that season. I finished second to Wilt in the MVP voting.

Despite all the problems, the Hawks did have a Lenny Wilkens Night for me, partly due to pressure in the black community. It had been a tradition to give a night to a player who had been with the team for a while. All the previous nights had been for white players. They gave me a color TV set, golf clubs, luggage, a silver tea set for my wife, a portrait of me by Cardinals outfielder and artist Curt Flood. Kerner even gave me a green Cadillac, and the Hawks said that I was a great guy, a real asset to the franchise and the community.

"Wilkens is among the top four guards in the league," Kerner told reporters. "I've got to believe that Lenny is the best backcourt man I've ever had (with the Hawks). He's got a million dollars worth of class."

In the end, all of that wasn't worth two cents.

I had made $35,000 that year, which was well below the market value of a player of my caliber. It was now the summer of 1968, and the American Basketball Association had come into existence, competing with the NBA and causing salaries to rise. An All-Star guard with Philadelphia, Hal Greer, had just signed for $60,000. The great Oscar Robertson had a new $80,000 contract, as did Jerry West. I thought I should get paid somewhere between those guys. At the very least, I wanted a raise to Greer's level of $60,000.

I met with Marty Blake, the Hawks general manager. Actually, I listened, and Blake yammered away.

"Do you believe these salaries?" he asked, not waiting for an answer. "Guys want $75,000 . . . $80,000. If that's what you're looking for, then there's nothing for us to talk about. But $75,000?"

"That sounds like a nice number to me," I said.

"If you feel that way, then we have nothing to talk about," Blake said.

I didn't go into the meeting with the intention of building a wall between myself and the Hawks, but it was obvious that Blake had no real intention of negotiating with me. He didn't treat me with respect. He just wanted to complain about the high salaries, kind of a strange way to convince me that I wasn't worth whatever I was asking—although he had no idea how much I had in mind.

I realized it was futile for me to talk to the Hawks, or at least to Blake. The Hawks came back and tried to sign me to a $45,000 deal with a $2,500 bonus. Then they said they wanted to trade me to Boston. I liked the idea of playing for the Celtics, but I knew that $45,000 was much less than I was worth. I also didn't trust them to make the deal. I asked to talk to Celtics president Red Auerbach, figuring I could work out a contract with him—and help the deal go through. That's common today when a name player is about to be traded near the end of his contract—the player's agent talks to the team trying to make the trade, and they come to a contract agreement. Then the deal is announced. But that rarely—if ever—happened in 1968.

The Hawks refused to let me speak to Auerbach. I refused to sign their contract. The trade collapsed. I sat home in St. Louis.

Then the team was sold to a group in Atlanta. As the team prepared to play the next season in a new city, Atlanta decided to host a booster club meeting and a media gathering to introduce the players to the fans and writers. Every Hawks player was invited to attend—except me. That decision was made by the Hawks management. I wasn't signed, but I was still part of the team and they should have invited me. I guess they didn't want me there because I was still unsigned, and they figured that eventually they'd trade me. This was in the era when there was virtually no free agency; a player's contract would expire, but his rights still belonged to the original team. The only leverage a player had to try to secure a better contract was to hold out during training camp, which I did. They began to fine me $100, then $150, for each day of training camp I missed. Of course, I wasn't signed, and I wasn't being paid by them, so how could they take my money?

The front office started a whispering campaign against me. They said I wouldn't report to Atlanta because it was a southern city, and I considered it to be prejudiced.

That was untrue.

Then they said I was jealous of Guerin and some of the players.

That wasn't true, either.

Then former owner Ben Kerner said I was just plain selfish.

That was an utter lie.

Kerner was ripping me, even though he no longer owned the team, and even though I was his favorite guard only a few months earlier. The new Hawks ownership wanted to meet with me, so Marilyn and I flew to Atlanta and checked into the Marriott Hotel. Then something strange happened: Marilyn was reading a book in our room and I was looking at the newspaper when we heard someone rattling around the door with a key. The person entered our room, looked up, apologized, and slinked away.

A few hours later, I was at the Hawks' office and I saw the same guy who had come into my room! He worked for the team. He offered a lame apology about the room. He offered no explanation of how he ended up with a key to my room. The Hawks had set up a black real-estate agent to show us around town, and he led us to one area. Silas and Beaty had already bought homes there. The agent made it clear that this was the best part of town for us, meaning black people.

That didn't thrill us, but our real problem wasn't with the city of Atlanta, it was with Marty Blake and his approach to the negotiations. He didn't want to pay me anything near my market value, and I'm sure Marty had orders limiting how much he could offer. But the Hawks floated rumors that I didn't want to play in Atlanta because of the "racial situation," and that began to appear in the local newspapers. That was really poor strategy, because what if I *had* decided to sign with the Hawks? Why trash your own player to the press? But it continued, as stories were written about my being jealous of Richie Guerin, and then a rehash of the old Tour controversy.

I requested a meeting with Tom Cousins, the new Hawks owner. I told him that I wanted to play for the Hawks, but my contract was important to me.

"If you really want to know my worth, call some other NBA general managers," I said.

He said he'd do that.

A few weeks later, Cousins called back and said what I was asking for was fair. So he offered me $75,000 on something stipulated as an "attitude contract." My base pay would be $50,000, and I'd receive another $25,000 at the end of the year if Guerin decided I had been a good soldier and was worth it. I was insulted. After eight years with the franchise, suddenly I was a headcase who needed to be held in line by the threat of losing $25,000? Then I met with Guerin, who sat in a dark room at O'Hare Airport wearing sunglasses the entire time and swearing it wasn't he who wanted the attitude clause, it was ownership.

That led to my turning everything over to Larry Fleischer, who had been general counsel for the Players Association. I'd never had an agent until that moment, although Larry had advised me about the kind of salary I should expect. This only hardened feelings on both sides: Fleischer believed that the Hawks' contract offer as structured was ridiculous. And the Hawks were angry that I had hired Fleischer to represent me, because this was 1968 and few players had agents or lawyers.

Then I received a call from Dick Vertlieb, the general manager of the Seattle Supersonics. He wanted to know if I was interested in playing for his team. The Sonics were an expansion team; they'd had a 23–59 record in their first year, and now they wanted to trade Walt Hazzard for me. I had them talk to Fleischer, and they agreed to pay me $75,000 annually for two years. I approved the contract, and the deal was made. This happened at the end of training camp. I hadn't signed and wasn't playing. I had been to Seattle only a few times, and it had always rained. Marilyn couldn't picture Seattle: She had never been there and thought it was up near Alaska with the Eskimos. I would have preferred to be traded to the Celtics or to another contender, but Seattle really did want me—and at this stage that was truly a refreshing feeling. The move proved to be one of the best things that ever happened to me.

CHAPTER NINE

THE CONVERSATION THAT CHANGED MY LIFE took place during the 1968–69 season, my first in Seattle. We were a second-year team, and not a very good one, but I was reasonably happy: I found Seattle to be a great place to live, and I was relieved to be out of the emotional quagmire that the Hawks had become. Even though the Sonics weren't a contender, their front office was much better to me than the one in St. Louis.

About midseason, Sonics general manager Dick Vertlieb asked me if I'd ever be interested in coaching. To me, it was one of those hypothetical things, something to think about while passing time.

"Some day, I'd like to try it," I said, not really believing it would ever happen.

He wanted to know if I'd always wanted to coach.

"Three years ago, I'd have said never," I said. "But once in a while now, I think about it."

And that was the end of it. It never occurred to me that I might be coaching within a year, and certainly not as a player-coach. Among other things, the only black coach in the NBA was Bill Russell, who was the player/coach of the Celtics, so it wasn't as if the door was open and the welcome mat was out for minorities to become head coaches. Russell had become the Celtics coach when Red Auerbach, emotionally spent from being both general manager and coach, realized he had to give up one of the jobs. He liked running the Celtics front office, and it dawned on him that no one could get as much out of Russell the player as Russell himself. It was a unique situation, hardly an indication that minorities were about to suddenly receive serious consideration for other coaching jobs.

Right after my first season in Seattle, Al Bianchi resigned as our coach. I didn't apply for the job. I didn't even think about applying for the job. I was like all the other players; I just wondered whom they'd hire next. One day, Vertlieb called and said he wanted to have dinner with Marilyn and me. We went to his house, had a nice meal, and talked some basketball, but nothing serious; I don't remember him saying anything about the next coach.

After we ate, Vertlieb asked if I wanted to play some pool. We went into another room, Marilyn staying with Joanna, Vertlieb's wife.

I took a couple of shots, and so did he.

Then he said, "I want you to be the player/coach."

"You have got to be crazy!" I said.

Then I laughed.

It had never crossed my mind that I might be the next Sonics coach. I was still in my prime as a player, and I figured they'd find another full-time coach.

"I'm serious about this," Vertlieb said.

"And you're still crazy," I said. "No way."

But Vertlieb persisted. He said he liked my maturity. He said he trusted my talent judgment. He said I had the respect of other players. He said I knew the league. It was an incredible sales job, and he was laying it on very thick—but in a way that made me believe it.

"Lenny," he said. "When you play, it's like you're coaching on the floor anyway. So why not just go ahead and be the coach?"

Then I started to think about some of the coaches I had played for in the NBA. To say the least, not all of them were the second coming of Red Auerbach. I had played in the same backcourt with Richie Guerin while he coached the Hawks; Richie did a decent job, but frankly, I didn't see anything that made me believe that the job of being a player/coach was beyond me. We won a lot of games in St. Louis with Richie as our coach.

My college coach, Joe Mullaney, used to tell stories about Fuzzy Levane when Levane coached the Knicks. During timeouts,

Levane, who often stuttered, allowed Carl Braun—one of his play-ers—to do most of the talking. After a while, Braun did all the talk-ing during every timeout.

One time, Levane said, "C-C-Carl, wait a min-min-ute. I-I-I'm the c-c-coach here."

Braun said, "OK, go ahead."

Then Levane looked into the eyes of his players and said, "C-C-Carl, you t-t-tell them what to do."

Another time, Levane tried to give the players a pep talk by showing them pictures of his family. "If we d-d-don't win, then I-I-I'll be outta work," he said. "And-and-and my wife and fa-fa-family will starve."

Later, I played for Fuzzy Levane. And I played for Paul Sey-mour. And I played for Harry "The Horse" Gallatin. And finally, Richie Guerin and Al Bianchi. I liked some of them better than oth-ers, but none of those guys made me think, "I could never do this."

Most of these coaches were former players themselves; their idea of practice was to scrimmage, then shoot some free throws. A scouting report was saying, "Hey, you've got Oscar Robertson tonight. He's a really good player, so you better be heads up." Players weren't taught, they were supposed to learn the game on their own.

When I played for Gallatin, he gave me a stack of forty differ-ent plays. I looked at them once, and that was it. Virtually all of them were to get the ball to Cliff Hagan and Bob Pettit. I already knew how and where on the court they wanted the ball; I knew the basic plays that worked best for our Hawks team. There was noth-ing new in Gallatin's strategy.

As for his approach to handling the team, when Harry was upset with us, he'd say, "If you don't like it, we'll go behind the barn and settle this."

That was pretty silly. What player would want to fight the coach, behind the barn or anywhere else? What would that prove? And why would the coach even say that, because suppose a player actually took him up on it? Then what? Gallatin was like most coaches of that era: When things went bad, they just screamed at you, challenging your manhood. They believed that was the only way to get you to play harder and better. Gallatin was a nut about physical fitness; during training camp, he made us run up and down stairs—on our toes! He had us do all these isometric exercises. Then we'd scrimmage—and scrimmage hard—for ninety minutes. By the end of training camp, we were exhausted. He nearly killed our star, Bob Pettit, who was coming to the end of his career, still playing forty-two minutes a night, and didn't need to be run into complete exhaustion during training camp. From Gallatin, I learned that you have to treat your players as individuals, even in training camp. Veterans with bad knees or other physical problems have a good idea of what it takes to get into shape. They don't have to take part in every drill and every practice. The idea is to get the most out of them during the season, not to wear them out as they try to keep up with the younger players.

Gallatin also worried about guys being out too late. He installed a curfew and then sat in the hotel lobby making sure that everyone arrived back in their rooms on time. Of course, guys found ways to sneak back out of the hotel to continue their nocturnal activities while Gallatin thought they were asleep. He also had some substitution patterns that made no sense, leaving some of our best players on the bench for long stretches in critical parts of the game. His idea of motivation was to write on the blackboard before a big game: IT'S NOT THE DOG IN THE FIGHT THAT COUNTS, IT'S THE FIGHT IN THE DOG.

I'm not trying just to be critical of Gallatin, but to give an idea of what coaching in the 1960s was like on most NBA teams. Guerin replaced Gallatin and eased up on some of the Mickey Mouse stuff such as curfews. But when he didn't know what to do, he just screamed at us. We were stupid. We were gutless. We were an embarrassment. We should be ashamed to cash our paychecks. Cowards, that's what we were. We were lucky that we weren't sweeping the street somewhere, because that's the only job we could do right. On and on, bellowing and insulting us just like his coaches had done to him—and doing it in some of the ugliest language you can imagine. He'd cuss a player out in front of the whole team, and do it while getting so red in the face, the veins in his neck bulging, you'd have sworn he was about to have a stroke right in front of you. While Guerin avoided some of the pitfalls of Gallatin, he eventually lost control of the team by playing favorites.

As I considered Vertlieb's offer, I thought about these coaches and asked myself, "Why can't I do the job?"

No one had taught me how to think like a coach, but I continually heard I was "the coach on the floor." Besides, no one had ever taught me how to play the pro game; I figured it out for myself, and I did pretty well. Strategy was very basic back then: I never even played for a coach who double-teamed on defense until my last year with the Hawks. Back then, you were told, "Jerry West is your man," and you covered Jerry West. You didn't expect anyone to help you defend Jerry West, and you didn't help anyone else defend his man.

The offense was simple: Keep moving. Keep moving without the ball. Keep moving the ball by passing it. Know your teammates. Know who likes the ball on the left side of the basket, who likes it on the right. Know who pouts if he doesn't touch the ball for a few possessions, and know who is unselfish and is willing to sacrifice his scoring to set picks and rebounds.

The more I thought about it, the more it made sense.

As I've said, Seattle was a recent expansion team, and not a very good one. Some of the players were Tommy Kron, whom we called Krash Kron because he really hustled; Rod Thorn, Plummer Lott, Dorie Murrey, Bob Kauffman, Art Harris, Bob Rule, and an aging Tom Meschery. There wasn't a lot of talent on the roster. Al Bianchi coached the team for the first two years. He was a study in patience. He kept our spirits up. He treated us as men. As the Sonics coach, he never even fined a single player. I averaged 22.4 points, 8.2 assists, and 6.2 rebounds for him, playing in every game and on the floor for forty-three minutes a night.

I later discovered that Vertlieb traded for me over the objections of Sonics owner Sam Schulman, who loved Walt Hazzard. But Vertlieb insisted I'd mean more to the franchise than Hazzard, and Schulman finally agreed to the deal.

And now, a year later, Vertlieb wanted to make me player/coach.

I was only thirty-two, the star of the team. I was in my prime as a player. It wasn't as if I'd demanded to coach: They came to me. It didn't take me long to realize that this wasn't just another job offer, it was an opportunity not only for myself, but for all the minorities in the future who would aspire to coaching. I didn't know all the problems I'd face as a player/coach, but I was sure I had to take the job. I had a moral obligation. Who knew when the chance would come for me—or any black man—to be a head coach again?

I met with Schulman, who had gone from hating the trade that brought me to Seattle to becoming my biggest fan. It was obvious that he wanted me to take the job. He asked me about different players in the league, about what the Sonics needed to become a contender and how I'd handle certain situations. I asked him if I'd be allowed to make a trade or draft a player, even if he didn't agree with it. He said if the coach and general manager wanted to make a certain move and he could afford it, then he'd give the OK. That made sense. He was the owner. He was paying the bills, so he must have the final say on business matters. But I also knew he respected his basketball people, as was evident when he allowed Vertlieb to trade Hazzard for me.

We agreed on a one-year contract for me to be the player/coach.

Think about this: Seattle wanted to give me a two-year deal, but I insisted on one year. The raise to be a coach was a small one, about $15,000. I figured if I did a good job in my first year as a player/coach, I'd have more leverage to negotiate a longer contract. Of course, if I flopped, it would be easy for them to fire or trade me because the contract was for only one year. I didn't think about that. I just assumed I'd perform well, and they'd want to keep me.

Today, it's standard for a coach to have at least a three-year contract, to protect you from an owner or general manager who might panic during a slow start and fire you in your first year. Having to pay a guy a lot of money over three years for *not* coaching at least makes them pause before dropping the axe.

But I wandered out on that precarious coaching limb with a one-year contract, and I didn't think twice. I was taking a one-year contract to coach a team that was only in its third year of existence, a team that had yet to make the playoffs and wasn't likely to do it in the near future.

Only now do I see the risk I was taking. But back then, I was sure it would work out. Either I was confident or I just didn't know any better, but I took the job with no fear.

At the press conference to announce my appointment, the Sonics praised my leadership, talked about how I'd been a coach on the floor, so why not just go ahead and make me the coach?

When I spoke, I said, "I've seen the player/coach role work. Bill Russell did a good job in Boston. I learned a lot from Richie Guerin, and he was successful, too. The big thing Russell did as player/coach was to give 100 percent as a player. The coach who can give a good effort on the floor can demand more from his players. My teammates know I give up the ball. If they're open, I'll pass it to them. I'll handle my players with respect and treat them as men."

My hiring was greeted with varying degrees of enthusiasm. Sportswriters thought it was a good idea, at least worth a try. I received a telegram of congratulations from NBA commissioner Walter Kennedy. Other players and coaches sent their regards, expressing confidence in me.

Marilyn was very excited and proud, but she was worried, too. She'd been around the NBA long enough to know that my life was about to change. I'd no longer just have myself and my own game to worry about; I was responsible for all the players, for the team. She knew that some players would test me. Some players were lazy, some weren't very tough, and some wouldn't like anything I did because some players just don't like coaches, period. She knew it was easier for a player to shake off a hard loss than a coach, and now I'd feel it two ways—as a player, and as a coach. A player often has a wife or friends who tell him, "It wasn't your fault your team lost, the coach screwed up." But no one can say that to the coach.

Or they might say, "Don't take the loss so hard, you played a good game. You did all you could." But when you coach, your job is to win every game. And when you lose, you invariably look back and ask yourself, "Could I have done something else, something better?"

I went from being responsible for just myself and accountable only to my coach, to being responsible for twelve players, to having to answer to ownership and the front office, and to being second-

With the Providence College Friars—in what I thought would be my last basketball uniform.

The sign of arrival as a pro: Getting Bill Russell in the air (and driving past Bob Cousy) in my early years with the St. Louis Hawks.

1

2

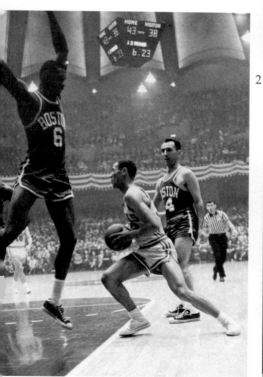

3

A left-handed (of course) hook shot during my next stop, the Seattle Supersonics, in the city where I still make my home.

The fans greeted me warmly, but it was a bittersweet homecoming to
return to Seattle with the Cavaliers after being traded by the Sonics.

A good point guard knows when to give up the ball. When you're triple-teamed, as I am here with the Cavs, is one of those times.

Older and wiser, an ex-player by now, the tides of the NBA brought me back to Seattle, where I got to coach my only league champion—so far.

With Wayne Embry, the man who hired me to come back to Cleveland—people do seem to keep asking me to come back places—with a cup commemorating my 600th NBA coaching victory.

Making a point in the Cavs huddle, with the team that could have been a Finals fixture if not for Michael Jordan—and might have anyway if we all could have stayed together.   8

On the sidelines with the 1992 Dream Team: I'm sitting between Magic Johnson, who's watching intently, and Chuck Daly, who can't help being nervous.

Sharing a Dreamers laugh with Clyde Drexler.

In the 1996 Olympics it was my team, and my turn to fight nerves. Listening to the national anthem with (from right) Penny Hardaway, Gary Payton, Mitch Richmond, and David Robinson.

How could I resist a victory cigar the night I passed Red Auerbach in career coaching victories?

13

With Father Thomas Mannion—my mentor, my dear friend, the man who was such an important influence on me as a boy, and remained so throughout my life.

14

Our family—me, my daughter Leesha, my wife Marilyn, Marilyn's mother Zaida Reed, my daughter Jamee, Leesha's husband Craig, and my son Randy—at Zaida's eighty-seventh birthday.

With my beautiful grandchildren, Ashlee and Nicholle.

15

It's getting to be a habit: At the Basketball Hall of Fame, when I was enshrined for the second time, in 1998, as a coach—nine years after I was elected as a player.

Here with Marilyn, the only woman I could want by my side through all these wonderful years.

guessed by the media and fans. Intellectually I knew this, but there is no way to feel the full impact of that change until you take the job.

I hired Tom Meschery to be my assistant. He was near the end of his playing career, and I respected Tom for his intensity and his knowledge of the game. I needed someone whom the players respected to be my eyes, ears, and voice on the bench. I also needed someone to keep track of the basics such as fouls, timeouts, and how many minutes certain players had been on the floor so they didn't become too fatigued.

I also knew that I'd need a friend.

As the coach, I could no longer hang out with the players after the game. There had to be some separation. If I started going out to eat with a couple of players on a regular basis, the other guys would assume I was playing favorites, especially if it seemed "my pets" were playing a lot or taking too many shots. If I learned anything about coaching from my final years in St. Louis with Richie Guerin, it was not to try to be friends with the players. A coach can't do that, at least not the kind of buddy/buddy relationship that players have with each other. A coach can't have a beer with the players. He can't play cards with them. He can give them advice, but he can't loan them money. You're no longer on equal terms with them; you're their boss. It's sometimes hard, and a little cold. John Tresvant was a friend of mine from our playing days; now that I was his coach, he still wanted to be buddies. Soon he was asking for special favors, wanting to come a little late to practice, not big things—but I saw a problem developing, and we eventually had to trade him.

No matter how prepared, how ready you think you are for your first coaching job, I have news for you:

You are never ready.

As a rookie player/coach, I expected to have Dick Vertlieb as my guide. He was the one who traded for me, the one who made the decision to make me the coach, and he was also a fine general manager and a good man.

I was hired on August 5, 1969, as coach.

In October 1969, Vertlieb resigned as general manager to take another job.

When training camp opened, we had five—yes, *five*—holdouts. One of them was Bob Boozer, a very good forward whom we acquired from Chicago in a trade. When he finally did report to camp, he was out of shape.

Suddenly, I found myself worrying about our front office getting my players signed.

I worried about Boozer's weight.

I worried about Meschery, who had developed a blood problem and couldn't play as much as we'd hoped.

I worried about Bob Rule, who was a very gifted player and was expected to be our starting center. But Rule liked the nightlife and was another player who wasn't in top physical condition. And then he hurt his ankle.

Suddenly, I realized how vulnerable a coach can be, because he can look at one team on paper and then watch it disintegrate right before his eyes because of injuries, contract squabbles, or a lack of dedication from some guys. I was aware of these things during my playing career, but I never fully understood the impact of them on a coach until I became one. Besides, as a player, my first responsibility was to play as well as I could; if a player has a good season and the team still loses because several of his teammates were hurt, well, he's done his job. But for the coach it's a different story. Furthermore, I was a rookie coach without a general manager to help him. For the first two months of the season, I also had to be the guy to talk trades.

Within a few months, I had gone from being a thirty-two-year-old point guard to being a coach and general manager, making the personnel decisions. Early in the season, Phoenix general manager Jerry Colangelo called me about a deal. He wanted Art Harris, one of our guards. I liked Dick Snyder, one of Phoenix's guards. We agreed on the trade. Then I had to tell Harris about the deal, and he nearly broke into tears. He was devastated, and I felt awful because I was not just the one delivering the news, but I also had made the decision. I was his teammate, and I was telling him I wanted someone else in his spot. It was the correct move, and it was easy to do when I talked to another executive on the phone, when the player was just a name on a piece of paper. But it was different when that player sat in front of me . . . I've been traded myself and realize how traumatic that is to the player and his family. You aren't just sending a player to a new job, you're uprooting his wife and kids, too.

And we lost our first six games.

Part of the problem was the point guard. The point guard was thinking too much like a coach, working too hard to get the other players involved in the offense. The point guard who averaged 22 points the year before was passing up shots that he needed to take. And the point guard had no one to tell him that, because that point guard was me.

Finally, on October 31, 1969, I got my first coaching victory. We beat Cincinnati, 129–121. Before the game, the coach had a talk with the point guard. He told the point guard, "If we're ever going to win a game, you better start scoring or I'm not going to be coaching for very long." I had 38 points that night, and I felt an enormous sense of relief to know that I wasn't about to finish the season with an 0–82 record.

Next, I found myself yelling at my players.

I wasn't as bad as Richie Guerin and some of my other coaches, but I started ripping into them too much. Telling a guy that he stinks doesn't make him a better player if you don't tell him *why* he stinks and *what* he needs to do to become a better player. After one of our losses, I fined the entire team $100—including myself—for a lack of effort. Another time, I hit Rule with a $500 fine for missing a team flight. Early that season, I was frustrated because we were losing. I was frustrated because Vertlieb was gone and it wasn't until January that we hired a general manager. I wasn't playing well, and I knew my game had tailed off because I had too many things on my mind, and it was taking away from my concentration as a player.

At home, I was very quiet, almost sullen, taking out the losses on poor Marilyn and our kids. Then we lost a game on a night when my wife had some friends in town. As I came out of the dressing room, I heard her telling them, "Well, we can forget about going out to eat tonight."

"Why?" they asked.

"Because of the game," she said. "Lenny is not going to be in the mood."

That really bothered me. I was letting basketball dominate my life, even at home. That wasn't right. My wife's evening shouldn't be spoiled because my team lost a game. I shouldn't be a distant father or husband because my team played poorly. I didn't want basketball to consume me and my family. I'd spent my life saying the most important things to me were God and my family, and here I was, putting basketball in front of all that. If I'd been on the road for a week and had just come home, it was natural that Marilyn would want to go out to eat: She'd been home with the kids all that time, while I was eating out. She was taking care of everything at home, twenty-four hours a day. She deserved a break.

This all hit me when I overheard her tell her friends about forgetting dinner.

"No," I said. "Let's go out."

I've seen coaches put their families through a mental meatgrinder, with the entire family's mood dependent upon how the team played. When I saw it in someone else, I knew it was ridiculous. When it began to creep into my own family, I had to stand up and put a stop to it. The family feels helpless. They can't play. They can't coach. They can't do anything but sit back, watch, and maybe pray the team will win so Dad won't be in a lousy mood. On that night, I vowed not to take work home to the extent that it got in the way of my family. When I realized the pain I was putting them through because of my approach to coaching, it really hurt me. They didn't lose the game. They didn't forget to rebound or play defense. All they did was love me, win or lose, and that was the least I could do for them.

The lessons continued.

One day, a college coach named Marv Harshman was at a practice. I really lit into one of my players because he couldn't get the ball to one of our big men at the low post. I let him have it: How dumb could he be? Didn't he see the man open? Didn't he want to get him the ball?

In some ways, I was acting just like Guerin and my other coaches without even realizing it.

After practice, Harshman told me, "Lenny, you know that you're a very gifted player."

I waited, knowing Marv had something on his mind.

"You really see the floor," he said. "It's easy for you to make that play, to get the ball to the low post. But not everyone sees the game the same as you."

I was starting to get the message.

"You have to show them, to teach them," he said. "You can't assume everyone knows the game like you do. Show them that there's more than one way to make that play."

I nodded.

Of course, *teach them*. It sounds obvious as I talk about it now, but teaching wasn't the norm for NBA coaching back then. It was screaming. What Marv told me made sense. I thought back to my rookie year with the Hawks, and how no one really taught me anything. Few people even said a word, unless it was to yell at me. I was acting just like my former coaches, who figured, "Hey, I know how to make that play, so you should, too."

But why would the players know how to play the pro game, especially the rookies? Even some of the veterans had real blind spots in their games, because no one bothered to show them how to make certain plays. If you didn't pick it up on your own, the assumption was that you couldn't do it.

About midseason, I really started coaching the guys. We went back to the basics. And I felt better because of something else that came out of that conversation with Marv Harshman: I didn't have to yell all the time. Screaming was never a part of my personality, so I was glad that I could coach more like myself. Talk quietly. Listen. Teach. Be patient. Admittedly, not all of this happened at once, but slowly I began to feel comfortable as a coach.

And we began to win.

After a rocky start, we went 18–12 to finish the season with a 36–46 record, which was an improvement from the 30–52 mark the year before. Bob Houbregs had been named general manager. He asked me to return as player/coach, and Schulman gave me a two-year contract.

☐

When your star players are injured, it doesn't matter if you're a great coach. You lose.

I always knew that was true, but I learned it the hard way in my second season as the Sonics coach. It began with Bob Rule, my talented but troubled center who was holding out. He rarely played in top physical condition, and he liked to party, yet he still averaged 20 points and 10 rebounds for me. Now, as the 1970–71 training camp opened, he wasn't signed, and I knew he was getting fat. I gave him a weight and said he'd be fined $100 per pound if he failed to meet it. It took a long time for him to sign, but he finally did right before the season. He nearly starved himself, but he showed up close to his designated weight. Rule was brilliant early in the season, and we moved into first place.

Then he blew an Achilles tendon and was out for the rest of the season.

We had acquired Don Smith, a forward, right before the season opened. After Rule got hurt, I moved Smith to center. In the next twelve games, he averaged close to 19 points and 17 rebounds. He was outstanding. We were winning. Then his chest began to hurt. It turned out that Smith had pericarditis, an inflamation of the heart lining. He was out for several months, and when he did play again, he wasn't the force that he once was under the basket.

You lose your top two big guys, you lose.

It's that simple, even if the coach is also an All-Star point guard. In fact, I was the MVP of the 1971 All-Star game, scoring 21 points in twenty minutes. But without my big people, I was a coach who wasn't going to win a lot of games.

Schulman tried to alleviate the situation by signing Spencer Haywood, who had been a star in the rival American Basketball Association. The NBA and the ABA never competed on the court, but they tried to sign the same players out of college, and they also tried to convince players to jump leagues. Rick Barry was the first to do it, going from the NBA's San Francisco Warriors to the Oakland Oaks of the ABA. Part of the reason was that Oakland hired Bruce Hale as its coach; Hale just happened to be Barry's former college coach and his current father-in-law.

Schulman was the first NBA owner to attempt to sign a player from the ABA. Haywood was six-foot-nine, and he averaged 30 points and 19 rebounds in his first year with Denver in the ABA.

But there was a problem. The ABA claimed Haywood was still under contract to its Denver franchise. Some of the NBA teams were unhappy with what they considered Schulman's "raid" of Haywood from the ABA, mostly because they didn't think of it first. The league owners even voted, 15–2, to take some sort of disciplinary action against Schulman. Naturally, lawsuits were filed from several different directions.

I kept hearing that Haywood would soon be playing for us. Then he wasn't. Then he was. Oh, no, not just yet. Then the lawyer said this, the judge said that. This was all new, because pro basketball was changing. None of my old coaches ever had to face the prospect of players jumping to a team at midseason, or a star coming to a team in the middle of the year—assuming a judge said it was OK. This was disturbing to the players, who didn't know when Haywood would come, or if he'd fit in with the team. They also knew he would be paid more money than any of them, and that caused another problem—jealousy. Who was this new guy who had never played a minute in the NBA and was going to be the highest-paid player on the team?

The blessing was that when Haywood was finally cleared to play, it was obvious that he had great talent. In thirty-three games for us, he averaged 20 points and 12 rebounds. He also was a decent guy, and the players accepted him.

There was one rough spot. Rod Thorn had become my assistant, and one night he chastised Haywood for forcing too many shots, not passing to open teammates. This was at halftime. So in the second half, Haywood pouted and refused to shoot, which really hurt our team. We lost the game.

I really wanted to blast Haywood in the dressing room in front of the other players. But this wasn't my way, and I realized it would just make the situation worse. Times were changing. This was 1970, and it wasn't going to motivate someone if I embarrassed him in front of other people.

I let things calm down, and then I approached Spencer away from the other players.

"Spencer, did you learn anything tonight?" I asked.

He looked at me strangely. "What do you mean?"

"Rod was just trying to give you some constructive criticism about sharing the ball," I said. "But you copped an attitude about it. You were out to show us, right?"

He said nothing, but I knew he was listening.

"You wanted to make a point, but what did you really do?" I asked. "You hurt the whole team. Yes, you showed us that we need you to score. But by not shooting, you saw what happened. We lost, right?"

Haywood looked me right in the eye. He nodded. I could tell he understood.

After that day, I had no real problems with Spencer Haywood. But we just weren't a very good team. Still, despite the injuries and controversies, we finished with a 38–44 record, a two-game improvement over my first season as player/coach.

I was upbeat entering the next season, my third as coach of the Sonics, and we ended up with a 47–35 record for the first winning season in the history of the franchise. We did it even though Haywood slipped on a wet floor and injured his knee, Don Smith missed the final 13 games with an ankle problem, and Dick Snyder hurt a finger on his shooting hand in the same game in which we lost Haywood and was through for the season.

We played the final nine games without three starters, and we failed to make the playoffs. But I thought we played well, given the injuries and another set of legal battles. We had signed another player from the ABA, Jim McDaniels, and that led to more lawsuits and more problems as I was supposed to work him into the lineup even though he joined us at midseason and wasn't in shape and didn't understand our system. He also wasn't nearly a player of Haywood's caliber, and the money McDaniels received to jump leagues bothered some of our players, who were feeling underpaid and underappreciated as the front office continued to pursue these players from the ABA.

In that context, 47 victories and a home attendance that set a franchise record of eleven thousand per game was a good year—at the very least worthy of my being retained as coach. The team even had a "Lenny Wilkens Night," on February 26, 1972, where I received a variety of gifts along with $500 bonds for each of my three children. The only downside was that we didn't make the playoffs, but in the early 1970s only the top three teams in each division made the playoffs. So even though we were 12 games over .500, we missed the postseason.

But I was concerned about Bob Houbregs, the general manager who replaced Vertlieb. He had been a star at the University of Washington and was working for the Converse Shoe Company when the Sonics hired him as GM. At first, we got along well, but in that third season I sensed a distance between us. I wasn't sure why, but he just didn't seem as open to me.

Then, near the end of the season, I received in the mail a clipping of a story from the Tacoma newspaper. In it, Houbregs was quoted as saying that he thought my play had slipped, that I had been "a one-on-one player," and I was slowing down. That made no sense, since I had never been a "one-on-one player." He also wondered if trying to do both jobs was taking too much out of me.

This bothered me because Houbregs had never come to me with these concerns. When I saw the comments, I had to wonder if he had some deeper agenda that I hadn't realized. I had a very close relationship with Sam Schulman, the team owner; Houbregs may have been upset by this. Also, he hadn't hired me, and general managers usually like to hire their own coaches.

When the season was over, Houbregs convinced Schulman that being a player/coach was too much for me. They wanted to hire Tom Nissalke as the coach and asked me to be strictly a point guard. I didn't agree with that evaluation of my coaching, but I was willing to return to being a full-time player and help Tom Nissalke in any way that I could. I even met with Nissalke, and we seemed to be on the same page.

Instead, I was handed a plane ticket out of town.

CHAPTER TEN

I'LL NEVER FORGET THE SIGN: *THIS IS LENNY'S COUNTRY.*

That was what greeted me, along with a sellout crowd chanting my name, at the old Seattle Coliseum when I returned to play there as a member of the Cleveland Cavaliers.

Yes, the Cleveland Cavaliers.

I went from being player/coach of the Seattle Sonics to being a point guard with the Cavs. I went from a former expansion team on the rise to an even newer expansion team. I went from a team where I was the coach, a team that won a franchise-record 47 games, to a team that had won only 38 games total in its first two years of existence. I went to a team that some players called "Devil's Island," a team where some of my new teammates dubbed me a Prisoner of War.

That's because my new Cleveland teammates saw things much as I did. They couldn't figure out why Seattle would fire me as coach, much less why the Sonics would trade me. The way the Sonics treated me was inexplicable: I was first assured that I would not be traded; then, when I heard I was headed to Chicago, another struggling franchise, I was told, "No way, we'd never trade you to a team like that." If they were going to deal me, it would be to a contender. Told me that right to my face. They also said they'd keep me informed about any possible deals, so I wouldn't be surprised by anything.

Yet the first person to hear I was traded to Cleveland was my father-in-law. And he lived in New York. And he heard it on the radio!

The next was Marilyn, who first received a call from her father, and she couldn't believe the report was true. Then the Sonics called, saying they couldn't find me and had to reach me as soon as possible. She told them that I was playing golf with Dr. Jack Nichols, the Sonics team dentist. It was a mess. The Sonics had to have been talking about this deal for several days. You don't make a trade of this magnitude in five minutes. Barry Clemens and I were being sent to Cleveland for Butch Beard. I was an All-Star. Beard was considered the Cavs' best young player. Then the Sonics insisted they still couldn't find me even after Marilyn told them I was out playing golf; that was a joke, because Bob Houbregs knew where I usually played—since Houbregs and I played at the same country club.

Finally, Marilyn tracked me down on the course and told me about the trade to Cleveland.

I was stunned. I knew it was true, but I couldn't believe it. I had been lied to. The Sonics knew that Seattle had become a real home to us. They knew that I wanted to play for a contender, or at least for a West Coast team so I could be closer to home.

Instead, they traded me to Cleveland. I had nothing against Cleveland; I later coached the Cavs and loved the fans, the area, everything about it. But that was from 1986 to 1993.

This was 1972. Cleveland was not near the West Coast. Cleveland had the worst record in the NBA over the previous two years. I was going to be thirty-five by the start of the season, and I knew I only had a few good years left as a player. I wanted to spend them with a team where I'd have a real chance to win an NBA title. Cleveland was not that team.

The Sonics had just dumped me. They didn't want me to play for a West Coast team, where I would come back several times a season and help beat them. They didn't want me to play for a contender, because it would look bad for them if I ended up on a team that won a title the year after they traded me. They wanted me as far out of sight and off their radar screen as they could find in the NBA.

That was Cleveland.

And they didn't inform me of the deal in advance because they were afraid that I'd call Bill Fitch from the Cavs and tell him that I really didn't want to play for Cleveland, and that would kill the trade.

To the Sonics, this was just business.

To me, it was a lack of respect. It gave no consideration to what I had done for the franchise, and how the team had improved in the three years I was there. It didn't matter to them that I was entrenched in Seattle, a part of the community. Nor did they take my word that I would help new coach Tom Nissalke any way I could, that I had no desire to undercut him. I'd be an All-Star point guard for him. My real desire was for the Sonics to win.

Then I thought of something else: Toward the end of my final year with Seattle, the Sonics had a night for me, saying that I was a great guy, an asset to the community.

A few months later, they traded me.

That had also happened in St. Louis. Near the end of my final season with the Hawks, they had a night for me. Again, I was a wonderful guy, an asset to the town and the franchise.

And a few months later, I was gone—and so was the team.

I didn't think I could survive too many more "nights."

The Sonics were right about one thing: At first, I didn't want to play for Cleveland.

It was nothing against the city, the franchise, or Bill Fitch. I was angry about how the trade had been handled. I felt betrayed because I heard that Golden State wanted to deal for me, and that would have been a good situation. The Warriors had a promising team with Nate Thurmond at center. They had a 51–31 record. I respected the coach, Al Attles. And San Francisco wasn't nearly as far from Seattle as Cleveland.

Yet the Sonics sent me to the Cavs.

I considered not reporting to Cleveland. I hoped that they might trade me to a contender if they knew how upset I was about the deal. But Bill Fitch flew to Seattle to meet with me. Then owner Nick Mileti came to see me. Both made it clear the Cavs planned to keep me. They offered me a new contract.

Marilyn and I talked about it, and then Marilyn said, "Are you ready to retire?"

I'd had some nice offers to go into business in Seattle. But Marilyn went right to the heart of the matter. Even though I liked business and loved Seattle, was I ready to walk away from basketball? The year before, I averaged 18 points and led the league with nearly 10 assists per game.

"I still I want to play," I said.

And we both knew that if I wanted to play, then I had to play in Cleveland.

I always appreciated what Joe Tait said about me during my first stint in Cleveland.

"Lenny was the first true professional basketball player we had," said the man who also was the first radio voice of the Cavs and remains in that job to this day.

The Cavs came into the NBA in 1970–71. They opened that season with 15 losses in a row, then finally won a game. They immediately went into a 12-game losing streak. They won again. Then they lost nine more in a row. That's a 2–36 start. Their final record was 15–67. They had a guard named John Warren who scored a basket—for the other team! They had a player named Gary Suiter who was cut because he ate a hot dog right before a game. He might have gotten away with it if he hadn't bought it at the concession stand, waiting in line wearing his warmups. Virtually all of the players were castoffs from other teams, and it didn't take long to find out why they were available: They were either too old, too hurt, too young, or too something to be very effective.

Fitch was new to the NBA. He had coached at Minnesota, Bowling Green, North Dakota, and Coe College. In his first press conference in Cleveland, he reminded the writers, "The name is Fitch, not Houdini."

Well, not even Moses could have led the Cavs to a winning season in those early years. They were coming off a 23–59 season when I arrived. They played at the old Cleveland Arena, which was on Euclid Avenue and East Thirtieth Street. As Joe Tait once said, "It wasn't an arena, it was a cave. It was dark, damp, cold, and empty. The locker rooms were so bad the visiting teams would dress in their rooms at the Sheraton Hotel, then they'd walk across Euclid Avenue wearing their warmups."

For those Cavaliers, a good crowd was five thousand. Often there were fewer than twenty-five hundred fans in the seats. On some nights, you could dribble the ball and hear the bounce echoing all over the empty arena.

"It was the black hole of the NBA," said Tait.

So I was traded to the worst team in the NBA that played in the worst arena with perhaps the worst fan support. I had a choice: I could pout and perhaps try to force a trade. Or I could make the best of what many would consider a bad situation. I thought of something Martin Luther King once said, "The measure of a man is not where he stands in moments of comfort and convenience, but where he stands in times of challenge and controversy."

Another saying that always meant a lot to me was, "Failure is only the opportunity to begin again, only more intelligently."

I knew I didn't fail in Seattle, but Cleveland was a chance to begin again. It also was a challenge, something completely out of my comfort zone. In a sense, it was a test: What kind of person would I be? How would I react to a coach whose playing experience was limited to little Coe College? A coach who was three years older than me, and a coach who had a worse record than I did? How would I handle playing for a losing team in a strange city in front of small crowds?

Once I decided to report to the Cavs, I was determined to be a top-flight point guard and to help Bill Fitch any way I could. When I arrived in Cleveland, I spent my first week in town staying in Fitch's home; he said he'd help me get settled and find a place to live. Actually, he wanted me to watch film of the team with him. We watched hour after hour, game after game, play after play.

Over and over it went.

I had used a little bit of film work with my team in Seattle. It was just in the infant stage as a coaching tool back then. But Fitch was obsessed with game films. I really liked and respected him, but after a while, there's only so much film you can watch. It doesn't hurt to shut off the projector and get a little sleep. I told Bill that, and we still laugh about it to this day. But this also shows how different the NBA of 1972 was from today. Now, a coach would never have a player spend a week in his home. Even if the coach wanted to, the player probably would decide it was best to stay elsewhere; certainly, with what the players are paid today, they can afford it. Or the teams would pay a player's hotel bill. But in 1972, the Cavs didn't have a lot of money. Fitch was a young coach who had enough confidence in himself to bring a veteran player into his home and pick his brain. And the player went along with it, because he thought it was best for the team.

The Cavs were a young team with the likes of Bingo Smith, Austin Carr, Steve Patterson, Rick Roberson, and John Johnson. Three years later, the 1975–76 Cavs would reach the Eastern Conference Finals.

But this team wasn't ready to win. As Joe Tait once told me, "Fitch traded for you because he needed a veteran to show his young players how to act. You were a role model for that team, and Fitch also wanted to have you around to learn what he could from you."

Fitch would ask my opinion, and he really listened. He didn't get upset or insecure when I said something that wasn't exactly what he wanted to hear. One day, we had just returned from a road trip: We'd lost most of our games, and I missed one of those games with a bad knee. We came home on a commercial flight, and he had the bus waiting for us at the Cleveland airport. We went straight from the airport to the gym, because Fitch wanted to have practice. Everyone was tired from the grueling trip, in which we'd played in five cities in eight days, and from the cross-country flight that had worn us out. Now Fitch had us on the court, and he was really pushing us hard, lots of demanding drills and a tough scrimmage. He didn't like how we were playing, but our legs were gone. When the tank is empty, the car doesn't run, no matter how much you try to tune up the engine.

Then Fitch stopped the practice and told us to run sprints.

First, the centers ran from one end of the court to the other.

Then he had the forwards do it.

Finally, the guards. All of us were dragging. My sore knee was killing me, and I sort of limped through the sprint.

Then, I just sat down.

Understand that no one sat down during a Bill Fitch practice. His personality was such that you'd never even consider it. But with my knee, I could barely stand up. Besides, these sprints served no purpose.

Yet Fitch was going for another round of running.

The centers ran.

The forwards ran.

Then he looked at me. The guards were supposed to run. I didn't stand up.

"OK," he said. "That's it, practice is over."

We went downstairs to clean up and change clothes. All of the players were grumbling about the practice, complaining about Fitch. The locker room was ripe for a mutiny, and I knew if I said anything against the coach, the situation would become very ugly.

I didn't utter a word. I respected Fitch too much to do that, even though I didn't agree with the practice. As I left the gym, Fitch was waiting for me.

"Let's have a cup of coffee," he said.

So we sat down for some coffee.

"All right," he said. "What's on your mind?"

"Well," I said, "what did you teach us today?"

He looked strangely at me, and I could tell he just didn't get it.

"What did you teach us?" I repeated.

"What do you mean?" he asked.

"You punished us today because we're not a very good team," I said. "But you didn't teach us anything. I'll run through a wall for you. So will the other guys, but you have to teach us something, not just punish us because we're not very talented."

He kind of shook his head. At the time, I'm not sure he understood exactly what I meant. But in some practices later in the season, when he saw my knee was bothering me, he'd tell our trainer, Ron Culp, "Take Lenny and work on his knee a little bit."

Then he'd go back and make the rest of the team run. So all he learned at that point in his career was not to run me into the ground.

But I learned a lot from Bill Fitch.

His assistant was Jimmy Rodgers, and I was shocked to see the scouting reports that Jimmy assembled for us. They were so detailed about each key opposing player and his tendencies that I was impressed. None of my pro coaches had ever put together reports that even approached the ones used by the Cavs. As I read them, I was amazed by their accuracy. I knew the league and the players very well at that point in my career, so I could judge if the information in the reports was worthwhile. I began to make mental notes that I'd want these kinds of reports the next time I coached in the NBA—and I was sure that I would coach again.

Fitch thought so, too. When we were on planes, Bill had me sit next to him. We went over the reports. We talked about the team. I give Bill credit for really wanting to know what I had on my mind. He'd constantly diagram plays and then ask me if I thought they'd work. Some of my teammates would say I was being held hostage by the coach, which went back to my being a POW in Cleveland.

When Bill was ejected from a game, he'd have me take over the team. I thought Jimmy Rodgers should do it, because he was Bill's assistant, but Bill insisted that I coach when he did something such as throw a chair at an official, which he did one night at the old Cleveland Arena. The official's name was Bob Rakel. He'd called something against us. The next thing I knew, Bill had grabbed the folding chair that he had been sitting on and flung it across the floor. Thank God it didn't hit anyone. Then Bill ran on the floor after Rakel. I suddenly realized that no one was going to stop him, so I sprinted over and grabbed Bill from behind, pinning his arms behind his back and telling him to calm down before he got in real trouble. I don't think Bill wanted to hit Rakel with the chair, but seeing it bang off the floor and Fitch being ejected was another lesson to me: Don't let your temper get so far out of control that you end up doing something you'd regret for the rest of your life. Bill understood that, too; he coached in the NBA for twenty-five years and never again did anything even remotely close to throwing a chair. By the way, he still has that chair—all dented up—in the study of his home outside Houston.

While I have been ejected from games—far more often than most people realize—I'm proud that I've never done anything that embarrassed me or my family. I just don't think it serves any purpose to lose control and act like a wild man. I don't believe it really fires up your team, and it can hurt you with the officials. They're human; if you're acting like a complete maniac, they're not going to cut your team any breaks on those key calls that can go either way.

Which calls are those?

Your player drives into the middle of the lane. At the last second, a defender steps in front of him. Your player flips up a shot that drops into the net. At the same moment, your player and the defender collide.

Is it a charge on your player, or a foul on the defender?

It all happened so fast, it's hard to know. But in a tight game, a call like this is crucial. If you've been screaming at an official all night, arguing even the most obvious calls, then you could be in trouble when it comes to a critical decision like this. Not with every official, but some guys. As I said, they're people. They have to make difficult, split-second decisions, calls that really can go either way. I like to keep everything in my favor when that happens.

Something else I learned from Fitch was how to use game films with the players. Bill was obsessed with films; he'd watch them for four to six hours a night. He had long film sessions with the team. I remember one day, he had the film on for quite a while. This was in the days of the sixteen-millimeter films played on a movie projector, so you'd turn the lights out. Well, with the lights out and the same plays being shown over and over, it didn't take long for some of the players to fall asleep. You can reach a point of diminishing returns.

When I use films—today, it's videos—I'm very careful how much I have the players watch. Usually, it's only a quarter of a game. Certainly no more than a half. And I have our video coordinator put together a certain sequence of plays that highlights what I want our team to learn. I might concentrate on how our big men are

not blocking out while rebounding, or highlight our ball movement, or something else we needed to do on defense. If I'm meeting
with an individual player, I'll prepare a tape for him to show what I
want him to improve in his game. Of course, technology is far advanced today compared to what it was when Bill Fitch had to haul
around that clunky projector and all those old reels of game films.
You couldn't put together a tape of nothing but screen-and-roll
plays or guys rebounding; you just had to keep rewinding the same
play and showing it over and over.

From Fitch, I saw how effective a game tape can be, because the
players see what happened. It's one thing to tell them that they
aren't hustling back on defense: They may believe you, or maybe
not, but when you show them on tape that they're loafing they can't
deny it. In a case such as this, the picture is worth a million words.
Sometimes I don't have to say much of anything. I'll call a player in
and remind him of something that happened in a game—and show
him the tape to make my point. Then I wait to see what he has to
say. Rather than having me scream and pound the table, five minutes of tape can speak eloquently about what that player has to do to
get better. When he sees it, he knows you're not just picking on him.

As a player, I tried not to become too emotional. I wanted to see
the game clearly, make decisions based upon what was best for the
team. The point guard can't get caught up in any personal battles on
the court: That can destroy the flow of the offense, because you become so intent on scoring—on beating your man—that you take
your teammates out of the game. They end up as spectators. For a
point guard, that's a cardinal sin. When I played, my goal wasn't just
to play the best that I could, but to get all my teammates to perform
at the top of their games, too.

But when the Cavs played in Seattle for the first time after I
was traded, it was a very special evening to me. It was personal.
When I came on the court for warmups, I received a standing ovation. I mean, they stood and cheered just because I stepped on the
floor. And I was with the other team!

The Sonics were off to a poor start. Their attendance was down,
falling nearly twenty-five hundred a game from my final season as

coach. But on this night, a sellout crowd of 13,174 was at the Coliseum.

And there were signs everywhere:

> THIS IS LENNY'S COUNTRY.
> WITH WILKENS, WE'D WIN.
> WE LOVE YOU, LENNY.
> BOMB TOM! COME HOME LENNY.

The last sign was a reference to new coach Tom Nissalke, who was taking the heat for the team's slow start.

"The funny thing about that game was how the Sonics management had put up all these banners supporting their team," recalled Joe Tait. "But the fans came in with their homemade signs for Lenny and put them right over the signs the team had made. Then, every time Lenny made a shot in the pregame drills, he got a huge cheer. They went crazy when he made a layup, and the game hadn't even begun. I knew Lenny was popular in Seattle, but I had no clue how strongly the fans there felt about him. But he was the first great player in the history of that franchise, just as he was for the Cavaliers. And like a lot of cases in Lenny's career, he never truly was appreciated until he was gone."

I had sat out the game before with a sore knee. But when we got to Seattle, the adrenaline took over. I had never been more nervous for a game as a player, but the butterflies also took all the pain in my knee away. I could have been on one leg, but I was going to play! Everywhere I've played, fans have been great to me. But I never had a night where I experienced such support, where I felt as if everyone in the stands was my best friend and wanted to carry me to the best performance of my career.

The fans started all kinds of chants:

> COME HOME, LENNY, COME HOME!
> WE LOVE YOU, LENNY!
> TRADE NISSALKE! TRADE NISSALKE!

While I've never cried in public, this was as close as I came. People cheered whenever I touched the ball. They about tore down the roof when I scored, and they cheered for the Cavs as if we were the home team.

At halftime, we had a 60–46 lead and we went on to win, 113–107.

"That game remains one of my favorite memories of Cavs basketball," said Joe Tait. "Those early Cavs never had support like that at home. The Seattle fans were not about to let Lenny lose to the Sonics. Lenny was like always, cool and collected. He played his usual controlled, savvy game. But on the inside, I knew it had to be a real vindication for him."

When it became clear that we had the game in hand, I remember a fan stood up and played "Taps" on his bugle, indicating the Sonics were dead, at least on this night. I did enjoy that. The Sonic players were very friendly to me. I still had a number of friends on that team. But the people from the front office avoided me, as if they were afraid to even speak to me. That was disappointing, after I gave them four very good years.

Here's what Gil Lyons wrote in the *Seattle Times:*

"Only the hanging judge was missing as Lenny Wilkens and the Cleveland Cavaliers rode a tidal wave of Seattle cheers to victory over the home-town Sonics in one of the most nerve-shattering sports spectacles of all time.

"A crowd of 13,174, the second largest home gathering in team history, goaded on the Cavs, booed the Sonics and chanted for Coach Tom Nissalke's scalp in a spiteful outpouring of vengeance. . . . Nissalke's plight might have been eased a trifle had the Sonics escaped their seventh loss in a row, and this one was to a team that had never beaten Seattle before in eight previous tries.

"Wilkens, whose trade to Cleveland caused the eruption of sympathy and hatred, scored 14 of his 22 points in the first half. . . . He also contributed nine assists, nine rebounds and four steals."

In my first season with the Cavs, I averaged 20 points and 8.4 assists. We won 32 games, up from 23 the season before. Our crowds at that old dungeon of an arena were small, but the fans were very warm to me. I continually grew in admiration for Bill Fitch, as I watched him mature as a coach. I spent one more year in Cleveland, 1973–74, averaging 16.4 points and 7.4 assists. I was now thirty-seven years old, and near the end of my playing career. I wanted another crack at coaching.

Portland had fired Jack McCloskey and was in the market for a new coach. The Blazers job appealed to me because Portland was very close to my home in Seattle. I also was thinking of retiring as a player. At a charity dinner, Blazers owner Herman Saskowski talked to me all night about taking the Blazers job. Finally, I said I was interested, and I told him to talk to my agent. The Cavaliers allowed me to pursue the opening in Portland, and the Blazers gave me a three-year contract as coach.

At first, that was all I was supposed to do—coach. But when training camp opened, we had only one veteran guard, Geoff Petrie. The other guards were players such as Phil Lumpkin, Larry Steele, Dan Anderson, and Bernie Fryer, who later became an NBA official. The Blazers front office wanted me to play one more year, and I did so against my better judgment. I knew that coaching was a full-time job—but I also knew that I'd be a better coach if I had a better point guard, and even at the age of thirty-seven, I was the best point guard in camp. Portland added a fourth year to my coaching contract as a way to help convince me to play. We also had just drafted a center out of UCLA named Bill Walton, and I thought it would be fun not only to coach Walton, but to play with him.

Besides, this team was yet another expansion team. It entered the NBA in 1970, just like the Cavs. In 1973–74, Portland had a 27–55 record. It needed all the help it could get.

The first time I met Bill Walton, he was in a hospital. That was a perfect symbol of my two years as coach in Portland. Bill had a bone chip floating in his foot, and that was only the start of his physical problems.

Portland was a difficult situation. We never knew when Walton would be able to play. He had knee problems in college. He soon developed the stress fractures in his feet that plagued him throughout his career. Because Walton had been such a dominating player at UCLA, the assumption was that we'd immediately become a contender. That assumption led the Blazers to give him a $2.5 million contract, a staggering amount for 1974. But it wasn't about to happen, not with him hurt, and not with a roster that just wasn't very deep.

Walton played only 35 of our 82 games as a rookie. He averaged close to 13 points and 13 rebounds, but there were very few games where he was 100 percent. We never knew if he would be able to play or practice. With Walton out, Sidney Wicks was our most talented player, but the other players considered him selfish. His attitude bothered some of the guys. When your key player is hurt, a team needs to pull together; Wicks would put up good statistics, but he just didn't make his teammates better. We tried to trade Wicks a couple of times, but the deals all fell through.

We finished the season with a 38–44 record, up from 27–55 the year before. I had played my last season, averaging only 6.4 points. I realized that I had to concentrate on coaching, and I was looking forward to my second year with the Blazers, especially since Walton was supposed to be healthy.

But nothing went right.

We still couldn't trade Wicks. He wanted his contract renegotiated. The front office refused, and he showed up with an even worse attitude than the year before. He was angry with his teammates whenever he wasn't getting enough shots, and that made everyone's life miserable. I learned from dealing with Wicks that when a player is truly unhappy, he makes the other players anxious and easily disgruntled. There's only one thing you can do: Trade him. Keeping a malcontent around doesn't make him any better, it just makes the entire situation worse. No matter what you get in return, you benefit from the addition by subtraction.

In his second year, Walton played in 51 games, but he was only himself in perhaps 30 of those. He couldn't stay healthy. I sensed that if we could get Walton healed and make a few other moves, Portland was not far from being a contender.

But the front office was not willing to be patient, at least not with me. We went 37–45, one victory fewer than the season before, still not bad for a team that had never won more than 29 games in a season until I arrived. I thought I'd earned the right to finish off the remaining two years on my contract, because the Blazers were in far better shape than when I arrived. But they let me go, which turned out to be a blessing. It enabled us to move back to Seattle full-time, where my kids were happiest in school and where Marilyn and I felt most comfortable. I was hired by CBS for a year to work on their pro basketball telecasts. It was a good time for me to sit back and watch all the teams in the league without being in the pressure cooker of playing and coaching.

It also set the stage for me to come home to the Sonics.

CHAPTER ELEVEN

FIVE YEARS LATER, Seattle became Lenny's Country once again.

That wasn't what I was thinking about in May 1977 when Sam Schulman approached me about returning to the Sonics as general manager. I had just finished my first year with CBS. I enjoyed television, but I still wanted to coach again. Bill Russell had just quit as the Sonics general manager and coach, but I didn't apply for the job; Seattle planned to promote Russell's assistant, Bob Hopkins, to head coach. Hopkins was also Russell's cousin.

I thought I'd work for CBS once again. The last thing I ever expected to be was a general manager, or as my official title stated: Director of Player Personnel.

I was at a big charity banquet in Seattle when Schulman approached me. We talked about his team, and Sam apologized for how my trade was handled. He explained that he wanted to give Tom Nissalke freedom to build the team in his own way and thought it might be a little difficult with the former head coach still on the roster as a point guard. I understood that part, because as a coach, I'd want that same control. But Sam also knew that his front office didn't level with me about the deal to Cleveland. He admitted it was a huge mistake.

In my last season with the Sonics, their record was 47–35.

Nissalke didn't even survive his first season, as the record dropped to 26–56. Russell coached the team for four years, and the Sonics' best record was 43–39.

So my 47–35 season remained the best in the ten-year history of the franchise as I talked to Schulman at that banquet. I knew the fans were unhappy, that attendance was down, and some of the players were disenchanted. Russell had seemed to lose interest in coaching toward the end of his tenure, and the Sonics were coming off a 40–42 season.

"You do need help," I told Schulman.

"No kidding," he said. "That's why I want you to be a part of the organization, but not as a coach." Schulman said he was committed to Hopkins. "He did a lot of the coaching for Russell, and he deserves a chance."

I didn't know Hopkins, and I wasn't after his job. Even though I'd never considered being a general manager, when Schulman asked me if I wanted that job, I was intrigued. I still had a home in Seattle. Despite the bitter ending, the Sonics were a team that was close to my heart. I liked the idea of being in charge of the basketball operations, of putting together the kind of team that could win.

Over and over, Schulman told me that they already had a coach, that they really liked Bob Hopkins, that my job was in the front office.

"Sam, I do understand," I said.

Under the old system, Russell had been both GM and coach. Zollie Volchok was in charge of the business side of the front office. Schulman wanted Zollie to keep his position, but for me to take care of the basketball side. I met with Hopkins and assured him that I was there to help any way I could. He seemed content with the changes. Besides, he had never played or been a head coach in the NBA before, so this was a tremendous opportunity for him.

On May 13, 1977, the new front-office setup was announced and was greeted enthusiastically by the media and the fans. I was really excited. Part of me always assumed that somehow, some way, I'd end up back with the Sonics. Seattle really did feel like "Lenny's Country" to me.

When I took over the front office, the first question I asked was, "Where are we?"

By that I meant, where was the team in terms of trades? Draft preparation? Contracts with the players?

I was told the Sonics were close to trading guard Fred Brown to the Lakers for Earl Tatum.

"You mean you're trading Fred Brown straight up for this guy?" I asked.

Yes, they were.

"No, you're not," I said. "I've seen Earl Tatum. He's not the kind of player you think. You better get a lot more than Earl Tatum for Fred Brown. And as far as that goes, Fred Brown is a great, great shooter. How many guys in the NBA can shoot like Fred Brown? You don't just give away a guy like him."

I took over the trade talks.

"Wait a minute," said Lakers general manager Bill Sharman. "Bob Hopkins is all for this deal."

"Bob Hopkins is not the general manager," I said. "I am. And as long as I'm general manager, we are not trading Fred Brown for Earl Tatum. If you want to talk about a first-round pick and another player—then, maybe, we'll talk about Fred Brown."

"But your coach . . ." Bill said.

"The deal doesn't make any sense," I said. "The way you want it, there is no deal."

"That's how we want it," he said.

"No deal," I said.

That was one of those cases where some of the best trades are the ones you never make.

I later discovered that Russell and Fred Brown didn't get along. Russell thought Brown was overweight. Brown had one of those fireplug bodies, and he had to watch his weight. I also knew that if you talked to Fred the right way, he would get himself in good shape. The main thing was that Fred Brown could shoot the basketball, and I wanted a shooter like that on my team.

Next, the Sonics were thinking of trading Tom Burleson, their seven-foot-four center. Burleson was not especially mobile. He averaged 9.7 points and 6.7 rebounds. But he was seven-foot-four and he did block shots.

"We have a deal for Burleson pending," they told me.

"Who?" I asked.

"George Johnson," they said.

"Wait a minute," I said. "George Johnson is not a bad player, but he's only about six-foot-eight. He's not a center. If we trade Burleson, we lose our defensive presence in the middle."

Obviously, the people in Seattle thought they were limited as a team with Burleson at center, and I didn't disagree with that. But I also knew that if you were going to improve in the pivot, you didn't just trade your current center for a thin, six-foot-eight forward. You had to get a center in return.

"What about Marvin Webster?" I asked.

I liked Webster, who was a physical, six-foot-ten presence in the middle. He had long arms. He liked to block shots, and his nickname in college was "The Human Eraser." He also was a good rebounder, and he didn't need the ball a lot on offense. He was content to let his teammates score. In my mind, he was like Burleson, only better.

I talked to Denver about Webster and Burleson, and the Nuggets were receptive. Webster's contract was up at the end of the season and they were concerned that they couldn't sign him. They wanted to trade him a year early, to make sure they at least received something in return. Contract considerations also were behind our wanting to move Burleson: He had five years left on a deal that looked very expensive, at least compared to his production. As I talked to Denver, I realized they were very anxious to move Webster. I started asking for other players in the deal, especially Paul Silas. I had played with Silas in St. Louis, and I knew he was another tough rebounder. I could see us becoming a team that would really defend the basket and get the ball off the boards if we could add Silas and Webster. I also knew that Denver was disenchanted with Silas. They thought he was washed up, but I knew that they didn't use Silas correctly. They wanted him to score. Even in the prime of his career, Silas was never an offensive player; now that he was past thirty, he wasn't going to suddenly turn into an offensive machine. But we didn't need Silas to score, just to defend and rebound. I also saw Silas as a veteran coming off the bench, maybe playing half the game. We threw around a few more names, and Denver agreed to send us Webster, Silas, and Willie Wise (a throw-in who was at the end of his career) for Burleson and Bobby Wilkerson. Denver wanted Dennis Johnson, but I thought Dennis had a tremendous future, especially compared to Wilkerson.

Anyway, the deal was done.

I found I really enjoyed the trading part of it, and I also knew that we had to make several deals or our team wasn't going anywhere.

One day, Sam Schulman stopped me in the hallway and said, "You've been busy."

I nodded.

"Well, I brought you back here because you know where the players are that we need," he said.

"That's right," I said.

I suppose Sam was a little surprised how I immediately began acting like the general manager. I had spent my entire adult life in the NBA as a player and a coach. I was confident in my background and my talent judgment, which came into play when the decision was made to draft Jack Sikma.

Hopkins had scouted the college players, and he had also projected the draft to where it looked as if we'd have a choice between Ernie Grunfeld and Sikma. Hopkins liked both players, and so did I. Grunfeld was a forward at Tennessee; he played in the same front court as Bernard King, and they both scored a lot. He was everybody's All-American and played in a high-profile program.

Sikma was a lanky, six-foot-eleven center from little Illinois Wesleyan College, an NAIA school. I had seen a lot of Grunfeld, because Tennessee was often on TV. But little was known about Sikma, because his school was small and had virtually no media exposure. I watched Sikma in the NAIA national tournament in Kansas City, and I was intrigued. He had this strange, fall-away step-back move. He'd catch the ball, turn, and face the defender. As his man attempted to block his shot, Jack would take a step back. That created some space. Then he sort of hesitated before he shot the ball, almost as if he had a hitch in his shot. This destroyed the timing of the guy trying to block his shot, and it often led to him drawing fouls. I didn't care that Sikma played at a tiny school mostly against players who were usually much shorter; I could see him being a very good player in the NBA. I was thrilled that Hopkins had found him and spoke so highly of a kid who, until that point, had been on only a few NBA teams' radar screens.

"You're right," I told Hopkins. "I really like Sikma."

"I don't know," said Hopkins. "Maybe we should go with Grunfeld."

I knew what was happening. Hopkins was worried about the public and media reaction to drafting a player whom no one had ever seen, at least no one in Seattle. Especially when a star like Grunfeld was available.

"Bob, you did all the work on Sikma," I said. "I'm just confirming what you originally saw."

"I know, but . . ." he said, his voice trailing off.

The more Hopkins wavered, the more I was sold on Sikma. Not because Hopkins was backing off, but because I could see Sikma as a guy who'd score 15 to 20 points a night, especially because that strange hesitation shot would enable him to draw a lot of fouls, and he was very good at the free throw line. He also should get close to 10 rebounds a game.

We needed a center, because we didn't know if we'd be able to sign Webster at the end of the season. We had already traded Burleson, our starting center from the previous year.

So on draft day, I stood up and announced that we were picking Jack Sikma. The reaction of most media and fans was summed up in this headline from one of our local newspapers: JACK WHO?

I could tell that Sam Schulman was concerned. He was trying to sell tickets. A player such as Grunfeld would have helped. In fact, I tried to work a deal with Milwaukee: The Bucks had three first-round picks, and I thought for a while that we could acquire one of them. Then we'd pick both Grunfeld and Sikma, but the Bucks changed their minds and kept the picks.

So JACK WHO? was our marquee draft pick. To Schulman's credit, he allowed me to make the choice. He didn't meddle as some owners do, owners who are too worried about the opinions of the fans and reporters rather than trusting their basketball people to make the decisions that would be best for the team—even if they're unpopular.

We signed Sikma in August, and he played for our summer league team in Los Angeles. Jack had celebrated being our top pick and knowing that he had a big contract to come by playing golf most of the summer. So he was in lousy shape, and for his first summer pro game, he was matched up against Moses Malone.

I knew it wasn't going to be pretty.

Moses just blistered Sikma. I think he had 39 points. He pounded Sikma on the boards. It was a nightmare.

I was sitting between Hopkins and Schulman. Sam could be very emotional, and when Moses dunked over Sikma, Sam started screaming, *"This is our first-round pick?!"*

"Lenny wanted him," said Hopkins, before I could even say a word.

I was a little surprised at how fast Hopkins had jumped off Sikma's ship, especially since he was the one who put Sikma's boat in the water to begin with by bringing Jack to my attention.

Anyway, I sat there, gritted my teeth, and said, "That's right, he's our first-round pick. Sam, he's going to be fine. This is just his first summer league game, for heaven's sake. Give him time."

"OK," barked Schulman, but I could tell that he had his doubts.

Meanwhile, Hopkins sat there, saying nothing. I knew what he was thinking: "We should have drafted Grunfeld." I also was beginning to realize that while Hopkins had decent basketball instincts, he was very insecure. He had never played in the NBA, nor had he been a head coach in the league. He had coached at Loyola of New Orleans, which wasn't a big-time college program. He was a friend of Russell's, and that's why he was hired to be an assistant in Seattle. If I was going to mess up, I could tell that Hopkins wanted to put some distance between himself and my decisions.

I admit, it was hard to watch Sikma play so poorly in the summer league, but I believed in him. I also knew that the combination of Webster and Sikma was a major upgrade at center over Burleson. I was sure Silas would help us, too. And I was positive that Fred Brown was a better player than Earl Tatum, so we were better there just by standing still.

But I knew we had to do more.

We needed another guard, and I considered Jimmy Cleamons, a free agent who had been a solid point man with Cleveland. But as I looked at the free agent list, I spotted Gus Williams's name. This was in the age when you could sign a free agent, but then you had to work out some sort of compensation with the free agent's old team. Williams had been an explosive scorer in the backcourt for Golden State. I loved his speed and enthusiasm, even if he sometimes took bad shots. Signing him cost us only a second-round draft choice, and we agreed to pick up about $200,000 in deferred money on Williams's original contract with Golden State. That money would be paid several years after Williams retired, so it was of no immediate concern to us.

We had holdovers Slick Watts, Dennis Johnson, Fred Brown, and now Williams in the backcourt.

We had Webster and Sikma in the middle.

We had Bruce Seals and Silas at forward. Webster also could play there. Hopkins wanted someone else and suggested Sidney Wicks. After what I'd endured with Wicks in Portland, there was no way I was going to bring him to Seattle. Instead, I worked a deal for John Johnson, who was with Houston. I had played with Johnson (called J.J.) in Cleveland. He was a strong-willed small forward who played so hard every night that you'd swear he absolutely hated the man he was going against. He also was a very good passer. Our backcourt was loaded with scorers, guys who were going to take a lot of shots, so I knew I'd better find a forward who liked to pass, and J.J. was available for two second-round draft picks. It was an easy decision.

As the season began, I didn't think we were a championship-caliber team, but I thought we'd be much better than people expected. I was eager to sit back and watch all the pieces come together.

Instead, the team fell apart.

In some respects, that wasn't a shock. We had a lot of new players, and they needed time to mesh. But Hopkins was taking each loss as if it were the end of the world. Every few days he was going to see Zollie Volchok, complaining about the players we had and wanting to trade for someone else. First of all, Zollie was in charge of the business side, not basketball, so Hopkins knew he was talking to the wrong guy: He should have come to me, but he didn't. Maybe he thought I was after his job. What Hopkins didn't know was that Schulman wanted to fire him about six games into the season. A week later, Sam again wanted to fire Hopkins.

"Sam, give him some time," I said. "It's early."

What I didn't tell Sam was that I saw Hopkins making a very critical mistake: He was continually ripping his own players in the newspapers. I mean, he was killing the guys. The reporters loved it because it made their jobs easy, so they were writing that Hopkins had no chance to win with the talent he was given. Meanwhile, the players kept reading in the paper every day that their own coach thought they stunk.

They figured, "Hey, if the coach thinks we can't play, then maybe he's right."

And they lost confidence.

Even if a coach is dealt a weak hand of talent by the front office, he can't keep going public with it. I'm not saying you should lie to the press. You can say, "We need to get a better performance out of player X." Or you criticize your team in general terms, saying how *everyone* has to play better defense. But you don't try to make yourself look good at the expense of the players.

I confronted Hopkins about this. I told him, "If you want to chew out a guy, that's your business. But take him in the locker room and do it in private. Then the players will respect you. But don't tell reporters that you think some guy is a stiff or he's stupid. It may sound funny to the people reading the paper, but not to your players. They don't like it, and if I played for you, I wouldn't like it, either. That crap belongs in the garbage can."

I'm not sure Hopkins fully understood what I was saying. He probably thought I was second-guessing him, but I was trying to help him, to save his job. I wasn't running around telling everyone what I thought of how Bob handled the players and the press: I went right to him, man-to-man.

But Hopkins's insecurity just became worse.

Finally, Schulman set up a meeting with Hopkins, Zollie Volchok, and myself. Things were bleak, as our record was something like 1–6.

"I want to clear the air," Schulman said.

The idea was for Hopkins to say exactly what was on his mind, and he started up about the Fred Brown deal, how he wished we had Earl Tatum.

"Listen," I said. "Every time we talk about Fred Brown, I hear the same thing . . . what he can't do. It's always negative. What about the positive? What does Fred Brown do better than about any guard in the league? He shoots the ball. He's in decent shape. Fred can help us because he can put the ball in the basket."

Hopkins seemed to accept that.

"But Silas isn't helping us," he said. "The only reason he's on the team is that he's your friend."

That really set me off. I have a lot of friends. I don't trade for a guy because he's a friend, but because he can play. I said that.

"Paul needs to get in better shape," I admitted. "So you need to play him some. Not all the time, but some. We have to find out about him. If you play him and we see he can't perform, I'll trade him. If my mother was on the team and she couldn't get the job done and you wanted to trade her, well, I'd trade her. I won't stop loving her, but I'd trade her. My friendship with Silas won't change if I have to trade him, but I'm telling you, Paul can be an asset."

We talked a little more. Hopkins was trying to grab on to anything that would take the heat off him.

"You know who the real screw-up is?" he asked. "Slick Watts. It's Slick. Right, it's Slick. He's the problem."

I sat there, dumbfounded. First it was Fred Brown. Then it was Silas. Now it was Slick Watts. I saw Sam look at Zollie. They were beginning to understand the problem, how Hopkins desperately needed a scapegoat.

"Bob," I said, "the only time we really disagreed was when I wouldn't trade Fred Brown for Earl Tatum. You told me that you agreed with the other moves. You can't say that you're stuck with all these players that you didn't want."

Hopkins said nothing after that. The meeting ended, and Hopkins went out to practice.

"Well," said Schulman, "what do you think?"

"You have to give him a chance to pull the team together," I said. "You hired him, so give him some time."

☐

Time didn't help Hopkins.

Ten games into the season, Sam wanted to fire him again.

"I just don't think it would be fair to do it so soon," I said, and I managed to keep Sam at bay for another week.

But Zollie kept coming to me, asking if I'd coach the team. I kept insisting that Hopkins was the coach. Our record went to 5–13 . . . 5–14.

Zollie asked me again about coaching. I knew Schulman was behind it.

"I'm very happy doing what I'm doing," I said.

"Think about it," he said.

Later, I told Marilyn what Zollie and Sam had on their minds. She was against it. She didn't want me to end up doing everything, being the GM and coach. She was still upset by what had happened the first time I coached in Seattle, and then in Portland. Both places, the team and record improved while I was there, yet I still was let go as coach.

"Someone is always second-guessing you, no matter how good a job you do," she said. "I don't want to see you go through that again."

Marilyn was right. As a coach, you're the one out front; you end up being responsible for just about everything with the team, even when a lot of that is out of your control.

We lost again. The record was 5–15.

"We still want you to coach," Zollie said. "But I don't blame you if you decide against it."

Now I seriously thought about coaching the team. I had either traded for or drafted most of the players. These were my guys. I kept telling Marilyn that I thought they could develop into a good team. If I was afraid to coach them, then something was wrong.

We lost again, and the record dropped to 5–16.

That game was against the New Jersey Nets, who were just awful. It happened at the Seattle Coliseum, and our fans booed us for much of the night. I was not at the game. Several months earlier, I had agreed to be at a restaurant opening in Tacoma. Schulman and Zollie knew that I was going to miss the game. When I arrived home, there were five messages, three from Sam and two from Zollie. They wanted to meet with me the next morning. I then called Les Habegger, who was our assistant coach, and he said what a miserable game it was, and how it seemed the players had given up.

The next morning, Sam was livid. He was yelling, "He's got to go! You hear me, *he's got to go!*"

I told Sam that I heard him. I could have been on Mars, and I'd have heard him.

"You drafted the players," he said. "You traded for them. You coach them."

To me, this was a challenge. Did I believe in the talent that I'd assembled?

"I'll take the job," I said. "Under two conditions. I want an adjustment in my salary. And if I don't like it at the end of the season, I can have my old job back."

Sam quickly agreed.

The team was playing that night in Denver, but it was too late for me to fly there and make the game. So I planned to catch up with the team the following evening for the game in Kansas City.

We lost again, the record falling to 5–17. After that game, Denver general manager Carl Scheer said we were one of the worst teams he'd ever seen. Some of the Denver players said the same thing.

I didn't believe that, but I also didn't know how fast you could turn around a team that was totally disheartened, a team with a 5–17 record.

Zollie told Hopkins that we were changing coaches. According to Zollie, Hopkins was relieved to hear the news. He just wanted out of the mess. We let him scout for us for the rest of the season, and he was content to do that because the pressure was off him.

I took over the team in Kansas City. I went with the same lineup that Hopkins had used the previous night: Fred Brown, Slick Watts, Bruce Seals, Marvin Webster, and Paul Silas. I had my doubts about the lineup, but I didn't want to make big changes without at least having a practice to work in my ideas. My first goal was to instill some confidence in the players, because they were a discouraged group, about ready to just go through the motions for the final 60 games.

"Tonight, let's just run the plays you believe in," I said before that first game. "If you don't think a certain play will work, let's not use it. And let's let our quickness show. If you see a fast break, take it."

What often happens when a team changes coaches is that the players receive an immediate infusion of energy. That's why so many teams win their first game after bringing in a new coach. The adrenaline doesn't carry over for long, but for one night, it can really fire up a team.

We jumped on Kansas City for a 17-point lead. Then we started to fall back. That had happened a lot during the season. We'd put together a nice lead, then blow it. But this time, we hung on to win a close game.

That meant a lot to our morale.

Our next game was in Boston, but we had a couple of days to practice. I didn't like the lineup that Hopkins had been using: It wasn't our strongest defensive lineup, and it also couldn't score a lot. The only guy I wanted to keep as a starter was Marvin Webster.

I called a team meeting in Boston and explained the lineup changes. Watts and Brown were going to come off the bench. Dennis Johnson and Gus Williams were going to start in the backcourt. I could see that Watts was hurt by this, but there wasn't much I could do: He simply wasn't good enough to start. To Fred Brown, I explained the sixth-man role that I envisioned for him, how he could come off the bench shooting, instant offense. Fred wasn't completely sold on the idea, but he was very receptive and willing to give it a try if I was convinced it would help the team.

I then told Silas and Seals, our forwards, that I wanted them to come off the bench. I would start John Johnson and Jack Sikma.

The players bought into the changes because they had been losing so much and were tired of being told they were terrible. Everyone was telling them that they were the worst team in the league. I came into the job very upbeat, saying they could win; all it would take was some adjustments, and the losing had made them very open to suggestions.

I wanted a team that stressed quickness and defense.

I knew with Williams and Dennis Johnson in the backcourt, we could really run. And they'd defend the opposing guards, play the kind of pressure, man-to-man defense where they nearly crawled right inside the other player's shirt.

But Dennis Johnson and Gus Williams both liked to shoot the ball. Neither was a natural point guard, and if I asked them to radically change their games and pass a lot more, that would take away from their strengths. I needed someone else to set up the offense and pass, and that someone was John Johnson. Former Milwaukee coach Don Nelson talked a lot about his "point forward" concept in the 1980s with Paul Pressey, but we did it with John Johnson in 1977. J.J. loved to pass. He was the ultimate team man. Dennis Johnson and Gus Williams could just take off down the court for a fast break, and J.J. could dribble the ball up and set up the offense if we couldn't get the break working. J.J. took the pressure of having to handle the ball off our guards, which made them more effective.

The Sonics had a lot of good pieces; I just had to put them in the right places and make sure everything fit together.

I knew Webster would rebound and block shots. I believed in Sikma and knew that he just needed playing time to become a real inside scoring threat.

When I looked down my bench, I saw Fred Brown, Paul Silas, Slick Watts, and Bruce Seals. That was pretty decent depth, because we wouldn't lose much when they came into the game. Also, Silas and Brown—who still could start for several teams—would be matched up against bench guys when they came into the game, and how many teams had reserves who could guard Silas or Brown? Most coaches just want to keep the score where it is when they substitute; I wanted to create the kind of bench strength that enabled us to pick up ground when we went to the bench. That's why I often keep a player capable of starting as a sixth man, just to make the bench better. I want a guy who can come into a game and make an immediate impact, a real splash—not just have us tread water.

At this point in my career, I also felt more confident in myself as a coach. It was a relief not to have to play, too, just to coach the team. That helped. I had a lot of faith in my vision of what a team could be, a faith that was reinforced when Portland won the championship just a year after they let me go. I could see how those Blazers were developing and what they had to do: I'd told them to trade Sidney Wicks, and they did, picking up Maurice Lucas. I pushed for Portland to trade for Dave Twardzik. I drafted Bobby Gross and Lionel Hollins, then played them as rookies so they'd get experience. The key was that Walton finally was healthy. That they won a championship after I'd left confirmed in my mind that I had the team on the right track. I recognized the kind of players needed to win, and that experience in Portland was paying off for me in Seattle.

We won our game in Boston by 28 points. The Celtics were having a down year, but how many times did any team win a game in Boston Garden by 28 points? The next stop was Buffalo, and we won there, too. So we came home on a three-game winning streak, and then beat Atlanta in front of our fans. That was a huge game in my mind, because we needed to get the fans back behind us. We had to win that game, and when we did, our home-court advantage returned.

We won six more in a row, stretching that streak to ten straight.

It wasn't hard to figure out what had happened. The atmosphere was negative, hopeless, before I took over. The guys knew that I really did believe in them, because I was the one who had acquired them. It wasn't as if I was some coach who came in from the outside and was saddled with all these players. Furthermore, the guys knew me as a former player. I had been out of the league for only two years, so I either played with or against most of them. I was only thirty-nine and still in good shape, and some days, I'd scrimmage with them. They could see I still had some of my game left. I understood what it took to play in the league, and the guys knew and appreciated that. You don't have to be a former player to be a good coach, but it helps. It gives you immediate credibility with the players. You have respect, and then it's up to you to make sure you don't lose it. A coach who never played in the league has to prove to his players that he knows what he's doing. They watch every move he makes and bear down on every word he says. He receives far more scrutiny than a former player, at least in the beginning of his coaching career. Then, if the coach shows he can win, the players will back him.

Another advantage I had was that I'd played and coached in Seattle. This was home for me. The fans quickly embraced me, because they knew me. They didn't know Bob Hopkins. I admit, playing in the NBA came relatively easy to me. I didn't have to work at seeing the entire floor, or finding the open man; it just came naturally. So did understanding different offensive and defensive schemes. It wasn't difficult for me to visualize those Xs and Os on the blackboard and translate that into what it meant on the court. This was an asset to me when I coached. As a player, I was a point guard, so I viewed the game not just from my perspective, but for what was best for the entire team. The coach does the same thing. It also never hurts to have some immediate success. Players are far more willing to sacrifice, to come off the bench, when they look up at the scoreboard at the end of the game and see that it paid off with a victory. Once most players taste winning, it just makes them want more and more. They hunger for it. They make even more of a commitment to a system that's working. Suddenly, I sounded like a prophet. I said we could be a good team, and we win 10 in a row. That made them pay attention to the other things I wanted them to do.

Except for Slick Watts.

Slick was a colorful character in Seattle, a little guard with a shaved head and an electric smile. He wore different headbands each night. He was the one Seattle player during the Russell Era who made tons of public appearances. He signed thousands of autographs. He loved the fans, and they embraced him. Some fans even wore headbands to the game, just like Slick. But Slick was only our fourth-best guard, behind Dennis Johnson, Williams, and Brown. And that meant his playing time was being slashed.

In the middle of our winning streak, he came to me and said, "Coach, I need more time."

"Slick, we're winning," I said. "I like our guard rotation right now."

"But Coach," he said, "my public needs to see me play."

"Slick, if we lose, the public isn't going to want to see any of us," I said. "Right now, we're winning. It doesn't make any sense to change. Any time you feel it's too much for you and you want to be traded, come to me and I'll do what I can. Or come, and we'll just talk about things."

Slick was OK for a few days, but then it began to really eat away at him. His ego took a beating, because it wasn't just that I had benched him—he also saw that the players in front of him were better.

In practices, he began to sulk a bit. His playing time became even shorter. He discovered that while the fans still liked him, they were adopting some of our new players as their favorites. That happens when a team starts to win: The fans gravitate to whoever is playing well and make those players their heroes. This really bothered Slick.

Then he came to me and asked for a trade. He assumed I could work something out within a few days.

It took a while. Slick's estimation of his own ability didn't match that of the other general managers. There just wasn't much of a market for a six-foot-one guard who played with a lot of enthusiasm, but shot only 42 percent from the field, 60 percent at the foul line, and didn't always make the wisest decisions when handling the ball.

Slick took his frustration to the media, saying, "I've been letting Coach Wilkens handle getting me out of here, but if something doesn't happen pretty soon, I'm going to have to take it over myself."

I read that and didn't know if I should laugh or take an aspirin.

Just how was Slick going to "take it over myself"? The poor guy's ego would have been smashed if he had heard what other general managers were saying about him. Slick thought he was a terrific player, a starter. Most teams saw him as I did—a fourth guard on a winning team. I sensed that Slick wanted to use his popularity with the fans to put pressure on me to make a trade, but at this point, Slick was not the main concern for the fans. They had quickly embraced our team, because of the winning and the exciting style we played. Slick was learning the hard way that some fans have very short memories.

Finally, I was able to trade Slick to New Orleans for a first-round pick, and Slick was surprised to see that there wasn't much of an outcry when he was traded. The fans just wished him well with his new team and went back to cheering for the Sonics who were on the floor.

Within two years, Slick Watts was out of the NBA at the age of twenty-eight.

We finished the year at 47–35, which tied for the franchise best (set in 1971–72, my last season the first time around).

But the real story was we had a 42–18 record after the coaching change.

When the playoffs began, no one gave us much chance of winning. I didn't know if we'd make the Finals, but I was sure we'd play well. Every week, our team was getting better. We opened against the Lakers and Kareem Abdul-Jabbar, and we upset them. Marvin Webster had a tremendous series against Kareem, contesting that famed hook shot and just being a bear on the boards and blocking shots. In the deciding game, Sikma had 24 points, and Webster snared 18 rebounds.

In the next round we faced Portland, my old team. They were the defending champions and had a 58–24 record, best in the NBA that season. But as I was to later learn, it's very, very hard to play at the top level the year after you've won a title. We simply had more desire to win, more sense of a mission, than Portland. We upset them, too, winning the series in six games. I'm not one to gloat: What happened to Portland that season is the same thing that happened to me when I coached there. Walton was hurting again, in and out of the lineup. You never knew what you'd get from him or some of the other guys from one night to the next. Jack Ramsay was an outstanding coach, but none of us are good enough coaches to overcome serious injuries to key players. But I was thrilled when Sikma made the winning shot in Game Six to ice the series. I was proud of him, because Maurice Lucas had been just pounding on Sikma, but our rookie held his own. Sikma averaged 10 points and 8.3 rebounds during the regular season, and that went up to 14 points and 8.1 rebounds in the playoffs. So much for a kid from a small school not being able to play in big games, as some of his critics said when we drafted him.

The Portland series brought some national attention to us. *Sports Illustrated* wrote, "Was Seattle's Lenny Wilkens some kind of a) miracle worker b) faith healer c) just plain lucky?"

Actually, we were d) a very good team that no one knew about.

In the Western Conference Finals, we knocked off Denver in six games. Fred Brown came off the bench to score 26 points in that Game Six to clinch it.

Sports Illustrated described Brown as "an elderly, bent-over codger with a goatee who enters stage left and hurls the ball from the unlikeliest places—Puget Sound, Mount Rainier, you name it."

Or as Denver coach Larry Brown said of Fred, "We handcheck him, we body him, we double up on him in the corner and he still gets away. Sometimes, he throws it up without looking, and the ball still goes down. They all go down, but that's his nickname, right?"

Yes, it was: "Downtown" Fred Brown, and our fans about blew the roof off when he came into the game. In fact, our fans were crazy about the entire team. *Sports Illustrated* called it "Sonicsteria," the magazine adding, "the good people of Seattle blow their lungs out over a team they call the bionic Sonics."

Dennis Johnson was "a stocky child who refers to himself as 'the black kid with freckles and bags under his eyes,' and he puts the defensive clamps on the opposition's hero."

We moved into the Finals against Washington—and discovered a problem: The Seattle Coliseum was booked for other events. The last thing anyone expected was for us to make the Finals. We had to move our home games to the huge Kingdome, which took away some of the home-court advantage we had developed with our sellouts of thirteen thousand fans right on top of the opposition. We took the Series to seven games, but in the end, Washington had too much experience for us with Wes Unseld, Elvin Hayes, Bob Dandridge, and Kevin Grevey.

But to take a Seattle team to the Finals in a season where we started 5–17, that told me that the next year would be even better. Most of our team was young; they had grown together, learned to trust each other and to have confidence in the coaching staff. If we were ever going to win a championship, I knew it could happen the following season.

CHAPTER TWELVE

I KNEW WE COULD WIN THE NBA TITLE in 1979. We had done so much in so little time the previous season that I knew, just knew, that we could get back to the Finals—and this time, we would win.

So why was I depressed immediately after we lost in the 1978 Finals?

Because it came down to the seventh game, a couple of key plays, a couple of crucial toots of the whistle. So close. And even more than my players, I knew how hard it was just to reach the Finals. In my fifteen years as an NBA player, I had gotten there only once—in my rookie year with the Hawks. It takes some luck, even when you've got a team that's coming together the way the Sonics were. The chemistry was there. The key players stayed relatively healthy. Just about everything was in place. And we still fell just short.

There was a critical play near the end of the seventh game. We had made a gutsy comeback to cut Washington's lead to four points. There was a loose ball on the floor. I mean, it rolled right past three of our guys. Washington's Mitch Kupchak picked it up, laid it in the basket—and was fouled. That four-point lead went to seven, and it was like someone punched us in the stomach. All the air came out of us. The final score was 105–99.

When the Finals were over, I actually had dreams about that play. I saw it as if it were happening all over again, saw it in slow motion. I found myself thinking, "If only we had picked that ball up . . ."

I also was utterly exhausted. I never realized how physically and mentally draining it is when your team goes all the way to the final game, the final quarter, the final few minutes . . . when a championship is so close, you can almost see the banner hanging from the ceiling . . . and you lose.

It feels as if you've left every drop of blood on the arena floor. When two teams have a series like we did with Washington, and it comes down to a final game, the team that has the better night wins. That sounds obvious, but think about it for a moment: You start training camp at the end of September. You play into the month of June. That's over 100 games, over 150 practices. That's nine months of injuries, agonies, and controversies that are a part of any season, even a great one. Then it comes down to who has the best night?

Yes, one night.

And Washington had the better night.

In some ways, that's hard to accept.

Yes, everyone was very gracious and upbeat after the season. Over and over, people were so excited that we had simply made it to the playoffs, that we came back from the basketball dead after that 5–17 start. Logically, I felt the same way. But emotionally, part of me wondered if we would ever get that chance again, if we could ever come so close to a championship again. So much had to go right for us to reach the Finals, and so much can go wrong in any given season.

I didn't feel as if my best friend had died, but there was this sense of a deep personal loss after that last game. Once training camp starts, there never is a day off, never a day when a coach doesn't have to do something—watch videotape, make telephone calls to other teams and scouts, prepare for the next practice or game. But after you lose that last game . . . Bam! . . . it's over. It's like you hit a wall. Suddenly, there are no more games, no more practices. It seems like your life shifts from going a million miles an hour . . . to . . . nothing. Everything just stops. You feel like you should be getting ready for another game, but there are no more games. When that sets in, you're drained. Right after the playoffs, there were days when I didn't get out of bed until 10:00 A.M.—for me, that's sleeping very late. Despite working what amounts to an afternoon shift, I tend to get up around 7:00 or 8:00 A.M. After a week, I was back to normal.

But I also was disappointed that I received so little consideration for the NBA Coach of the Year, an award that I never won until 1994. If there ever was a season when the voting should have gone my way, it was 1977–78. I know that the NBA writers have to vote before the playoffs, so perhaps I might have won if they could have voted later, after the Finals. About the only support I received was from the Seattle writers. Atlanta's Hubie Brown was voted the award. His Hawks had a 41–41 record, up from 31–51 the previous season. Hubie did a good job, but I didn't think it was that much better than what we accomplished in Seattle. Furthermore, since I acquired most of the players on that team, I also could have received some serious consideration for that as part of the Coach of the Year award, or even for Executive of the Year, but that didn't happen either.

I didn't dwell on it; I had already recognized that the combination of my not being a self-promoter along with coaching in a distant market such as Seattle meant I wouldn't get much national recognition. Is it fair? Of course not, but who ever said life was fair? You take what comes, and you move on or you drive yourself crazy worrying about things you can't control. I learned that very early in my coaching career. It's also part of my faith in God. I have to believe that He is in control, that everything will work out according to His will. Over the years, I've learned to trust God, and that has helped me handle things as a coach.

A coach can't take a poor team and turn it into a great one. But a coach can have an impact on the game. The fans see the obvious: They know when a coach calls a time out, when a coach makes a substitution, or when a coach changes the lineup. But there is much more to it than that, especially for me in those days with the Sonics.

We had no superstar. Jack Sikma, Dennis Johnson, and Gus Williams were all very good players, but there's no Magic Johnson, Larry Bird, or Michael Jordan among them. None of those players could individually dominate game after game and win it for us.

When I took over the Sonics, I asked the players to consider not just their own strengths and weaknesses, but the strengths and weaknesses of everyone else on the team.

For example, Fred Brown was a great outside shooter. Maybe as good as anyone in the NBA back then. I told the players, "When Fred comes into the game, I want him shooting the ball. Not taking bad shots, but if he's open, no hesitation, get him the ball."

And I told Fred that if his teammates were going to look for him to score, it was up to him to keep moving, to get himself free of the defense so he had an open shot.

"If Fred takes a couple of bad shots, don't get uptight," I told the players. "I'll handle it."

And there were times when Fred turned into "Downtown" Brown, his nickname because he loved to shoot the ball from so far away. And sometimes, "Downtown" got a little carried away. The players understood that. They also knew that Brown was sacrificing by coming off the bench, rather than making a big stink about not starting. They respected him for that, so they gave him some freedom when it came to shot selection.

But I also told some of our players, "Look, when Fred goes off and starts forcing shots, don't yell at him. Just quietly say, 'Hey, Fred, give me a look, I'm open.' That's all, say it once. He'll hear, even if it looks as if he's not listening."

Fred's personality was such that getting screamed at just made the problem worse. A quiet approach worked better.

For Jack Sikma, there were certain spots where he liked to set up near the basket. When he established that position, throw him the ball. Don't hesitate, give him the ball!

Over and over, I urged our players to learn each other's games, their tendencies. If Paul Silas is open at the top of the key, you don't have to pass him the ball and expect him to shoot it; Silas is not an outside threat. But if it's Fred Brown open at the same spot, give him the ball—now!

This may seem obvious, but realize that most people—not just basketball players—worry about themselves first. They don't always think about what's best for the other guy. It's human nature for most of us to look out for number one, right? But that's not the best way to play basketball.

Before the 1978–79 season opened, I called the team together and said, "We don't have to love each other. It would look stupid if all twelve of us walked down the street, holding hands."

That drew a laugh.

"But we do have to respect each other," I said. "We *have* to play together. We *have* to learn from each other. I realize that certain guys will hang out together away from the court, and some other guys will go their own way. That's OK. We can't all be together all the time. But we have to be a family when we're at the gym. It's us against everyone else. When a teammate makes a suggestion to you, take it the right way. He's not trying to insult you, he's saying something to make the team better. And when you go to say something to a teammate, say it the right way. Don't insult the guy. Treat each other with respect."

I talked about how we went from a bunch of individuals with a 5–17 record to a true team that went to the seventh game of the NBA Finals. But I said we had to trust each other and sacrifice even a little more. We came so close, yes, so close to winning. Just a little more teamwork, that's what we needed.

The guys sat there, taking it in. You know how things get very quiet when a message is hitting home? How it gets so quiet, you can hear yourself breathe? That's how it was when I spoke to the team that day.

"There is only one ball," I said. "Each of us does something a little different with it. Some of us are better at shooting it, some at rebounding, some at driving on the fast break and some at defending, taking it away from the other team. The way we win is to get the ball to the guy with the hot hand, the guy who can do the most with it *right now*. That guy often changes from game to game, even quarter to quarter. We have to be unselfish enough to keep finding that guy."

Players working together is more than coach-speak, and the coach can't do everything. Early in our playoff series against Washington, Elvin Hayes was just pounding on Jack Sikma. Hayes knew Jack was a rookie and didn't know how to retaliate to all the elbows and shoves, at least not without being called for a foul. Paul Silas was watching this from the bench. He knew that Hayes was trying to physically intimidate Sikma, and he knew that Sikma lacked the experience to battle back. He also knew that if someone didn't challenge Hayes, Sikma was in big trouble. When Silas went into the game, Hayes leaned on him—and Silas nailed him in the chest with a right forearm. It happened so fast, no one saw it. But something happened, because suddenly, Hayes was staggering a bit under the basket. Hayes tried to shove Paul away from another rebound . . . and BAM! . . . Silas drilled him with another forearm. The officials never saw it, because Silas was too savvy to get caught. I didn't tell Silas to do this. He saw it on his own. And he took care of Hayes, who then backed off Sikma a bit.

This is part of what a coach means by chemistry. It's the players looking out for each other. It's veteran players spotting a young player who's spending too much time on the town, taking the kid aside, and explaining, "Hey, man, you gotta get your rest or you'll never last in this league." Young players want the respect of the veterans, and they're more likely to listen to a veteran player than they are to some coaches. That's just a fact. It comes down to peer pressure, and when it's used the right way, it's the best thing for any team. For a couple of years in Seattle, we had that.

In the summer of 1978, we lost Marvin Webster to New York via free agency. That meant we had to find some more size to help Sikma under the basket. There was still compensation for losing a free agent, either by agreement between the teams or by the decision of an arbitrator. In this case, the arbitrator said we could pick one of two New York players—Lonnie Shelton or Bob McAdoo.

McAdoo was the bigger name, but he was approaching the end of his career. He also was more of a scorer, and we already had an inside player who could score in Sikma. I needed the defensive presence that I'd lost in Webster, so that's why I went for Shelton, a burly, six-foot-eight, 270-pound forward. He was much like a grizzly bear, because he could be mean and strong, but he also was surprisingly quick and agile. I had always liked his game, dating back to when he played college ball at Oregon State. This deals with chemistry. In the eyes of most fans, McAdoo was the better player, but Shelton was the better player for us. If we had lost Sikma and kept

Webster, then maybe I'd have picked McAdoo for his offense. Shelton was also a very unselfish player; he could score inside, but he liked to set up his teammates. A reporter once said, "Lonnie Shelton is wide enough to set a pick on the sun." That was so true. The guy was huge. A guard could run his man into a Lonnie Shelton pick, and the guy would get wiped out. Lonnie's body would just engulf him.

I also picked up Dennis Awtrey, a veteran backup center, along with Dick Snyder, a veteran guard, and Wally Walker, a veteran forward. I knew we needed experience on the bench if we were going to win the title, and these guys would be content to play any role that I asked of them, especially if they knew they had a real chance at a championship ring.

As we went through training camp, I liked the looks of our team. Sikma was our center, and was no longer a rookie. He'd averaged over 15 points and 12 rebounds that first season. His confidence had grown, and he also understood the kind of conditioning and strength needed to survive an 82-game regular season schedule and another 20-some games in the playoffs. I originally had Tom LeGarde in my starting lineup, but he was injured.

I put Shelton in the lineup as a power forward, with John Johnson coming back as small forward, or point forward. J.J. was happy to handle the ball, to make sure that our guards, Gus Williams and Dennis Johnson, could use their speed to run down the court on the fast break.

On the bench were Silas, Dick Snyder, Dennis Awtrey, Wally Walker, and Fred Brown.

Expectations were high, at least in Seattle. Our fans were picking us to at least win the Western Conference and return to the NBA Finals. We couldn't sneak up on people, as we had the year before. I felt quite a bit of pressure because this was the first team that I ever coached that was supposed to win big.

I knew we were a good team, but not a classic basketball team. We had no prototype point guard. Both of our guards were scorers. The small forward is supposed to be an offensive position supplying 15 to 20 points a game, but we needed our small forward (John Johnson) to run the offense, like a point guard. After we lost Marvin

Webster, we also lost our shot blocker. Sikma had played power forward next to Webster, now he was taking over at center for Webster.
While Jack was a solid rebounder, he was neither a leaper nor a shot
blocker. No one was going to take a look at Sikma and think, "I'm
not driving down the lane on that guy." This is not to knock Jack, it's
just to put his game into the perspective of the rest of the team.
That's why Shelton was such a critical pickup: He didn't block a lot
of shots, but he blocked the path to the basket. He put his enormous
body in the middle of the lane, and he wasn't afraid to knock a guy
down who thought he could dunk on us. Silas gave us that same
kind of presence when he came off the bench. For us to win a championship, every piece had to fit just right. Every player had to buy
into a system that accented his strengths and covered his weaknesses. And more important, the players had to cover up for each
other. A lot of players say they're willing to do this, but they don't
carry it out. They start worrying about their scoring average, and
how they need good statistics for the next contract.

This team understood all that. If there was a mismatch, say
Sikma was being covered by a guard, right away, we passed the ball
to Sikma. This team recognized mismatches and continually made
them work to our advantage. It played tremendous team defense,
each player not just guarding his own man, but making sure that
the defense was like a glove—all five fingers were covered. To coach
a bunch of guys who were willing to put their egos aside and play
together the way this group did in that 1978–79 season was a pleasure. I believed in those guys, and they believed in each other. I don't
care if that sounds corny, that's at the heart of any winning team.
The guys believe in something bigger and more important than
themselves.

There is also a very strange element to the story of this season,
and only a few people know about it.

During the 1977–78 season, there was this lady who occasionally left messages for me. She claimed to be a clairvoyant, and she
said she had visions. I never bought into any of that stuff, so I ig-
nored it. But it turned out that she was a friend of my brother's

wife. She kept telling my sister-in-law that she needed to see me, that she had something important to tell me. My sister-in-law kept bugging me about it, saying this lady was special.

Finally, I agreed to let her come to our home. Marilyn and her parents were also there. The lady asked to see me in another room. We went to my den. She held both of my hands and began to speak in tongues. I wasn't real comfortable with this, but I was trying to be gracious. During part of it, my father-in-law walked by, shook his head, and obviously thought the entire thing was crazy.

Finally, she said, "I've wanted to talk with you for some time because I've seen things. I knew that last year would be good for you and the team, but this year is special. You will win a championship."

I said I hoped she was right, still not sure what to make of it.

She said she wanted nothing from me. She said she prayed for me and my family, and just asked that I occasionally pray for her.

That was fine with me. I didn't think a lot about it for quite a while.

The season began and we got off to a good start. Then Shelton and Brown were hurt, and we lost some games.

The lady called and asked me to stop by her house, that she had a vision. I went to her house, which was in the projects. She had candles everywhere, and started praying, speaking in tongues.

Then she said, "One of your players is hurt right now."

That wasn't exactly something visionary, because it had been in the newspaper, the injuries to Shelton and Brown.

"But one of your players is hurting now because he just changed to a different pair of shoes," she said.

I tried to think who that could be. Brown had an ankle injury, but I didn't know that he had done anything to his shoes.

"Go to that player," she said. "Tell him to put a lift in his new shoes, and he'll be back right after. Right now, he's favoring his leg."

I thanked her for the words, and left.

The next day at practice, I saw our trainer and said, "Did Fred change his shoes recently?"

"Yeah, he got new ones," he said.

"Did you take the lift out of his old shoes and put them in the new ones?" I asked.

"Fred said he didn't need the lift anymore," he said.

"Put it in anyway," I said.

The trainer put the lifts in the shoes. Our next game was against Denver. At first, Fred said he wasn't going to play, his ankle was still bothering him. Then he said he'd like to try it for a few minutes. He came off the bench, hit two or three quick shots. He only played about ten minutes that night, but by the next day, he said his ankle felt much better. We kept the lifts in those shoes, and he didn't have any more problems for the rest of the year.

The really weird thing is that I only heard from the lady one other time. It was a few years later. She told me, "I see a tire in your future. Yes, a tire. Rubber. That kind of thing."

I was still coaching in Seattle, so that made no sense to me.

But I remembered what she said a few years later, when I was coaching the Cavaliers . . . and living in Akron, which was once known as the Rubber City because so many great tire companies were located there.

We finished the regular season with a 52–30 record, good for first place in the Pacific Division.

Even though we'd made it to the Finals in 1978, then won the Pacific Division the following season, most "experts" didn't consider us serious contenders for the championship. They thought our success was a fluke.

As *Sports Illustrated* wrote, "When the Washington Bullets beat Seattle in the seventh game of the championship series, many felt justice had been served, that the Sonics were merely a group of average players who had rallied around their monster center, Marvin Webster, and happened to hit a hot spell at just the right time. Surely, after the team lost Webster, the Sonics would return to journeymanhood and the franchise would just disappear under one of Seattle's floating bridges."

That seemed especially true after Webster went to New York and we replaced him with Shelton—whose claim to fame in New York had been leading the league in personal fouls during his first two seasons.

But *Sports Illustrated* eventually figured out what we knew all along—we were a team in the best sense of the word. No one player "made us," or as *SI* wrote, "Marvin Webster didn't make the Sonics, they made him. Winning all those games and advancing through all those rounds of playoffs built trust and respect and a mutual confidence that one man's leave-taking could not erase—even if the man was the Human Eraser himself."

Our team was special. No one averaged 20 points a game, but seven guys scored at least 11 points a night. We also led the league in defense and—I believe—floor burns as we came up with so many loose balls.

Gus Williams was happy-go-lucky, and because he had such enthusiasm, such an engaging smile and love of the game, he could get away with taking some bad shots. His teammates respected Gus for how he flew up and down the court, sometimes becoming a one-man fast break. He had a knack for stealing the ball, for scoring lots of points in a hurry. But most of all, he was just so upbeat, so happy just to be playing basketball, that it rubbed off on the rest of the team.

Dennis Johnson was far more serious. He was a tremendous defensive player. When we needed to shut down a hot-shooting guard, Dennis put out the fire. He smothered the guy, and he liked doing that, taking on the other team's best scorer. And Dennis could score, too. He could be moody at times, wanting to be respected and worrying that he didn't receive the credit he was due. During the championship season, some of that anger worked for the good of the team, because Dennis was out to prove that he was a great player. Every game was a personal challenge to him, a chance to show everyone that he was an outstanding player.

Silas was a tough guy on the court. He'd knock you down to get a rebound. If the game got rough, he'd knock a guy's block off. But he was a very friendly man, and a tremendously unselfish player who came off the bench for us to rebound and set picks.

Shelton learned a lot from playing with Silas. In many ways, he was a young Paul Silas, a burly forward who didn't feel a need to shoot a lot. He could really defend and rebound. When we had Silas and Shelton on the court together, no team could muscle us. That's why I was amused later in my coaching career when I had a more skilled, finesse team in Cleveland with the likes of Mark Price, Larry Nance, Brad Daugherty, and John Williams, and some critics claimed that having a "soft team" was a reflection of my personality. No, it was due to the kind of players that I had to work with. Just as this team in Seattle was a rough, physical group thanks to Silas, Shelton, and Dennis Johnson.

John Johnson is another guy who could be ornery on the court. He would work himself into such a state before games that he absolutely despised the player he was to defend that night. He just got mad at the guy, period. But he kept that rage under control. And on offense, J.J. was unselfish. He was a small forward with the heart of a point guard, because he loved to pass, to find the open man, and to get us settled into our regular offense when the fast break wasn't available. He was the most underrated player on the team.

Sikma was very consistent. Almost every night, you could put 17 points and 10 rebounds next to his name. He had that strange step-back move that made him hard to guard. That move also helped him draw fouls, and he was an 80 percent shooter at the free throw line. He was a quiet guy who just came and did his job, no muss, no fuss.

Brown was the life of our party, coming off the bench and launching those jump shots from another area code. He was the best sixth man in the league. He brought our crowd to its feet. He never hesitated to shoot. He could miss 10 in a row and still be absolutely, positively convinced that the 11th shot would go in. I loved the energy he brought into the game every time he took off his warmups and headed to the scorer's table.

We faced Washington again in the Finals, and I knew we'd win this time. I just knew it. Our team was, to quote *Sports Illustrated,* "a superb club with relentless defense, a running, guard-oriented offense and backcourt talent unequaled in the NBA. . . . Unlike other so-called 'defensive' teams, the Sonics don't slow down the game to a frustrating crawl [but stop opponents] by textbook, body-hugging defense."

Our team had its own blend of a balanced attack. That season, Brown was the best outside shooter in the NBA. Dennis Johnson may have been the best all-around guard. Remember, this was the year before Magic Johnson came into the NBA, and long before Michael Jordan; D.J. not only could score 20 points, but he could take the top scorer on the other team and hold him under 10. Gus Williams was mercurial, perhaps the quickest guard in the league. No forward passed the ball better than John Johnson. Sikma had developed into a very good center, while Silas and Shelton were a pair of bearlike forwards who guarded the basket as if it were their den. Strong, quick, determined, and explosive. Those were the Sonics in the 1979 playoffs, as Washington could attest.

We lost the first game, then won the next four. Only once did the Bullets score more than 100 points against us. Gus Williams averaged 28 points in the series, while Dennis Johnson averaged 25 and "did everything but change the light bulbs in the 24-second clock," according to *Sports Illustrated*. D.J. was named the MVP of the Finals. Shelton and Silas combined to hold Elvin Hayes, Washington's star forward, to 39 percent shooting and a grand total of only 14 points in the fourth quarters of the five games.

It's a shame that the country really didn't get a chance to see all the games. Some of them were tape-delayed and shown after the 11:00 P.M. news in some markets. After the first game, which was on May 20, we had to sit for four more days before playing Game Two on May 24. Why the delay? Because CBS was showing *Blind Ambition*, the miniseries based on the book by Watergate figure John Dean. That just shows where the NBA was in the pecking order of the TV networks in 1979.

In Seattle, it was a different story. Our fans were wildly in love with us. Over twenty thousand of them were waiting for us at the airport when we came home from Washington, D.C. There were parades and parties and we were the toast of the town. The champagne seemed to flow for days. I can still see the parade, with over 250,000 people lining the streets of downtown Seattle. I still remember the feeling I had during the Finals, where I never worried about us losing. Even after we were beaten in the first game, I was confident that we'd win. This was our year. We were the right team in the right place at the right time.

After the season, I again wasn't voted NBA Coach of the Year. This time, the award went to Cotton Fitzsimmons, who had coached

Kansas City into the playoffs. But CBS gave me a "Coach of the Year" award, which I believe embarrassed the NBA; the network never gave another Coach of the Year award after that. The Congressional Black Congress also gave me a special Coach of the Year award, and had an incredible presentation for me with a lot of U.S. senators and representatives there. They thought it was unfair that I was slighted by the NBA for the award. I wasn't thrilled either, but I was starting to get used to it.

The season we won the title, I was forty years old. I was proud of our team and what we'd accomplished, but I was in no danger of letting my ego run away with me. I had too many people in my life who warned me about fame being fleeting. I had stayed in contact with Father Mannion, calling him several times a year, visiting when I was in New York. He kept me spiritually grounded and also gave me great confidence because he believed in me. Both my wife and Father Mannion were quite capable of telling me if I was becoming too full of myself.

Besides, I had been in the NBA for nineteen years when I got my first championship; I knew how hard it was to win, and I knew that I was very fortunate as a coach to have this group of players, and that they had stayed relatively healthy, especially in the playoffs. What I didn't know was how hard it would be to try to win the next season.

CHAPTER THIRTEEN

THEY DON'T TELL YOU what happens after you win a championship.

The champagne bubbles hadn't even gone flat before the problems started: Some guys retired. A couple got hung up on money. A few lost their focus and dedication. Everyone got a year older, and some of our players just didn't have any mileage left in their legs.

For our team to win the title, virtually everything had to go right. Each player had to be committed to his role, to be willing to put the team first. Our guys did that and it paid off. So I was surprised when some of them weren't willing to do it again the next season. To a coach, the game plan is obvious: Let's just do everything the same way, and we'll win again. This is the formula. We found the secret. Let's not change it.

But winning a title inevitably shakes things up—especially in the modern era of pro sports, where the money is so big, the distractions so overpowering, and the feelings of some of the athletes so delicate.

Our team was hit with what I call "Championship Fallout." Pat Riley called it "The Disease of Me." No matter the label, the point is that winning suddenly isn't enough. The players hug each other, hold up the championship trophy together, share the champagne—and suddenly ask, "Where's mine?"

"Mine" could be more money, more playing time, more public recognition. All of those things can be like worms eating away at the heart of a team, especially a team like ours that wasn't carried by a superstar. The teams that became NBA dynasties all had at least one great player who was the constant, who set the tone, demanded respect from the other players, and was willing to serve as a policeman in the dressing room. In Boston, the great player was Bill Russell. Later, it was Larry Bird. In Los Angeles, it was Magic Johnson. In Chicago, Michael Jordan. When Detroit won their back-to-back titles, the great player was Isiah Thomas.

Those guys were obsessed with winning. To them, winning meant more than money, more than fame, more than life itself. They not only drove themselves, they powered the entire team. They were like Supermen, and their teammates knew they had to grab on to that cape or they'd be left behind.

We didn't have that player. When I took over the Sonics, they'd never had a Rookie of the Year, an MVP, a scoring champion, or a Coach of the Year. When we won the title, the whole was far greater than the collection of the parts. In our title season, we had no one in the top ten in scoring. Sikma was fifth in rebounding, Fred Brown third in free throw percentage; those were our only players among the league leaders. Our top scorer was Gus Williams at 18.1, but we had seven players scoring at least 11 points per game. We were a true share-the-ball, share-the-wealth team.

Dennis Johnson was the MVP of the Finals, deservedly so. Dennis had a great, great series, especially on the defensive end. He led both teams with 11 blocked shots, an amazing feat for a guard. During the entire playoffs, he averaged 20 points and came up with 6.1 rebounds per game—from the guard position! In that 1978–79 season, Dennis made his first All-Star team. When we won the title, he was twenty-five years old, a tough-as-rusty-nails six-foot-four, two-hundred-pounder. It was the kind of season that Dennis had later in his career with the Boston Celtics, a season in which Larry Bird was inspired to say, "Dennis Johnson is the best guy I've ever played with."

Winning the championship and the MVP award in the Finals meant a lot to Dennis. It was a sign of respect to a player who craved it desperately. He was one of sixteen children from Compton, California. His father was a cement mason, his mother a social worker. Because there were so many kids, they often spent time at a grandmother's house. Dennis said he was blessed to have two parents at home, even if they weren't wealthy.

The amazing part of Dennis's story is his basketball career. He was cut from the teams in seventh and eighth grade. When he was a senior in high school, he made the team but sat on the bench. He was only five-foot-nine.

He graduated from high school and went to work, first as a stockboy at a liquor store, then driving a forklift in a warehouse. But the year after high school, he grew to six-foot-three.

Suddenly, basketball became a much easier game for him. He was quick, tall, and strong, especially for a guard. He was spotted in a pickup game by Jim White, who was the coach at Harbor Junior College. Dennis struggled with the discipline of organized basketball; according to his old coach, he was nearly kicked off the team on three different occasions, mostly because he would miss practice and not call in to explain. But in his sophomore season, Dennis averaged 20 points and a stunning 13 rebounds per game as Harbor won the California Junior College title. That earned him a scholarship to Pepperdine, where coach Gary Colson recruited him after seeing Dennis score 30 points, grab 15 rebounds, and out-jump a seven-foot-two center for a jump ball in a playoff game. Back then, his nickname was "Airplane," and for good reason.

Pepperdine was 22–6 in Dennis's first year. He decided to enter the NBA draft early, and Bill Russell picked him in the second round of the 1976 draft. He signed for a bonus of $27,500, which was very small—and he'd considered himself underpaid ever since.

Dennis was one of our lower-paid players during the championship season. That's because he wasn't a high draft pick, so he didn't command a big contract out of college. I admit that based on his performance, Dennis was underpaid. *Sports Illustrated* called him the "best all-around guard to come into the NBA since Jerry West." But he also had signed a long-term contract, and ownership did not want to renegotiate the deal. Sam Schulman was one of those guys who believed that since you signed your contract of your own free will, it was your obligation to live up to it. Sam thought, "If Dennis got hurt and couldn't play any more, I still had to pay him. That was my risk when I signed him to a long-term deal.

Dennis took the risk that he might end up a better player and be worth more than he was being paid."

All of that is good business sense, but this went from business to personal with Dennis. He became angry, sullen, withdrawn from the rest of the team. He thought the front office had taken advantage of him. I talked to Dennis. I listened to Dennis. I knew what the problem was and I was sympathetic, but I didn't write the checks. And Dennis was unable to separate his anger toward ownership from his feelings toward the rest of the team.

Sometimes, he was obsessive about not making as much as certain other players. He'd see a guy whom he considered half as good as he was, yet who was making twice as much—this would eat up Dennis inside, wreck his morale. And Dennis had the misfortune to have as a teammate the brilliant but one-dimensional Fred Brown.

The Seattle fans loved Downtown Fred Brown. He was fun to watch, because when Fred Brown was hot, few shooting guards could compare to him. He also played the game with a smile, with pure joy, and the fans related to that. Meanwhile, Dennis played with a controlled rage. He scowled. He gritted his teeth. He played as if someone were trying to take away his last meal. The fans respected Dennis for his effort, but they didn't warm to him as they did to Fred Brown.

And that bothered Dennis, who knew he was a better all-around player than Brown, but thought the fans preferred Brown. The lack of appreciation from the fans then became tied in Dennis's mind to the front office's refusal to give him a new contract. Gus Williams was also making twice as much as his backcourt mate, and that gnawed away at Dennis, because he considered himself to be the best player on the team. When a player is unhappy, it's easy for him to start playing for himself. He thinks, "Well, the team won't take care of me, so I better take care of me." Furthermore, his griping tells the other players that selfishness is creeping into his mindset. The pure magic of the game is five guys playing as one, five players fitting together like five fingers of one hand. For the hand to work right, all the fingers have to be operating for the same purpose.

There was a game where Paul Silas thought Dennis was holding the ball too long, that he was forcing shots instead of passing to open teammates. He said something to Dennis, and Dennis snapped back at Silas. This happened in the middle of the game. In the past, when Silas or another veteran said something, it was taken the right way—Silas just wanted what was best for the team and was not trying to attack Dennis personally. But Dennis was taking everything personally.

As a coach, there wasn't much I could do about it. Dennis wanted more money. The owner wouldn't give him more money. Dennis wanted more attention from the fans, but the fans liked Fred Brown best. Intellectually, Dennis didn't blame me or his teammates for this, but emotionally, he was wounded and couldn't stop the anger from gushing to the surface. Players are the first to know when a teammate is no longer on the same page with them. And it's easy for them to say, "Screw it; if that guy is going to shoot all the time, so am I."

As a coach, you try to head that off the best you can—and if the problem is just one guy, you stand a chance.

But there was also Lonnie Shelton.

All of the Sonic players were made to feel as if they owned Seattle after we won the title. They were invited to restaurants, parties, and bars. They never had to pay for anything. Men, women, everyone wanted to get close to them. Shelton's lifestyle changed. He got caught up in the nightlife. He put on weight. He lost some of the agility that made him such an impressive inside force on both ends of the floor. He also lost some of his desire. He just wasn't the same guy.

Dick Snyder, who came off the bench for us and could really make jump shots, decided to retire. So did Dennis Awtrey, who was very effective for us in spot duty guarding great centers such as Kareem Abdul-Jabbar. Paul Silas came back, but he was thirty-six and just not the same player. Age was taking its toll. The same was true of John Johnson, who was thirty-two and seemed to be battling one minor injury after another. He played, but he was hurting. As if that wasn't enough, John Johnson injured his Achilles tendon. So it wasn't just one thing that brought us down, it was a lot of things.

But we still won 56 games, which was a franchise record. It was four more victories than our title season the year before. But suddenly it wasn't as much fun. We won more but enjoyed it less because of all the internal problems: Every day, I was reminded how fragile it was, how just the slightest little thing could throw an entire team off course. Fred Brown told the truth in a *Sports Illustrated* article that season when he said, "We're not as hungry. Last year, we were building a mountain, and when you're working that hard, you can't help but be hungry. This season has been different."

It's the old story of how much harder it is to stay on top than to get there. When we tried to repeat in 1980, no NBA team had done it since Bill Russell's Celtics of 1968–69. In the previous two years, we'd played defense as well as any NBA team ever had. By that, I mean all the guys worked together and trusted each other on the court. That was why we became champions, even without having a shot blocker in the middle. But it's hard for a team to do that after a title. The temptation is for the players to think they can relax during the season and just turn up the defensive intensity in the playoffs. But that doesn't work. Sometimes a team gets better in time for the playoffs, but that only happens when you're coming together for the first time, when you've been playing hard all along and then you suddenly understand how to play effectively, too. You can't turn the effort on and off. A coach can talk about this, can stress the need to play with the same urgency every night, but in the end, the players have to do it. And we didn't.

Despite all this, we still could have repeated as NBA champions, except for one thing—Magic Johnson.

He joined the Lakers as a rookie that year, and his leadership changed that team—and the entire Western Conference. He took a Laker team that had won 47 games without him, and they jumped to 60 wins with Magic as a rookie. We knew we'd have to get past the Lakers to return to the Finals.

We beat Portland in the first round of the playoffs. Then we won a tough seven-game series against Milwaukee. Then something crazy happened: We had the Lakers in the Western Conference Finals, but we lost our home court again. For some reason, they booked the circus or something at the Seattle Coliseum. How dumb was that? Two years before, it was a surprise when we went to the NBA Finals, so it was almost understandable. But this time? When we were defending champions? How does that happen? With our regular home court, I still don't know if we could have beaten the Lakers that year. But to not even have it? It was ridiculous. These are the kinds of things that really bother players, because they wonder what the front office is doing: Are they paying attention, doing everything they can to help us win? It's a distraction no team needs, especially after the rather rocky season we'd just endured. Anyway, our home games were moved to the University of Washington's court, and we lost the edge that comes from playing in a place that feels like your backyard.

We lost the best-of-seven series in five games. The Lakers had the same kind of attitude that we had the year before, that incredible desire to win a title. Abdul-Jabbar seemed revived by the presence of Magic, who found ways not only to get him the ball, but to score enough so that Kareem knew that the entire offense didn't rest on his skyhook.

While I didn't admit it publicly, in my heart I had a bad feeling: I saw the future of the Western Conference, and its name was Magic Johnson. Meanwhile, I saw more problems ahead for my team.

Fans don't like to hear this, but it's the truth: Either you have a superstar, or you don't.

Seattle did not have a superstar. The Lakers did, in Magic. And the Celtics did in Larry Bird. And that's why those two teams dominated the NBA for most of the 1980s. You must have someone on your team who demands the respect of the players and has earned that respect by what he does on the court. The coach can only do so much; then it's up to the players.

Kareem was one of the greatest players ever, but he was not that guy. He won a title with Milwaukee in 1971, when an aging Oscar Robertson came in to join him, and then he didn't win again until Magic arrived in 1980. Kareem is a thoughtful, quiet man. He is not the kind of vocal leader who can inspire a team, despite his greatness on the court.

A great player in basketball can tilt the game in his direction because there are only five players on the court at any given moment. His impact is greater there than in football, where eleven play at a time, or in baseball, where nine play at a time and where the offense doesn't control the ball. When he played minor league baseball, Michael Jordan talked about how frustrated he was because he couldn't control the game; he had to wait until it was his turn to bat, or for someone to hit the ball to him in the outfield. In basketball, a great player doesn't have to wait to get the ball. At any point, the coach can set up a play for him to receive a pass, or the player can just steal the ball, get a rebound, do something to get the ball *now!* The great player can impose his will on the game and affect it constantly.

In Seattle, we didn't have that guy.

Dennis Johnson's contract situation continued to fester until the front office felt that he had to be traded. I agreed with the decision, and we sent him to Phoenix for Paul Westphal, who was an All-Star guard—but Westphal broke his foot, and he played only 36 games for us in 1980–81. Now, I would handle this situation differently. I would have spent more time with Dennis after we were eliminated from the 1980 playoffs. I would have listened to him, talked to him, let him know that I was sympathetic—and then I would have pushed harder with ownership to try to convince them to rework Dennis's contract. I would have been the go-between for both parties, try to get them talking again and maybe get the thing resolved. But I was still a relatively young coach, only forty-one. And Dennis was a very young twenty-five. Instead, emotions boiled over.

When we traded Dennis, I was talking with a sportswriter. He said, "One bad apple can spoil the whole barrel." I didn't want to use that analogy, but I just made it worse by saying, "That's right. If a person has a cancer, you remove it, right? You don't let it spread and affect the whole body. So if something doesn't work, you try to address it."

That wasn't smart, as I realized when I saw the headline the next day reading: WILKENS CALLS JOHNSON A CANCER. It ran first in a Denver paper, because Silas had called him a cancer before I did. Then the whole thing spread, and I ended up in the middle of it. It was a mess. We lost Dennis. Westphal was hurt. Shelton continued to be distracted by personal problems. Then Gus Williams became unhappy with his contract, and he held out. He sat out the entire 1980–81 season in a dispute with the front office.

Again, money was changing everything. First, it forced us to trade Dennis; then we lost Gus for the whole year. And we went from winning 56 games in 1979–80, to a 34–48 record in 1980–81. It was hard to believe how fast everything disintegrated, but it did. We were never able to put that same chemistry together again. In 1981–82, we signed Gus to a new deal and won 52 games, which was the second-best record in franchise history. But we lost to San Antonio in the second round of the playoffs.

Another by-product of winning is low draft choices. The more you win, the lower you draft. So we didn't have an influx of young talent to replace the aging veterans such as Silas, John Johnson, and Fred Brown. We traded for players such as Tom Chambers and drafted James Donaldson who helped us, but we were in the same Pacific Division as the Lakers, the same as Magic Johnson. And we weren't going to beat them, period.

Over the next three years we slipped to 48 wins, then 42, then 31; we couldn't get past the first round of the playoffs in 1982–83 or 1983–84, and then missed out on them altogether in my last season coaching the Sonics, 1984–85. I spent the next year strictly as a general manager, but I found I missed being a coach. I couldn't bear to watch the ends of close games in the arena; I had to go somewhere and watch on TV. I wanted to be in the huddle, trying to come up with a play to help us win. In some respects, it was good for me to have a year away from coaching. It recharged my batteries and allowed me to fully concentrate on my job as a general manager. For most of my time in Seattle, I was doing both jobs—although Les Habegger had that position in my final year as coach. Owner Barry Ackerley asked me to be the GM, and I knew I needed a break from coaching. I made some good deals that year, shipping Al Wood to Dallas for Dale Ellis and drafting Nate McMillan in the second round. Our number one pick, Xavier McDaniel, had a strong rookie season and became a very good NBA player. But we were working on a limited budget in Seattle. I wanted us to re-sign Fred Brown for one more year, to offer him about $100,000 to come back and play if he wanted, even though Fred was at the end of his career. It was the respectful thing to do. But the front office refused, and that became a media fiasco because it looked as if we were kicking Fred Brown out the door.

As I spent that year as general manager, people kept asking me if I wanted to coach again. A number of them, like my friend Dick Helm, said I really should coach. I ran into Wayne Embry, who had just taken over as the Cleveland Cavaliers general manager, and he asked me if I was interested in coaching. I had hired Bernie Bicker-staff to replace me in Seattle; his record was 31–51, but it wouldn't have been fair or made any sense for me to come down and replace Bernie after only one season. We were rebuilding, and Bernie de-served a chance to put things together his own way.

The last thing I did before leaving Seattle was to trade Jack Sikma. I didn't want to do it, but Jack wanted to play for a contender; Milwaukee was interested in him because the Bucks had been searching for a center for years.

The Bucks orginally offered a first-round pick and a player for Sikma. I talked to Bickerstaff about that, and he said he needed someone to play center if Sikma was traded.

"How about Alton Lister?" I asked.

Bernie liked that idea. Lister wasn't great, but he was service-able, about six-foot-eleven, with long arms, and he liked to block shots.

I told Don Nelson we wanted Lister. Nelson was both coach and general manager.

"That's a possibility," he said.

"I want two first-round picks and Lister for Sikma," I said.

"That's *crazy!!!*" he screamed.

"Nelly," I said, "I've got to get two first-rounders in this deal."

"*I'll never trade two first-rounders!*" he screamed again.

"That's the way it is," I said. "Sikma is an All-Star-caliber player. If you want him, that's what it will cost you."

Nelson still refused. The conversation ended, and the next day I went to Cleveland to interview for the Cavaliers coaching job.

I came back the next day, and Nelson called.

"We've got a deal," he said.

"What do you mean, we have a deal?" I asked. "We didn't when I left."

"We do now," he said. "I just talked to [Seattle owner] Barry Ackerley and he said he'd do it for Lister and a first-rounder."

"That's crap," I said. "You know that Barry doesn't make the deals, I do."

"I'm telling you that Barry said—"

"I don't care what he said," I roared. "There's no deal."

Then I hung up the phone and went to Ackerley. He said he didn't agree to any trade with Nelson; he said Nelson pressured him, but he didn't say it was a deal.

I called Nelson back and said, "Ackerley told me that he never agreed to anything."

Nelson was naturally upset. Then he got Bucks owner Herb Kohl on the line. Kohl also was a U.S. senator from Wisconsin.

"Lenny," he said, "I know you are an honorable person. I know what you wanted in the deal. But I'm telling you, this guy said he'd make the trade for Lister and a first-round pick. I just want you to know that. But I also know what you wanted in the deal."

"I'm sorry that happened," I said. "But I told both you and Nelly that I needed two first-rounders in the deal."

Finally, we agreed to Milwaukee sending us Lister and first-round picks in 1987 and 1989 for Sikma and two future second-round picks.

That gave Seattle five first-round picks in the next three drafts. I could have said that I was probably leaving the Sonics anyway, that it looked as if I had the Cleveland job wrapped up, so why fight for that last draft pick? But I always loved the Sonics, and I felt I owed it to the fans to leave the team in the best possible shape to become a contender again, which I felt I did.

CHAPTER FOURTEEN

ONE OF THE BEST THINGS that ever happened to me was the chance to coach the Cleveland Cavaliers. It came at a perfect time in my career, when I needed a change of scenery and some good players to coach. Even better, I had a chance to work for a wonderful owner in Gordon Gund and a good general manager in Wayne Embry.

For that, I'll always be thankful.

When I remember my seven years in Cleveland, I'm filled with pride. We won a lot of games. We won with excellent people. We won for fans who appreciated our players and our style of play. Yet I still think about what could have been, and I have a feeling of incompleteness. In my heart, I believe we could have won a title in Cleveland—even in the era of Michael Jordan.

In the summer of 1986, the Cavaliers were looking for a new coach. Then again, it seemed the Cavs were always looking for a new coach. In the first six seasons of that decade, the Cavs changed coaches eight times! Some of them like Bill Musselman did two tours of duty. Here's a list of men who coached the Cavs from January 1980 until I was hired in July 1986: Gene Littles, George Karl, Tom Nissalke, Chuck Daly, Don Delaney, Bob Kloppenburg, Stan Albeck, and two courses of Musselman.

Why would I even want a job in a place like that?

Because things were changing. Gordon Gund bought the Cavs from Ted Stepien in 1983. The Stepien regime was a constant swirl of coaches and players, coming and going. The trades were so questionable that for a while, the NBA office stepped in and said it had to approve all deals—a way of protecting the Cavs from themselves. During the early 1980s, Stepien's Cavs were called "The Cadavers," for obvious reasons having to do with their dismal records and their horrible attendance. At times, the twenty-thousand-seat Richfield Coliseum seemed like the world's largest tomb. You could hear the ball echo all over the building as it was dribbled up the court.

By the summer of 1986, Wayne Embry had just been hired as general manager. I didn't know Wayne well, but I had played against him. Wayne was a huge center, about six-foot-eight and 270 pounds. He set bone-rattling picks for Oscar Robertson in Cincinnati. He later backed up Bill Russell for two years in Boston, then finished his career with the Milwaukee Bucks. He also was general manager of the Bucks for six years, turning them into a contender and a consistent winner. Too many people automatically assume Wayne and I are great friends, because we're black. And they assume Wayne hired me in Cleveland because of that friendship, which supposedly was based on race. That's insulting to both of us. I played against Wayne for many years, but never had any in-depth conversations with him. In fact, the man who was the Cavs general manager before Wayne, Harry Weltman, was the first to ask me about coaching the Cavs. Weltman has since told friends he fully intended to hire me—only he was fired in May 1986. Then Wayne was hired, and he talked to me about the job. I was interested not only because I trusted Wayne, but because I saw the moves he and the rest of the front office made in the 1986 draft. They picked Brad Daugherty, Ron Harper, Mark Price, and Johnny Newman. John "Hot Rod" Williams had been drafted in 1985 by Weltman, but had to sit out a season because he was indicted in a point-shaving case from his days at Tulane; in June 1986, Hot Rod was cleared of all charges and allowed to play.

So it didn't matter to me that the Cavs hadn't had a winning season in eight years. Nor did the small crowds bother me: I knew that Cleveland was a rabid sports town if the team was a winner. When I played with the Cavs in the early 1970s our crowds were small, but the fans who did come were very vocal and loyal. We just needed more of them. Also, that old Cleveland Arena on East Thirtieth and Euclid Avenue was a dump. The Richfield Coliseum was way out between Cleveland and Akron; one writer nicknamed it "The Big House on the Prairie," but it was a sparkling palace near several interstates that made it easy for the fans from the Cleveland suburbs and Akron area to come to our games. They just had to have a reason to show up. The building also had a practice court and a weight room, which meant a lot to me because I never had that situation in Seattle. It allowed us to use the locker rooms and all the equipment every day, not just for games. That's standard in many arenas today, but it was rare back in the middle 1980s. I sensed with Wayne Embry and Gordon Gund running the team, combined with the attractive building and the young players they had acquired, that something very special could happen in Cleveland—and I wanted to be a part of it.

When I interviewed with the Cavs, I knew they were as excited about me as I was about coaching their team. I met with Gordon Gund, who has been blind since the age of thirty because of a disease called retinitis pigmentosa. It's interesting that this white man who hired a black general manager/coach combination is blind. Of course, Wayne recommended me to Gordon, but in the end Gordon had to approve. Race was never an issue in my interviews with the Cavs. Gordon hired both Wayne and me for all the right reasons— we were the best men available, period. In a sense, this was the American Dream, Martin Luther King's dream. The world had changed. When I broke in with St. Louis in the early 1960s I couldn't eat or buy a house in some areas. Now I was being hired to coach an NBA team, and to work for an African-American general manager. And the best part was that no one dwelt on the racial aspect, we were all just there to try to do a job, to make the franchise into a winner.

The only concern Gordon had was that I remember Wayne was the general manager: I reported to Wayne, and Wayne reported to Gordon. That was a point Gordon made several times to me. He was worried because I had been a general manager in Seattle, but I assured Gordon that I wasn't interested in running the front office. I was forty-eight years old and in excellent health, and the year in Seattle's front office had left me eager to coach again, especially in a brand-new situation with a young team. Besides, the business side of the NBA had evolved and become more complicated because of salary caps, free agency, and other issues to the point where you need a full-time GM. I was glad I didn't have to worry about making trades or draft picks, nor was I in constant contact with the owner. A good general manager is a real shield between the coach and the owner, keeping both informed while not making the coach feel any more pressure than the enormous amount that already comes with the job. Wayne Embry was the ideal general manager when it came to juggling all those things, and I'm happiest when I can just focus on coaching.

At the time, the Cavs had a guy running their business operation who wanted me to take a psychological exam, which was something they gave to people they were considering for key positions in their organization.

I said, "Listen, I'm the coach. I'll be the one who gives the tests."

Gordon caught my humor and laughed, but the others around the table sat there stone-faced.

"No, I do the testing," I insisted.

Gordon said that was fine with him, and I was able to skip the test. I really liked Gordon. He came from a very wealthy family; his father was the man who discovered the formula for what became decaffeinated coffee. Then the family ventured into the banking business, and Gordon also owned a company that bought ailing corporations, put them back on their financial feet, then sold them. In fact, they purchased the Richfield Coliseum from some banks that had taken over the building because of financial troubles. With my interest in business and economics, Gordon and I had more than basketball to talk about. He is just an amazing guy. Yes, he is blind, but when he greets you, he shakes your hand and says, "Good to see you." I think he intentionally uses those words to put people at ease about his blindness. He could be sitting at a table with seven different people, and after everyone has said hello, he memorizes where you are and looks right at you as he speaks—even though he has no way of seeing you. He just remembers where he heard your voice. He'd sit at the games and cheer, listening to the broadcast on his headphones. The Cavs' radio voice is Joe Tait, one of the best broadcasters in NBA history, and a very good friend dating back to when I played for the Cavs. He was Gordon's eyes at the games. Gordon listened very intently to everything Joe said on the air. In meetings with Gordon, he'd ask probing, intelligent questions. I respected him for how he dealt with his blindness, how he refused to just take his family's money and sit on the sidelines of life. Instead, he pressed on, attacking life with a passion that impresses virtually everyone who meets him.

Some people wondered how I could leave Seattle. Between 1968 and 1986, I had spent all but two years playing or coaching in that city. Marilyn and I had a wonderful home there, plenty of friends, and we felt entrenched in the community. We never did sell our home in Seattle, because Seattle will always be just that to us— home. But I had come to the end of the line with the Sonics. And I wanted to coach.

I believe there are times in all our lives when God opens up a door for us, when an opportunity beckons. This was it. When I looked at the 1986 Cavs roster, I thought, "We could do the same things here we did in Seattle."

The Cavs had a rookie center in Brad Daugherty with great passing skills and a soft touch near the basket. He was seven feet tall and still growing—because he was only twenty years old. I heard that he was a little immature and not real serious about basketball, but that wasn't the case; he was just twenty, and all of us at twenty have some growing up to do, physically and mentally. Brad wasn't afraid of hard work. He played at North Carolina for Dean Smith, and really was team-oriented. If anything, he sometimes was too unselfish, because he was a gifted scorer who didn't shoot as much as he should. He wasn't a leaper and he didn't block many shots, but he was a decent rebounder and a skilled pivotman, which was rare back then and is nearly extinct today.

We had a power forward in John Williams, who had long arms and a knack for blocking shots, and who would have been a lottery pick in 1985 had it not been for the point-shaving accusations that caused him to sit out a year.

We had a shooting guard in Ron Harper, who was a pure athlete at six-foot-six with long arms, pogo sticks for legs, and a knack for getting to the basket. This is not to put him in the same class as Julius Erving, but Harper grew up watching videos of Doctor J. and he had more than a few of Erving's superb moves to the basket. Ron also had charisma. He acted as if he was too cool to listen to you, but he heard everything you said. Because Ron had a stuttering problem, some people assumed he wasn't very smart. Just the opposite: He knew where every player on the court was to be on every play, not just where he was supposed to go. The same was true of John Williams.

We had a point guard in Mark Price, although no one knew it at the time. Price was a second-round pick out of Georgia Tech, where most scouts saw him as a shooting guard in a six-foot point guard's body. Some scouts said he was too slow to be anything more than a role player, a Kyle Macy type, but they typecast Mark instead of really watching him play. I remember arguing with a few scouts, saying Mark would be a good point guard because he had a great cross-over dribble. Maybe he didn't have tremendous sprinter's speed running in a straight line, but he was just as fast dribbling the ball as when he ran without it—a key to judging the real speed of any point guard. He was always very shifty, able to move quickly from side to side, which enabled him to fake and shake the defense, to get open for his shot or to drive to the basket. I knew if I could teach him to split the double-team on the pick-and-roll play, to dribble through the two defenders who try to squeeze him, Mark could team up with Brad to become the key to our offense. That's eventually what happened.

But when we went to camp in October 1986, we were young. Daugherty, Price, Williams, Harper, and a reserve named Johnny Newman were all rookies. Price held out and didn't report until two weeks after camp started, and then he wasn't in top shape.

As for veterans, we only had a few who could help us. Most Cavs fans don't remember, but that year it was John Bagley who started at point guard, with Price as the backup. Our small forward was Phil Hubbard, one of my all-time favorite players because of his relentless work ethic and his dedication to putting the team first.

But Hubbard was not a classic small forward. He was six-foot-seven, but had some major knee injuries early in his career and was nearing the end of his time in the NBA. He really couldn't jump, but his best moves were to post-up inside and make this odd righthanded layup from the left side of the basket. Usually you want your small forward to be a scorer, a sky-walker who plays above the rim or a deadly jump shooter from the perimeter. Hubbard was neither. He was a classic, feet-on-the-floor small forward who scored 10 points a game, grabbed 5 rebounds, and set countless picks and played gritty defense. Larry Bird once listed Hubbard as one of the five toughest players ever to guard him. I respected Phil so much that I later hired him as my assistant when I coached in Atlanta.

The one thing we never had in my time with the Cavs was a small forward who fit the usual NBA job description. Most of the guys who played there after Hubbard, among them Mike Sanders and Winston Bennett, were guys who sacrificed their bodies to play team defense and set picks in Hubbard's tradition. You hear about blue-collar players, but usually at power forward. Not with us. We had Williams and later Larry Nance at power forward, and they could score. Nance also developed a very accurate fifteen-foot jumper. So we had to alter our offense, make the small forward into the guy doing the grunt work while the power forward did some shooting. Because of unselfish players such as Hubbard, Bennett, and Sanders, we made it work.

That first year with the Cavs, we started three rookies in Harper, Daugherty, and Williams. Price came off the bench, often as the sixth man. When four of your top six players are rookies, you lose. That was especially true when some of the veterans were Melvin Turpin and Keith Lee: Turpin had weight problems, Lee had horrible knees, and neither had a notable NBA career.

In the middle of that season, Price had an appendix attack and we needed another guard. That was when Wayne Embry and Gary Fitzsimmons, our player personnel director, made what appeared to be a little move that turned out to be crucial for us. They found Craig Ehlo playing for the Mississippi Jets of the Continental Basketball Association. Ehlo was signed to a ten-day contract while Price recovered from his surgery, and he ended up becoming a starter for us after the Ron Harper trade in 1989.

I didn't mind taking a beating that first year because I knew we'd get better, that all our players needed was experience. Some coaches believe they have to win every game no matter what, so they'll play a veteran over a young player even when it's in the best interest of the franchise to make sure the kid plays and matures. Sometimes the coach is worried that if he loses today he won't be around for that better tomorrow. But some coaches just can't take the losing. Listen, I hate losing as much as anyone, but I also understand development. You can't improve sitting on the bench. I also was fortunate because Wayne Embry and Gordon Gund wanted our young players on the floor; if we lost some games because of that, so be it. Actually, we had a 31–51 record in 1986–87, which wasn't bad given the youth on the roster. That season showed us the players' strengths and weaknesses, and it revealed what we needed to do to improve the roster.

The only thing we didn't find out about that first season in Cleveland was Price. We could see that Daugherty and Harper had star potential, and that Williams would be a very good pro. But Price never could get on track as a rookie. He had a couple of nice games, but between his holdout and his appendix problem, it was pretty much a lost year. So when the 1987 draft came along and we had a chance to pick a top point guard in Kevin Johnson from the University of California, we didn't hesitate. I was still positive about Mark; if everything went right, we'd have two good point guards, and at least one of them was bound to come through. Well, that summer after his rookie year, Price worked extremely hard on his shooting, conditioning, and ballhandling. Like most rookies, Kevin Johnson didn't understand the kind of physical shape a player needs to be in to compete at his peak level in training camp. Mark just dominated Kevin, winning the job easily. But that was fine. We had Kevin Johnson to back up Price. Furthermore, we were adding assets for possible trades.

But that created a problem—a nice problem, but still a problem. We had two young point guards, both good enough to start. This was a much different situation than in my final years with the Cavs, when Price was a veteran and we had a young Terrell Brandon playing behind him. It was clear that in a few years, Brandon would be ready to take over as the starter because Price was coming to the end of his career. But back in 1987, we had Price and Johnson, both in their early twenties, and neither wanting to be the backup. Furthermore, Price had dominated Johnson that year. I loved Mark's outside shooting, his quickness, and his growth as a ballhandler. Meanwhile, Wayne Embry was looking to acquire a veteran small forward. Phil Hubbard's knees were aching and he was coming to the end of his career. We wanted to trade Kevin Johnson for Eddie Johnson, a small forward for Phoenix who would have been perfect for us. He could really shoot, and that was exactly what we needed.

But as Wayne talked to the Suns, the trade changed. Phoenix was in the midst of a massive rebuilding movement, and they wanted to trade Larry Nance—not because they had anything against Nance, but because Nance would bring them the most back in a deal. Phoenix needed a lot of young players.

Wayne called me and said, "We can get Larry Nance."

I said, "What happened to Eddie Johnson?"

Wayne said, "Larry is a great player. It's not often you can get a guy like this."

In that respect, Wayne was right. Nance was six-foot-ten, with long arms and tremendous leaping ability, and was a magnificent shot blocker. He averaged 20 points and a little over 8 rebounds per game for Phoenix.

"I know Nance can really play," I said, "but Wayne, he's not a small forward."

"What do you mean he's not a small forward?" he asked.

"Wayne, I've coached in the Western Conference," I said. "I've watched the guy for years. He's a power forward. He's a great player, but a power forward."

"I think he can play small forward," he said.

"Wayne, I don't know," I said. "He's always been a power forward."

"He's athletic enough to cover the smaller forwards away from the basket, and he's tall enough so they won't be able to defend him inside," Embry said.

I wasn't sure if that was true, but I knew that Larry Nance would make us a better team regardless of where he played. My only reservation was that I had six-foot-eleven John Williams at power forward, and I really needed a small forward.

Anyway, the trade was made. We sent Kevin Johnson, Tyrone Corbin, and Mark West to Phoenix for Nance and Mike Sanders, who was the Suns' backup small forward. What I didn't find out until later was that we also agreed to flop number one draft picks. At the time, it didn't sound like a major sticking point, but it turned out to be a big deal to the Suns: With that pick (which originally belonged to us), the Suns drafted Dan Majerle, who became an All-Star. With the Suns' pick, we took Randolph Keys, another in the long line of guys we tried at small forward who never worked out. Majerle would have made us a much better team, because he was capable of playing either small forward or shooting guard. But I have a hard time being overly critical of the trade, even though we probably gave up too much. Larry Nance became a very important part of our team. He brought us instant credibility because his shot-blocking just shut down the lane. He was a great defensive player. He also developed a very good medium-range jump shot. He was a delight in the dressing room, the kind of veteran who'd take young players out to dinner on the road, or invite them to his home to fish in his pond. Larry supported me in everything I wanted to do with the team.

But he wasn't a small forward.

I tried to start a front line of Daugherty at center, with John Williams at power forward and Nance at small forward. From a physical standpoint it was impressive, with Nance the smallest at six-foot-ten, but we had trouble defensively. Both Nance and Williams liked to block shots, but to do that you need to be near the basket. When either of them were called upon to defend a small forward such as Dominique Wilkins, Scottie Pippen, or Eddie Johnson, they were fifteen to twenty feet away from the rim. Yes, they were taller than those players, but not as quick. So either Wilkins would drive past our small forwards or Nance would have to leave him open—play soft defense to protect against the drive—and surrender a jump shot.

That's when I realized I had to do something. I was not going to keep trying to pound a square peg into a round hole, forcing Nance to play small forward. So I asked myself, "Who is the better player, Williams or Nance? And who would be more suited to come off the bench?"

Nance was the superior player, but not by a lot. Williams had been our starting power forward in 1986–87 and made the all-rookie team as he averaged nearly 15 points and 8 rebounds. It's not easy to tell a player with those statistics that you want him to become the sixth man, but Williams was not an ordinary player. Hot Rod and I had become very close. He never had a father, and he almost looked at me that way. He called me "Coach Lenny," and it was a term of respect. He talked to me when he was going to buy a new house, and then showed me the blueprints. Hot Rod grew up very poor in Sorrento, Louisiana. He was abandoned before his first birthday and raised by a neighbor woman who just took him in: She heard the infant crying on a front porch, went over to offer some comfort, and ended up raising Hot Rod. She also was the one who gave him the "Hot Rod" nickname because he loved to play on the floor with toy cars, making motor sounds with his mouth.

So I approached Hot Rod about giving up his starting spot to Nance. Hot Rod was a shrewd player. He could see that our big front line wasn't working, that someone else had to be the small forward. We talked about it for a long time. I didn't just say, "Hot Rod, I want you to come off the bench," then end the conversation. That's not how you coach in the modern NBA. You have to treat players with respect, explain to them what you have in mind, then ask them what they think. And, most of all, you have to listen to them. As a coach, you want them to have a part in a decision that has a direct impact on them and their career.

"Hot Rod, the one thing we need is more energy and scoring off the bench," I said. "When I was in Seattle, I had Fred Brown do that. It turned out to be great for him, and great for the team."

Hot Rod was not an explosive scorer like Fred Brown, but he began to understand how he could help us.

"When I go to the bench, I don't want us just to tread water, to keep the score what it is," I said. "I want to develop a bench that helps us increase our lead when we substitute. To do that, we have to have someone coming off the bench who is good enough to start."

Hot Rod would have preferred to start, but he agreed to become the sixth man. At small forward, I started Mike Sanders, who had played that position in Phoenix with Nance. Sanders wasn't a big scorer, but he was a very physical defender, the kind of guy who defended you so close it was like he was your shirt. He also blocked out well, hit the floor for loose balls, and if you left Sanders open from fifteen feet he could drop in his jumper.

On most teams, the power forward is the guy whose speciality is physical defense and rebounding. Think of Charles Oakley, Horace Grant, or even Dennis Rodman. But with this Cavs team, our power forward was more of a scorer—like the conventional small forward. And the small forward played the role of the power forward.

Furthermore, Hot Rod became so versatile I could play him at all three frontcourt spots—both forwards and center. Yes, the Larry Nance trade took us from a .500 team to a team that won 57 games in 1988–89, but we never could have gotten there unless Hot Rod decided to sacrifice his own ego to come off the bench. Making it even better is that Hot Rod and Nance became very close friends. Both grew up in the rural South. Both had the same unselfish view of the game. Both were family men who didn't like the NBA party scene.

By my third season in Cleveland (1988–89), our young team was maturing. We probably had the best young backcourt in the league with Price and Harper, or at least the best that didn't have Magic Johnson or Michael Jordan. Daugherty was growing into a center who could put 20 points and 10 rebounds next to his name every night. We had Nance, Williams, Sanders, and Craig Ehlo, who came off the bench as a backup guard.

That season, we had a 57–25 record. Our ballhandling, spacing, and understanding of offense was beautiful. We had four players— Daugherty, Nance, Price, and Harper—who averaged between 17 and 19 points, and all of them shot at least 51 percent from the field. Hot Rod was our sixth man, and he scored 12 points a game. Magic Johnson predicted that the Cavs would become "the team of the 1990s." That may have been a bit of stretch as long as Magic, Michael, and Larry Bird were still playing, but it was an indication of the kind of respect we were gaining around the league. That season, only Detroit (63–19) won more games than we did.

We faced the Bulls in the first round of the playoffs, a five-game series. What most fans didn't realize was that we had a couple of injuries that worried me. Price was bothered by a hamstring, and Nance had something wrong with his ankle. All everyone saw was we had won 57 games, and we beat the Bulls all six times in the regular season. I thought we'd win, but any time you play a team with Jordan, you worry. And this was before Jordan had won his first ring, back when some people were wondering if Jordan would ever be the kind of player who'd lead his team to a title, or if he'd just be a great scorer. I had no doubts: Michael Jordan was both, a great scorer and a champion. It was just a matter of time. But on April 28, 1989, it seemed much closer to our time than Michael's. We opened that series at the Richfield Coliseum, which had become an enormous home-court advantage for us. Its critics could drone on about it being stuck in the middle of nowhere, but our fans loved it. They packed the Big House on the Prairie, and we had a 37–4 record there, the best home mark in the NBA.

But when it came time to play the Bulls, Price had to sit out with that hamstring muscle. We started Ehlo and Harper, and we just weren't the same team. Chicago upset us in the opener, 95–88. Price returned, but it was obvious that he wasn't 100 percent. He just didn't have that explosiveness when he tried to make his dribble moves to the basket. Nor did he have the lift on his jump shot. A pulled hamstring cuts the legs out from under a player. But we won two of the next three games, making the series 2–2.

That set up the fifth and deciding game at the Coliseum. It remains one of the best games in NBA history, picked as one of the Top 50 ever by ESPN. What most people remember is the final six seconds. The Bulls had a 99–98 lead, and we had the ball. I called timeout and set up a play.

This is the only time in my coaching career that I can say we ran an out-of-bounds play that worked *too well*, that was *too good*. Craig Ehlo passed the ball in and threw it to Nance. The plan was for Ehlo to cut to the basket, and if he was wide open, Nance should throw him the ball. I doubted that he'd be open, and we had other options. But no one even bothered to cover Ehlo. He passed the ball to Nance, broke to the basket, took a return pass from Nance and made a layup.

Cavs 100, Bulls 99.

The problem was there were still three seconds on the clock as the Bulls called timeout. Later, Ehlo would say, "I wish I was like Michael and I could have hung in the air for three seconds before I made that layup."

Ehlo played a lot of small forward for us that day, and he should have been the hero. He had one of the best games of his career, scoring 24 points.

But there were still three seconds left, and the Bulls still had Michael Jordan. During the timeout, I had to decide how we should defend Jordan. You didn't need to be Red Auerbach to know the ball was supposed to end up in his hands.

I had a choice: defend Brad Sellers as he passed the ball in-bounds and guard Michael with one man; or put two men on Michael and let Sellers have an open look as he passed the ball in-bounds.

I picked the second, because I didn't want Michael to end up with the ball.

This is one of the few times in my career where I've watched the video of a play over and over and over. I assigned Ehlo and Nance to stay with Michael. As the ball was handed to Sellers, Michael took a step as if he were going to set a pick to free Pippen. For a split second, Ehlo hesitated as if to follow Pippen, who was cutting across the floor. Then Michael slipped past Ehlo, shook Nance, caught the pass, drove to the top of the key—and swished a jumper as the horn blared.

I've never heard 20,273 people so painfully silent. It was one of those times when you could hear a heart break. We were all just stunned, staring in disbelief as Michael and his teammates celebrated on our court. A lot of Cavs fans believe if we had won that game, we would have gone on to an NBA title. I doubt it, because Detroit was the champion that year, and the Pistons were in their prime with Isiah Thomas, Joe Dumars, Vinny Johnson, and Bill Laimbeer, while we still had those injuries to Price and Nance. But over the next few years, we would be something very, very special. We were still a young team and we had time on our side.

In November 1989, Ron Harper was twenty-five years old. He had played with the Cavs for three years, averaging 19 points, shooting 47 percent, and even soaring for 5 rebounds per game from his shooting guard spot. He was six-foot-six, two hundred pounds, and on the verge of becoming an All-Star. Ron was a special player to me because he came to the Cavs as a talented but free-spirited player; as a rookie, he came within 10 turnovers of a league record. But Ron wanted to become a great player, even if he wasn't sure how to do it. More important, he was willing to listen, to watch film, to admit that he didn't know everything. That's the key to a young player growing into a guy who becomes a respected veteran, which is what Harper became by the end of his career. If we were ever going to beat Michael Jordan in a playoff series, we needed Harper's athleticism. He was about the same size as Michael, nearly as quick, and jumped almost as high. He wasn't Michael, but he was good.

Which is why I never would have traded him—and why I was shattered when the Cavs did. Especially when we ended up with Danny Ferry, who wasn't a shooting guard, in return. His best position was power forward, and that was the last thing we needed because we already had Larry Nance and John Williams.

So why trade Harper?

Late in the summer of 1989, I began hearing stories about Harper, that he was running around with some questionable characters in some places where he shouldn't have been. The people telling me these things made it sound as if Ron was about to be handcuffed and led away at any moment.

I remember talking about Harper to a guy who was working in private security.

"Did you ever see him sell drugs?" I asked.

"No," he said.

"Did you ever see him use drugs?" I asked.

"No," he said.

"So you saw him at this nightclub, but you saw some other athletes there, too, right?" I asked.

"Yes," he said.

"So we're really talking about guilt by association," I said. "Ron knows the guy who owns the club, and the guy is suspected of dealing drugs, or hanging out with drug dealers, right? It's just guilt by association."

"It is," he said. "But we have reason to believe . . ."

But the guy could never give me any proof.

Yet the stories continued to swirl. They reached Cavs owner Gordon Gund. This was at a time when the Cleveland Browns had a player who was arrested at a crack house. One of the TV news shows had the bust on tape, the guy led out of the house in handcuffs, the policeman grabbing the player by the back of the head and shoving him into the back of a squad car. It was a very embarrassing moment for the Browns as everyone saw it on the 11:00 P.M. news. The last thing the Cavs wanted was that kind of public-relations fiasco, which is why the rumors about Harper alarmed them.

Ron played seven games for us at the start of the 1989–90 season. He was averaging 22 points, and I noticed no problems with him. He was always on time. His personality seemed the same. His eyes were clear, he was attentive. I've been around players with drug problems, and you can tell if a guy is a heavy user. His attention span is nil. He tends to be late. He lets little things slide. But Ron was exactly the same as he'd always been.

Still, Gordon Gund was worried, and he called a meeting. I sat in a room with Gund, Embry, Cavs player personnel director Gary Fitzsimmons, and Dick Watson, the team lawyer. They would not allow me to bring my assistant coaches into the room.

"This is about Harper," said Gund. "We've got to get rid of him."

"I really don't want to trade Ron," I said, just repeating what I had already mentioned to them before when the rumors first arose.

"I want the SOB out of here!" Gund screamed, and that shocked me. I had never heard Gordon yell like that. He also dropped an obscenity into the sentence, and I'd never heard him swear. I had never seen him so agitated.

Even Gund seemed a bit stunned because he was quiet for a moment, the silence hanging over the room.

"Listen," he said, "if you guys don't make the trade, I'll make the trade."

Then he stared hard at me.

Remember, Gund is blind. But he also makes a point of knowing where everyone sits in a room, so he can look right at them as he talks.

"Gordon," I said, "it's your team. You can do what you want. But I'm the coach, and it's my job to win games. Ron helps us—"

"Can you guarantee that he'll change?" Gund said, interrupting me.

"First of all, I don't understand all that," I said. "Secondly, only God can change people, and I don't know that Ron is that bad."

"Well, I'll handle it," he said.

"It's your team," I said. "If you feel that's what you have to do, then you have to do it."

That ended the conversation. A few days later, Harper was traded to the Los Angeles Clippers along with two first-round picks for the rights to Danny Ferry and guard Reggie Williams.

After the deal was made, Harper told the *Akron Beacon Journal*, "They traded me because they didn't like my friends."

That was pretty much the truth. Ron had grown up in Dayton, in the inner city. Some of his friends had done time in prison. That's true of many NBA players who come from that kind of environment. Ron also was still a young man, just twenty-five, and still maturing. I'm sure that at the age of thirty-five, he probably doesn't go to the same places or see all the same people he did at twenty-five. But he never was in any trouble, never indicted or charged with anything, and was never a problem for any of his coaches.

That's why the trade hurt so much.

And I also had this sinking sense that whatever chances we had of winning an NBA title left town with Ron Harper. Not because he was our best player, but Harper joined with Price, Daugherty, Nance, and Williams to give us a great team. With Ron gone, we had to start Craig Ehlo, who was a role player. I had been around the NBA long enough to know how rare it is to find a player with Harper's talent, and I doubted we'd have another one in Cleveland in the near future.

I don't fault Embry for this. Wayne was put in a tough spot. When word came out that we were interested in trading Harper, it was a red flag to every team in the NBA. They couldn't figure out why we'd trade such a great young talent; then the rumors surfaced, and the trade offers dried up. Embry always liked Ferry, a six-foot-ten forward from Duke who had refused to sign with the Clippers, instead taking a $2 million deal to play in Italy. Embry was still looking for a small forward, and he hoped Ferry could fill the spot. I saw Danny in college and I thought he was a good shooter, but not a great one. My real concern was his quickness. He was six-foot-ten, and how was he supposed to defend small forwards? And I knew he wasn't good enough to start at power forward for us because he lacked the strength and the rebounding skills.

But the front office fell in love with Ferry. They saw him as the next Larry Bird. Publicly, they didn't say that, but I heard conversations to that effect. In the press release announcing the trade, the Cavs said they had to wait a season for Ferry to finish his contractual obligations playing in Italy. The press release also said, "Boston waited a year for Larry Bird. San Antonio waited a year for David Robinson. We think Danny Ferry will be worth the wait."

Then they gave Ferry a whopping ten-year, $33 million contract, which made him the highest-paid player on the team. I could never figure out why they paid Ferry so much. Yes, he was in Italy, and he could play another year in Europe, but everyone knew Ferry wanted to return to the United States; the only reason he went to Italy was that he didn't want to play for the Clippers, which was the worst franchise in the NBA. Yet the front office acted as if it was negotiating against someone who was going to take Ferry away, and they emptied the vault. I'll never understand that. As a coach, I'm not consulted on contract matters for players—which is fine with me. That's the domain of ownership and the general manager. But a coach has to deal with the consequences of a contract, especially a monster one given to a rookie who I wasn't sure really fit on our team. To the credit of our players, they didn't hold the money against Danny. We had an exceptional group in that regard, just wonderful people. The front office also reworked the contracts of some of our key players, trying to placate everyone. But none of them had a contract that was as rich or as long as Ferry's, and that was a fact. In a situation like that, the coach is supposed to play the guy as much as possible so the team can have a return on its investment.

The first alarm bells went off the summer before Danny joined the team. I was invited to lunch with this coach from Italy, and I brought my assistants—Dick Helm and Brian Winters—along. As we were talking, the Italian coach said, "Danny Ferry can't make your team."

I about fell out of my chair.

"I've watched him play all the time in Italy," said the coach. "I know your team, too. I've seen them on TV. Ferry can't beat out Nance. He can't beat out Hot Rod Williams. He's not a small forward. I don't see where he can play for you."

My assistants and I just sat there, staring at him, our lunches growing cold in front of us. I was in a state of utter disbelief. I wasn't sure how good Ferry was, but I thought he'd help us.

"Well, it's too late now," I said. "The deal is done."

But the coach turned out to be exactly right.

The front office wanted me to play Danny at small forward. But he came to camp with a knee problem left over from Italy. He played, but he couldn't move and it became very obvious that he would not be able to defend against the six-foot-seven pure athletes who usually play small forward. I had him on the floor about twenty minutes a game during the exhibition season, but his defensive problems were glaring. He was in constant foul trouble. While he made some shots, he didn't seem to be an outstanding shooter. And he was saddled with that incredible contract and the tag of being "The Next Larry Bird," which just made the situation worse.

In retrospect, Ferry came to the worst possible team for him. His best spot was power forward, where we were already strong. He was under the spotlight because of the magnitude of the trade and the contract he signed. Then, we were playing Ehlo at Harper's old spot—and it was clear we missed Harper terribly. Harper was scoring 20 points a game for the Clippers, although he did suffer a major knee injury. Nonetheless, he came back to remain a very potent scorer, and we never did replace him at shooting guard in my time with the Cavs—at least, not with a player of his talent. And some of that blame fell on Ferry, because he was sitting on our bench while Harper was putting up big numbers in Los Angeles. The front office wanted me to find time on the court for Ferry, but I wouldn't bench guys who were better than Danny just to make the front office happy: If a coach does that, he loses credibility in the dressing room with the players. I will give Gordon Gund and Wayne Embry credit for this; they allowed me to use Danny as I saw fit. Yes, they wanted him to play, but they never demanded that I play him. They respected me enough to let me use the players the way I thought best for the team, and that had to be hard for them because they were taking so much heat from the media and fans over the trade.

Danny Ferry is an excellent person, a dedicated worker and a useful NBA player coming off the bench. That's why he lasted all ten years of his contract with the Cavs. Yes, the contract made him hard to trade, but in the final few years with the Cavs, Danny had learned how to help a team by making some outside shots, passing the ball, and playing solid team defense. He never pouted. He never just sat on his money. He had one year where he averaged 14 points for the Cavs, and another season he was at 10 per game. That was in the late 1990s, after Nance and Williams had left the team. But he's just a player of average ability who averaged 8 points, 3 rebounds and shot 44 percent for his career. His outstanding character did enable him to handle all the pressure he was under with grace.

Despite the Harper trade, we had some terrific years in Cleveland. The best was 1991–92, when we won 57 games in the regular season, then beat New Jersey and Boston in the playoffs to reach the Eastern Conference Finals. We lost to the Bulls in six games, and there was no dishonor in that. Some people talk about my time with the Cavs and say, "You couldn't get by the Bulls." No kidding. Who did get past Michael Jordan? In the last six full seasons that he played, Michael's teams won NBA titles.

I'm proud of the teams we had in Cleveland. Daugherty developed into an All-Star center. Nance was an All-Star power forward, Price an All-Star point guard. Our teams played so smoothly, so unselfishly, I felt privileged to coach them. We were entertaining, from Price's long-range shooting to Nance and Williams blocking shots. Purists loved the way Daugherty passed the ball from the high post, or moved down to the low post and dropped in old-fashioned hook shots. They always talk about John Stockton and Karl Malone as being the epitome of how two guys should run the pick-and-roll play, and they are great—but in their prime, Price and Daugherty could match them. Their two-man games were a thing of beauty.

Our players lived year-round in the community and were seen in local churches and shopping malls. The fans embraced us because they liked the fact that we not only won games, but had good people and we never embarrassed them or the franchise. As time has passed, those teams in the late 1980s and early 1990s have become even more appreciated by Cavs fans because the team has tailed off since, as those players retired or were traded. In 1988–89 and 1991–92 we won 57 games, the most in franchise history. In 1992–93, my final season with the Cavs, the team won 54 games, which is the next-best record in franchise history.

Some fans and writers complained that we were a "soft" team, a finesse team. This was in the era of the Bad Boys, the Detroit Pistons who threw elbows and body checks as much as they did passes. The Pistons were the team that caused the NBA to bring in many of the strict rules the league now has against fighting, because they tried not only to beat you, but beat you up. And it was true, we weren't a physical team like Detroit. But how soft can a team be when it wins 57 games, or goes to the Eastern Conference Finals? I get tired of good people and good players like David Robinson or Brad Daugherty being labeled "soft." It's just not in their nature to knock a guy down and step on him. But a lot of so-called physical players develop that style because they don't have the skills of Robinson or Daugherty. Four times in my seven years in Cleveland, our teams were in the top six in NBA defense, so we must have been doing something right. I remember some guys writing and saying the reason we didn't win some titles was we didn't have a Rick Mahorn–type player.

I think the real reason was that we just happened to come along at the same time as Michael Jordan.

CHAPTER FIFTEEN

I WANTED TO BE THE HEAD COACH of the first Dream Team.

Few people know that. Few people understand that I had to swallow a little pride and take a deep breath before I accepted a spot on Chuck Daly's coaching staff for the 1992 Olympic team. That's because I mentioned my true feelings to only a few close friends.

I didn't want to sound as if I was whining, or was somehow playing the race card. That's not me. It's not what my life has been about. But when the decision was made to build a roster for the 1992 Olympic team with NBA players, I thought I would be the natural choice to coach that team. Between my playing and coaching careers, no one had been around the NBA any longer. I believed I had the respect of the players, and that I had been doing a good job as the head coach of the Cleveland Cavaliers.

Deep in my heart, I thought I deserved it.

But just as deep in my heart, I knew it would never happen. Maybe that goes back to my being slighted by the Olympic Committee back in 1960. But when it came to a head coach in 1992, my name was being mentioned, along with the likes of Chuck Daly and Don Nelson. I knew they were going to name a pro coach, because eleven of the twelve roster spots would go to NBA players. It made no sense to have a college coach in charge, because he wouldn't know the players, and even more important, the superstars wouldn't know—and perhaps wouldn't respect—a college coach, at least not compared to a veteran NBA coach. A pro coach was the logical choice, but I just didn't think the first coach of America's first Olympic Dream Team would be black.

And he wasn't.

The job went to Daly, who had just won back-to-back titles with Detroit and is an excellent coach. When I talk about my feelings of being passed over, it has nothing to do with Chuck Daly. He was recently voted into the Hall of Fame, and he deserved it. Perhaps race had nothing to do with it. Chuck was a good choice. I told myself that to cushion the disappointment.

Then Chuck Daly called and asked me to be his assistant.

There are times in life when all of us have our feelings hurt and we'd like to tell the world to just shove it, I don't want to play your game. For a moment, I wondered if Chuck really wanted me as his assistant, or if the Olympic Committee just wanted a black face on the coaching staff for racial balance. Or maybe they were throwing me a bone, because they knew I should have been named the head coach. All these things and more ran through my mind, and I was still a little angry about being snubbed for the head coaching job. A small part of me said, "If they don't want me to be the head coach, then maybe I don't want to be a part of the staff."

Then I took a mental timeout and thought about it.

That's always a good idea when you're angry. Don't make a snap decision. Don't lash out. Take time to consider all the factors, the people involved. I thought about Chuck Daly, whom I knew reasonably well: I respected him, and I knew he respected me. I use that word—respect—carefully, because it's very important to me. If the respect didn't run both ways between Chuck and me, then it made no sense for me to be his assistant. But I knew it did. His Detroit Pistons and my Cleveland Cavaliers had some great games in the late 1980s and early 1990s. We were competitors in the Central Conference. I liked Chuck. And I knew the 1992 Olympic team would be something special. I also had always wanted to represent my country.

"Well?" I asked myself. "Here's a chance."

Did I want to be on the coaching staff with a roster that included Magic Johnson, Michael Jordan, Larry Bird, David Robinson, Patrick Ewing, and all these other future Hall of Famers?

When I put it in that context, the answer was easy: I'd have been out of my mind to turn it down. From the moment I accepted the invitation, I put whatever bitterness I may have had aside and concentrated on enjoying the experience and being the best assistant I could for Chuck Daly.

It was one of the best decisions I've ever made.

It didn't take me long to learn something about Chuck Daly—he worries about everything.

I mean, *everything.*

Chuck worries when he can't find anything to worry about—because he figures he missed something, and something had to be going wrong if only he could find it. No wonder the *Boston Globe*'s Bob Ryan nicknamed him "The Prince of Pessimism."

But coaching the 1992 Dream Team left no reason to worry. I wish I had a dollar for every time I told Chuck that.

"Our guys could take these other teams too lightly," he'd say.

"Chuck," I'd say, "look who is on your team: Magic, Michael, Larry. All those guys. Do you think they're going to lose?"

"I know," said Daly. "But what if . . ."

"Chuck, there won't be anything that goes wrong," I said. "If one or two guys are cold, just put in someone else. You've got a bench full of 'go-to' guys. This is the greatest basketball team ever assembled."

Chuck would agree, but he'd still wrinkle his brow, shake his head, and look as if all he had was 50 cents in his pocket and he needed a dollar to get his car out of the parking lot.

He worried that the players might be too tired from the NBA season.

He worried they wouldn't feel like training again in the summer, especially since it came right after the playoffs.

He worried that our great players would take one look at some of the teams from the other countries and decide all they had to do was walk onto the court and win.

There was something else Chuck worried about, something that he never said out loud: If that team lost, the finger of blame would be pointed right at him. It didn't take much imagination to hear the critics saying, "The guy has Magic Johnson, Michael Jordan, Larry Bird, Karl Malone, and John Stockton—and he loses to Spain? Are you kidding?"

In a sense, Chuck was right about one thing—he was in a no-win position, coaching a team that was the most lopsided favorite to win, not just in the history of the Olympics, but in the history of sports.

I felt just the opposite from Chuck. I was extremely confident. Obviously, talent is one of the reasons the members of the Dream Team were superstars, but there was something else: pride. Those guys wanted to show the world they were the best. That was their motivation. They weren't about to lose. These were some of the most competitive, driven men in the history of sports. They knew the eyes of the world were upon them and they knew the stakes were high.

In my mind, there was no reason to wonder if they'd lose . . . because there was no way they'd allow that to happen. That team had too many great leaders, too many players of tremendous character to fail to win a gold medal.

At one of our first press conferences, our players noticed that some of the British reporters were very smug, as if they didn't think our team was anything special. Remember, the United States had lost in the 1987 Pan Am Games, then again in the 1988 Olympics. Of course, those were teams composed of our college kids. But some of the foreign reporters weren't knowledgeable enough to realize that. To them, those kids were the U.S. team. To us, they were a bunch of college kids who had been physically overpowered by men. The days when the United States could throw together a bunch of college players in a few months and beat some thirty-year-olds who had been playing pro ball in Europe . . . those days were over. European basketball had progressed a great deal, especially during the 1980s. I'd conducted coaching clinics in Europe; a lot of U.S. coaches had, and it showed. The coaches and players overseas were hungry for our basketball knowledge, and they soaked up everything we told them. Not only did the coaching improve, but so did the skill level—especially the outside shooting and the low-post moves of the big men. You see that today in the NBA, where so many centers are from Europe. Their big guys are well-schooled, with excellent footwork. They don't just rely on natural jumping ability, they practice those inside moves. That's why our college players no longer could beat them with their sheer running, jumping, and athleticism. The 3-point shot put an emphasis on outside shooting, and the best European teams had guys who could drill it with ease.

In 1991, I scouted the European championships with Chuck Daly. The atmosphere was fantastic. I loved how the fans waved flags, sang songs, whistled at the officials, and really loved their teams. You could sense the nationalism. Chuck sat there, creating scenarios in his head how Italy could beat us . . . Spain could beat us . . . anyone could beat us. I saw that European basketball had really improved, and right away, I could see why our college kids struggled against them.

But there was no way the Dream Team would lose. All the coaches had to do was make sure we had the opponents scouted and our guys prepared.

"If we all do our jobs, we have nothing to worry about," I told Chuck Daly.

He nodded as if to agree, but he was still worried.

The Dream Team opened its training camp in May in La Jolla, California. I arrived a few days late, because my Cleveland Cavaliers were involved in the 1992 Eastern Conference playoffs. That year, we had what I thought was the second-best team in the NBA; unfortunately, we were still in the same conference as the greatest player in the history of the game, and the Bulls beat us in six games. Then they eliminated Portland to win the title.

In one of the early scrimmages, we played a group of the top college players. It was very close, partly because many of our guys were just coming off their NBA seasons. Their legs were a little tired, and they probably weren't as focused as they should have been. We weren't keeping score, but if we had, the college players probably would have won by a few points. The college guys were making a big deal about it, and the pros were saying, "Wait until tomorrow."

The next day was the first glimpse of the real Dream Team. The score was 19–0 before the college players scored. Half the time, they couldn't even get the ball past midcourt. Our defense just swarmed them, then took away the ball, and then their confidence. You could see it in the college kids' eyes: the fear. The doubt. The awe. It was something we'd see in game after game once the Olympics began. When the greatest players in the world turned the intensity up a notch, no one had the slightest chance against them. These guys were all great athletes, as physically gifted as very few men ever have been when it came to quickness and strength. And they were also overachievers, obsessed with winning, and very smart players on top of all that. What happens when a great athlete is an over-achiever? You end up with a Michael Jordan, a Larry Bird, a Magic Johnson. True champions. Players who not only play great, but whose greatness lifts up their teammates. If you played with Michael, Magic, or Larry, you didn't want to let them down. It would be embarrassing to not play at the top level of your game when you saw the best player on the floor hustle so much that he left pools of sweat on the floor whenever he stopped for a moment. How could you not dive for a loose ball when Jordan does? How could you not pass to the open man when Magic does? How could you not crash the boards when Karl Malone and Charles Barkley do?

Our team breezed through the Tournament of the Americas, which was played in Portland. We beat several Latin American teams with ease. This was the first time the world saw a snapshot of the Dream Team, and no one appreciated our players more than our opponents. We'd beat them by 50 points, then they'd ask us to pose for pictures with them after the game. They wanted our autographs! I mean, the players from the other teams! I had never seen anything like it. To them, just being on the same court with our guys was a privilege. The foreign players knew that it was an honor to be close to such greatness, and they wanted to savor the moment.

Our next stop was Nice, on the French Riviera, where we'd practice for a while before the Olympics. Some of the players were just relaxing, playing golf, spending time in the casinos of Monte Carlo. They loved to play blackjack, and they weren't afraid to spend money. Some of our players gambled night after night, and that worried Chuck—not because of the gambling, but because he worried they didn't get enough rest. We also were being wined and dined by local dignitaries. We met some royalty from Monaco. It was the red carpet treatment, and some of the players had their families along. That worried Chuck, too.

"These guys don't have their heads in the game," he told me after one practice.

His face was turning gray from all the worry. I told Chuck to relax, the players had been off for a week, they had their families along and were taking it easy. They knew how to pace themselves and they'd be ready when the time came.

Chuck didn't want to hear any of it.

I mentioned to Magic Johnson that Chuck was concerned about the intensity level in practice. That was all that needed to be said. Magic had one team, Michael had another. They began to scrimmage, and Magic's team jumped to a big lead. He began to talk trash to Michael. At this point in their careers, Magic and Bird had more championship rings than Michael, and they weren't afraid to remind him of that.

Anyway, Magic got Michael's attention.

Playing on Magic's team was Clyde Drexler, who some media people said should be the MVP over Michael in 1992. Michael never said a word, but we all knew that really bothered him—even though he did win the award. In Michael's mind, he was the MVP every year. In 1992, he certainly proved it by leading his team past Drexler and Portland in the Finals. Now he was being covered again by Drexler, and you could sense the hairs on the back of Michael's neck standing up. His competitor's antenna was up. Everything about that game was up, from the emotion to the way the players jumped. Michael seemed obsessed that day. It was like the scrimmage was the 1992 title game all over again. His energy was contagious.

Michael's team was down by 15 points, and he went right at Drexler, scoring time after time. He destroyed Drexler, much as he did in a couple of those 1992 playoff games. Of course, Michael would destroy anyone when he was in one of those grooves. Fans know about his driving and dunking, but Michael's outside shooting has always been underrated, and it improved with age. If you backed off him to guard against a drive to the basket, he made a jump shot right over you. Climb up on him, and he drove past you. Michael looked lean, but he was very strong. It was hard to knock him down, and he could bull his way through a double-team, just put his shoulder down, see a crack of daylight, and dribble between two defenders without losing control of the ball. His dribbling was another underrated part of his game. After he had his way with Drexler, other players tried to defend Michael. No chance. Not on this day.

David Robinson was playing center for Michael's team, and Patrick Ewing was the center for Magic's team. Those guys were just pounding on each other. It wasn't dirty, no one wanted to injure someone else, but the elbows were out, the picks were hard, the teeth were rattling, and the sweat poured off their bodies. These guys were nailing each other. For a basketball fan, this was a dream game. The practice was so good, I think I saw Chuck Daly almost smile—I said, almost. At least, he wasn't frowning like some guy who'd just found a letter from the IRS auditors office in his mailbox.

Michael's team won that scrimmage by two points. The guys wanted to play some more, but we decided to end practice. The last thing we wanted was anyone getting hurt. I always wished there had been a tape of that practice, because it was better than any of the Olympic games, better and more intense than any All-Star game you've ever seen because it wasn't for show. It was for pride, and for the joy of playing hard at the highest level there is.

Our next stop was Barcelona, Spain, where the Olympics were held.

No matter where the Dream Team played, it would have been an event. But having these Olympics in Europe just added to the aura of the team. I was shocked to learn that the Europeans loved basketball. They not only knew the players, they knew what all the players looked like. Granted, tall black men in Barcelona weren't exactly going to be confused with the guy who cooked in a neighborhood restaurant, but even I was recognized everywhere. I had more people stop and talk to me in Barcelona than I did in Seattle, Cleveland, Atlanta, or anywhere else I've played or coached. That just amazed me.

I was overwhelmed by the attention, and I was just an assistant coach. It was ten times that for the players. After a while, we found it difficult to walk the streets. So many people wanted us to sign autographs and pose for pictures, we couldn't accommodate everyone. It was the first and only time in my life that I felt like a rock star. When we traveled to practice, there were three police cars in front of our bus, three police cars behind it. Still, we had to go a different route each time because people found out where we were headed and blocked the streets. They just wanted to wave at the bus . . . see the bus . . . take a picture of the bus! They couldn't see who was inside, but they still wanted to see the bus! People lined up behind police barricades as we walked into and out of the arenas. They yelled our names. They waved. They took our pictures. As the Olympics went on, our security force got bigger and bigger until it seemed that we had an army protecting us—not because any fans wanted to hurt us, but for fear they might smother us with their love.

We had only a couple of rough spots.

One day, I saw that Karl Malone looked really down in the dumps.

I talked to him for a while. At first, he said that nothing was wrong. We made some more small talk. Finally, he said he'd heard that Chuck Daly didn't like him as a player.

The more he talked about that, the more upset he became. People see Karl Malone as this huge man with rippling muscles, possibly the strongest man in the NBA, but he is a very sensitive man. I think he's felt underappreciated for much of his career, partly because he played in Utah and most of the country didn't get a chance to see the player he had become. This was especially true in 1992, because the Utah Jazz had yet to make it to the NBA Finals.

Astute basketball people knew of Karl's greatness, but the average fan probably didn't. That bothered Karl. And now, he had heard that Chuck didn't like him.

I assured him that wasn't the case, that I had never heard

Chuck say anything negative about him, and all the coaches were thrilled to have Karl Malone on the Dream Team.

He nodded, thinking about that for a while.

I again told him how happy we were to have him on the team. We talked a little more.

"Karl," I said, "this is the opportunity of a lifetime. You love your country, right? We are representing our country. They'll love you in Utah for doing this, and the whole world will get a chance to see what a great player you are."

He calmed down.

"Karl, this is a great chance for all of us," I said.

He agreed, and that was the last time I saw Karl Malone upset during the Olympics.

Part of Karl's unhappiness may have stemmed from the hotel where we stayed. They had just built a new one in Barcelona, especially for us. A lot of our guys had never been to Europe before. They didn't know that European hotels are different from those in America, especially the wonderful places we stay in when traveling around the NBA.

At our hotel, Larry Bird had a big suite. So did Magic Johnson and Michael Jordan. The people running the hotel knew those names were the biggest, and they gave them the best rooms.

The problem was that not all of the rooms for the players were suites.

In a word, some of them were—small.

The bathrooms seemed like closets. The beds were so tiny, the players' feet hung over the side. Some guys had their families along, and they had five people in that little room. I know that Malone, Stockton, and Drexler had very tiny rooms, and I found myself talking to them, calming them down.

These are men of tremendous pride, and they felt that if Magic and Michael had great rooms, then they all should have great rooms. They all were on the Dream Team, right? But the hotel just didn't have enough suites for everyone.

"Listen," I told some of the guys, "we only have to be here for a short time, and we'll be back home for the summer. What you'll always think about is not that you had a bad room, but that you were in the Olympics. You were part of the greatest team ever assembled."

There were some unhappy campers at that hotel, and I spent a fair amount of time smoothing over the trouble spots. I felt that was part of my job, a way I could help Chuck. The players respected me, and I knew that I could talk to them and they'd listen.

But other than those incidents, everything was fantastic.

Naturally, we won the gold medal, and I was very proud of that. But what I enjoyed the most was being around those great players so much. We usually ate together. It's one thing to see Michael Jordan playing against you, it's another thing to see how hard he practices. Same with Magic Johnson and the rest of those guys. Jordan, Drexler, and Scottie Pippen all reported a little late to the Olympic practices because their teams had been in the NBA Finals. They had just played over 110 basketball games, from the start of the exhibition season to the end of the playoffs. As a coaching staff, we talked about letting them rest for a few practices, not wearing their legs out.

"No, we're here to play," said Michael. "We want to practice with everyone else."

Drexler and Pippen said the same thing.

That impressed me, because if they'd wanted to take it easy for a while, no one would have objected. Heck, the coaching staff thought of the idea in the first place. But the Dream Team was too important to them. Same with Patrick Ewing, who had had thumb surgery. It was still sore, but he insisted on playing. Charles Barkley worked extremely hard. Now, we worried a little bit about Charles after practice, because he's such a social creature and you knew he was going to be out for most of the night. We coaches held our breath a bit, concerned that one night we'd get a call that Charles had had one of his scrapes and was in handcuffs. But that never happened. Charles knew the importance of the Dream Team, and none of these guys wanted to embarass themselves or our country. And when it came time to play, Charles Barkley was ready. They all were ready. Larry Bird's back was killing him. When he wasn't on the court playing, he was flat on the court—on his stomach, trying to cope with the pain. After the Olympics, he would have a spinal fusion and never play again. Larry Bird didn't play a lot, but with that back, he never should have played at all—but he wanted to be a part of it. We all wanted to be a part of it. In the end, it didn't matter that I had been passed over for the head coaching job; I was there, in Spain, with the greatest basketball team the world has ever seen.

CHAPTER SIXTEEN

THE DOCTORS WERE WORRIED. They thought I might die.

They never said that, but I could see it in their eyes. I could hear it in their voices, even though I couldn't make out most of the words. They worked quickly, efficiently, urgently.

No one told me what was wrong, but I knew:

Blood clots.

I knew the moment I heard they were giving me a drug called Heperin. It's a blood-thinner. They don't give you a blood-thinner unless they think your blood is clotting.

That's serious.

So was the fact that I was having a hard time trying to breathe. And that I felt dizzy. And that when the doctor told me to come to the hospital, they brought me straight in—the first time in my life that I was admitted to the hospital and didn't have to fill out some stupid forms. I got there and two doctors were waiting for me: not one doctor—two!

I was fifty-four years old, I had just come off that summer with the Dream Team, and I was preparing to coach the Cavaliers, a team that had won 57 games the year before and advanced to the Eastern Conference Finals. I had a wife who loved me, children who loved me, everything to live for.

And I had God.

You can make of this what you will, but I knew God was with me in that hospital room, just as God has been with me every step of my life. For that reason, I didn't think I'd die, not even after I found out that I had blood clots not just in one lung, but in both lungs. I was in pain and I was worried, but I wasn't going to die, not unless God wanted me to die. And I knew that He didn't think it was my time.

It's hard for some people to understand this, people who maybe have never taken God seriously. Maybe they went to church, but they never really prayed. Or perhaps some priest, minister, or Christian did something that turned them off to God. For whatever reason, they never really knew God.

I can say that I know God.

It's not like I've had visions or huge, emotional encounters with him. I wasn't awakened in the middle of the night by his voice. I wasn't healed miraculously. He just always has been a presence in my life, sort of a small, quiet voice guiding me, a light hand on my shoulder, telling me that He's there. In the hospital, I heard the voice, I felt the hand. Nothing dramatic, I just knew He was close by.

I think this comes from growing up in a Roman Catholic home, being an altar boy, seeing my mother go to all those Masses, say all those rosaries and all those novenas. As I said before, I don't believe anyone has ever been prayed for as much or as hard as my mother prayed for me. Prayer was always a part of my life. As a kid, I attended a Catholic elementary school, and the nuns had us pray, and they said all those novenas, just like my mother. I was taught that if you honored God with how you lived your life, He would honor you. That doesn't mean He'll make you rich, or that you'll never have pain, heartache, and setbacks. It just means He won't let you go through them alone.

I could have stared at the ceiling in that hospital bed, hooked up to all those monitors, feeling all those needles hooked up to my arms, and simply asked, "God, why me? What did I do to deserve this?"

I didn't ask that question. I'm not sure why, I just didn't. It probably had to do with my faith. Yes, I felt my mortality. There was one day in the hospital when, I swear, about all I did was stare at the clock on the wall. I watched the second hand move oh-so-slowly. I watched the minutes crawl by. As for the hour hand, I thought it would never move. Watching that clock gave me a real sense of my own mortality.

But I never was angry at God.

I wasn't thrilled with how all this had happened. A few weeks before, I had what was supposed to be a basic operation to repair a torn Achilles tendon. Nothing life-threatening. I mean, they operate on your foot, and you end up with blood clots in both lungs? How do you explain that?

I really should have known better.

I should have remembered I was fifty-four years old, about seventeen years past my playing career. I still played basketball, but only a few times a year. Those games were halfcourt, with a couple of sportswriters who covered the Cavs.

But these guys asked some of the Olympic coaches to play in a pickup basketball game with them. This was in Spain, and our team was two games away from the gold medal. It was the security force who wanted us to play with them, and they were a great group of guys. They'd protected us like the president, and anything we wanted, they were there to take care of it. The game was supposed to be our way of showing appreciation for them, so we put together a team of people from the NBA office, my son Randy, ex–NBA player Mike Bantom, and myself. I knew I was in pretty good shape; I played tennis regularly during the Olympics, and I knew to stretch, to watch myself, to keep my body under control. Why couldn't I play basketball with those guys? I wasn't going to try to be Michael Jordan or anything. No dunks. No tough moves. I'd run up and down the court a few times, throw some passes, maybe take a few outside shots.

No big deal.

I took my time stretching and loosening up. I felt fine, ready to go. Two minutes into the game, someone threw a pass that was over my head. I changed directions and reached out to try to grab it. That's when it felt like a rubber band in the back of my left ankle was stretched to the limit—then, POW! It snapped. I swear, it was like someone whacked the back of my foot with an axe. The pain was excruciating. I hopped on one foot for a moment, then tried to put my injured foot down. It was like the foot wouldn't work, it wouldn't listen to the orders from my brain. This all happened in a matter of a few seconds.

And I knew instantly that I had torn an Achilles tendon.

Some of the other players said it didn't look that bad, that maybe it was just a strain. But I knew.

I had blown an Achilles tendon. The pain disappeared into anger. I couldn't believe I did this: I blew out an Achilles tendon playing in a pickup basketball game with some security guys—and we still had two games left! How dumb! How could I do this? How was I going to get through the next two games? Why did I get involved in this game? I never play fullcourt basketball! I beat myself up mentally as they took me to the Olympic Village, where an American doctor was waiting to tell me what I already knew—I had completely severed the Achilles tendon. I needed surgery, and the best thing to do was operate immediately before the swelling became a real issue.

No way.

That's what I thought, and that's what I said.

No way was I going to have surgery and miss the last two games, the most important two games. There were four days left, and somehow I had to make it through the gold medal game. The doctor put me in a bulky cast up to my knee. On crutches, I returned to my hotel, where Marilyn saw me. She couldn't believe what had happened. How could I get hurt playing basketball? Well, I did. The real question was, what to do next? I called Dr. John Bergfeld in Cleveland. He's one of the best surgeons in the country, working with the Cavs through Cleveland Clinic. I told him what happened, and how I wanted him to do the surgery, but only after the Olympics were over. I was not coming home early. The Olympic doctors agreed to put my leg in a cast. Dr. Bergfeld told me to take only Tylenol 3, no other kind of pain medication. I was supposed to keep my leg elevated as much as possible. He'd make preparations for surgery in Cleveland as soon as I returned home. So there I was, on a blown Achilles, hobbling around on crutches during the last few practices and games. Chuck Daly would just look at me and shake his head. He didn't say a word about it, but the head shake said it all: "How could you do that?"

Well, I was asking myself the same thing, especially at night, when the pain was the worst. Sometimes, it felt like my leg would just explode inside that cast. The Tylenol didn't work very well, and I also hate taking medication, so I used it sparingly. Some people said not to worry about the team, go home and have the surgery. The gold medal was a lock. But after all the work and all the preparation, I had to be there for the last game—even if I was forced to grit my teeth through all those agonizing, sleepless nights until I got home. I knew it wouldn't kill me.

The players had fun with me. At first, they'd see me coming and run away, as if I were cursed and they didn't want to catch the injury bug from me. In the back of their minds was the possibility that they could rip up a knee, an ankle, an Achilles, or something else during these games. No one ever wants to get injured, but they sure didn't want that to happen in the summer. After that joke wore off, the players were great, very concerned. I already admired them tremendously, and my appreciation for them grew even more. My wife suggested that I have the Dream Team sign my cast, which had to make it the only leg cast in the history of the world signed by Magic Johnson, Larry Bird, and Michael Jordan. When the gold medal game came, I was not going out there on crutches. I can't explain why that was so important to me, I just wanted to be able to walk out there— or at least limp, dragging my foot and that cast behind me. I was tired of bothering people with my crutches. So I made it through the last two games. I received the gold medal without being held up on crutches. Then I flew back to Cleveland, assuming I'd have the surgery immediately. I figured I'd be in and out of there in a couple of days. I knew some people who'd had the Achilles surgery, and they usually were in the hospital for one night, maybe two. That's it.

No big deal, right?

Guess again.

Because I'd been dragging that foot around for nearly a week, then flew from Spain to New York to Cleveland, I really couldn't keep it elevated as much as I should have.

The thing was swollen like an overripe pumpkin by the time I made it to Cleveland Clinic. They made me stay in the hospital for three days with my leg elevated, just to get the swelling down so they could do the surgery. I was starting to pay the price for my stubbornness about staying for the final games. But that was OK; if I had to trade a few extra days in the hospital to be there for the gold medal, that was fine. I could handle it. Up to this point in my life, I'd never had a serious operation. I'd had some arthroscopic surgery on my knee, but that was eleven years after I quit playing: I had been very blessed to have had such a lengthy career and never suffer a major injury.

So I really wasn't fully prepared for the Achilles surgery, even though I understood what the procedure entailed. I had the operation and ended up spending eight days in Cleveland Clinic. For the first three weeks after the operation, I was in a cast up to my hip. They didn't want me to move that leg, for fear I'd reinjure the Achilles. Then they put me in a cast from below my knee, which made it a little easier to move around on crutches. The worst thing was having those bulky casts, which cause your skin to itch and your muscles to feel like soggy, useless noodles.

I spent the first month recovering from the surgery at my condo in the Akron area. When I was put in the short cast, I wanted to go to our regular home in Seattle. Marilyn was with me, and we had an awful flight. We had to go through Minneapolis. The plane was delayed, and then we finally left for Seattle. After any sort of leg surgery, what you discover is that your leg isn't happy when you don't elevate it periodically. When the leg is straight down—as it would be when sitting in an airplane seat—your leg feels as if it's burning, like all the blood is draining right out of it. When I got home, I was relieved. I'd been gone for over two months because of the Olympics and the surgery. I figured I could relax, put the leg up, rest, and in a few weeks I'd feel great.

By the second day at home, my back was killing me.

I didn't panic. I thought, "It's probably because I've spent so much time on crutches, all that strain on my arms and shoulders, that could mess up your back."

I'd be fine with a little rest, or so I thought.

Marilyn could see I was in pain. She kept saying, "Why don't you call the doctors? Call the trainer?"

The last thing I wanted to do was see another doctor. Maybe I was being macho, but athletes are taught to deal with pain. Besides, I thought once I was home for a while, I'd be fine. All I needed was rest.

The third day home, we were having dinner. But instead of feeling better, I was worse. I was more tired than ever. I wasn't hungry.

"Marilyn, I'm going to head upstairs and rest," I told her.

"I think you should call the doctor," she said.

"I'll be fine," I said.

When I got upstairs, I wasn't fine. I tried to lie down, but I couldn't make it. I couldn't even breathe. I felt like my lungs were on fire.

In the meantime, Marilyn had called the doctor. She put me on the phone, and I told him the symptoms I was having, the gasping for breath, the sore back.

"Get down here right away!" he said.

He wanted to send an ambulance, but my son Randy was home, and I said Randy could get me there faster than waiting for an ambulance to come to the house and then take me. When I arrived at the hospital, they were ready: They checked me and ran some tests, but couldn't conclusively prove there were blood clots. At first, I felt pain just on one side of my back. The next day, it was the other side. In fact, it was shifting back and forth. Right side, left side. Then left side, right side. I was having trouble breathing. I knew this was very serious. They decided to do an angiogram. It's a nerve-racking test, because you're flat on your back with this thing on your chest, the doctor looking through it, not saying much, and you're wondering what's going on. Hey, they're looking at your heart, right? What do they see?

What they saw was blood clots.

A blood clot in each lung.

"Good thing your wife called and you got here when you did," the doctor said, "or you'd have been in real trouble."

My wife had already been telling me that she saved my life by calling when she did, and it turned out she was right.

Even though I had the two blood clots, I thought everything was under control. I was in the hospital. The doctors knew what the problem was, and they would treat me. A couple of days, I'd be out of there.

Guess again.

I felt rotten. Tired. Weak. Sick. I had a headache that felt like a guy inside my skull trying to knock his way out with an axe. On the first day, they brought me food, I ate it—and vomited. After that, I didn't want to eat. When you don't eat, you feel weak and sick. But when I did eat, I got sick to my stomach. So what was I supposed to do? I began to realize that I was in pretty bad shape, much worse than even Marilyn knew. They wanted me to take pain medicine, but I refused. The first time I took it, I got sick to my stomach, really bad cramps, which was worse than the pain from the blood clots. But the pain kept me from sleeping. No matter how I moved my body in that bed, it hurt. No matter how I tried to rest, it hurt. No matter what I did, it hurt. Finally, a nurse—whose brother, coincidentally, I had met some twenty years earlier—suggested that we cut the dosage of the painkiller with distilled water. That worked, and I finally was able to get some sleep. The next morning, that same nurse came to see me. She had a picture of her brother and me taken about twenty years ago at the Seattle airport.

But no one really sleeps well in the hospital because every four hours they wake you up for something—take your temperature, give you a pill. Then they ask if you're resting. Well, you were resting until they woke you up.

During my first four days in the hospital, they had me using a bedpan. That was degrading. You feel like your dignity is gone. You also get a very good idea of what it's like to be old, to be bedridden. I hated the thought of it. They didn't want me walking on my Achilles, because my leg was still in a cast and I was so weak. On the fifth day, I got tired of the bedpan. I got out of bed, grabbed my crutches and headed to the bathroom. Then I discovered they had me hooked up with an IV to this thing that had a bag of medicine. The thing was on wheels. It took me forever, but I used the crutches and made it to the bathroom, dragging the medicine thing behind me.

Just as I sat down on the toilet, the nurse rushed in and yelled, "Are you all right?"

"I'm fine," I said. "Leave me alone."

It felt so good just to be in the bathroom, alone. I wanted to enjoy the little bit of freedom for as long as I could. Then I was determined to haul myself back to bed, and I felt very proud of myself for making it. I never thought that walking to and from the bathroom would be such a big deal, but it was my major accomplishment that week. I didn't spend a lot of time thinking about where the blood clots originated, or trying to blame anyone for what happened. Sometimes after surgery, there are blood clots: It's a risk. But I did spend a lot of time considering how I was feeling great and coaching in the Olympics only a few weeks before, and now I was in a hospital bed. It gave me a reminder of how thankful I am to have spent so much time in sports, to not only be physically fit, but mentally fit. The doctors said that was part of the reason I was able to recover, that I was in good shape physically and emotionally. My faith also had a lot to do with that. Because I believe in God, I'm generally an optimistic person. I believe He has a plan for me. I believe that some things are out of my control, but all things are in His control. My belief in God kept me from panicking in the hospital. I trusted Him to pull me through, or to do with me what He wanted. I'm not saying I was smiling every minute; there were times when I was in that bed, staring at the ceiling, and thinking, "This is a lousy way to come home from the Olympics." I'd think about the blood clots, wondering if they were breaking down as the doctors hoped. It's not like a bruise or a wound you can look at and see the healing: It's happening inside you, and you really have no idea what's going on. But my faith kept me out of any real depression, and I believe it also helped my healing.

I spent eight days in the hospital, and by the time I was released, it was nearly the opening of training camp with the Cavaliers. I was completely exhausted and drawn out. I had gone from the Eastern Conference Finals with the Cavs to the Olympics, to the Achilles surgery, to the hospital for the blood clots. Then I was told to stay home for a week and not do anything. No airplane trips. No leaving the house. Nothing. Just rest.

Before I was released from the hospital, they cut off the hard cast and then put my Achilles in a portable cast. Then they said I had to leave the hospital in a wheelchair.

I said, "Let me use the crutches and walk out."

They said, "Use the chair, or you don't go home."

I used the chair. When I got to the car and tried to get out of the chair and into the seat, I realized how weak I was. It turned out that I'd lost fifteen pounds in the hospital. When I got home, my appetite returned. My spirits rose. And from that day, I've never taken simple things for granted, things like walking or a good night's sleep. And I came away from that experience feeling even closer to my family and to God.

CHAPTER SEVENTEEN

I DIDN'T WANT TO TELL ANYONE how tired I was, how rotten I felt, how drained I was after the summer of 1992. I didn't open up to anyone except Marilyn about how it felt to be so close to death, or what those blood clots in my lungs did to me. Cavs trainer Gary Briggs may have been the only one who had an idea of what I was going through as I tried to recover while also rehabilitating my torn Achilles tendon. There were days when he'd ask me how I was doing in the kind of voice that said he knew I was in bad shape.

But I was determined to press on.

Now, I see that wasn't real smart. If I had to do it over again, I probably wouldn't have coached during the 1992–93 season. But at the time, I had no idea how long it would take for my body to recover from the clots and the surgery. I didn't understand the mental strain of sitting in a hospital bed, day after day, not knowing if those blood clots would choke off my lungs. I thought I could just shake it off, will my way through it. I knew that God had a plan for me, that He was there with me. But I was still scared, and I'll never forget the night I lay in that hospital bed, watching the hands of the clock slowly move for twenty-four straight hours.

When NBA training camp begins, it opens with a vengeance. The coaches work twelve- to fourteen-hour days because there are morning and early evening practice sessions. In between, the coaches meet, study practice films, plan out the next practice. After the morning practice, all I wanted to do was go home and sleep. After the evening practice, all I did was go home and sleep. Sometimes, I was so exhausted, I'd lie down in the dressing room. I was coaching out of a golf cart because I was still on crutches. I didn't want to admit what had happened to me. All I knew was that the Cavs had won 57 games and gone to the 1992 Eastern Conference Finals, and we were obsessed with trying to get past Michael Jordan and win an NBA title.

This would be the most demanding season of my coaching career because of my health problems and the rising expectations surrounding the team. As time passed, I moved from crutches and the golf cart to a walking boot. But anyone who has ever had Achilles tendon surgery will tell you that it takes a full year for the leg to heal. I'd coach the team in practice, then do rehab on my Achilles afterward. That sapped all my energy. So did the travel, the games, the practices—everything involved in the NBA, which is a seven-day-a-week lifestyle. I don't think I realized how much rest I'd need to recuperate from the combination of the surgery and the blood clots. And when I did feel the fatigue coming on, I fought it; I refused to admit that I wasn't my old self. I didn't want to give in to the fact that my body wasn't allowing me to coach with the same energy.

We still won 54 games that season, third-best in the history of the franchise—behind the 57 games we won in 1988–89 and 1991–92. So we still had a good year, but we weren't quite as sharp as the season before. I was under a lot of stress because I felt we just weren't at the top of our game, both the team and myself. When I'm not feeling well, I tend to withdraw a bit, so some of the people around me may not have understood all that I was going through.

In the playoffs, we won a tough five-game series with New Jersey. The Nets had some injuries, but Derrick Coleman decided to play, and when he sets his mind to it, Coleman is a great player. He carried the Nets to that fifth game, before we prevailed. Then we faced the Bulls in the second round and were swept in four games. A couple of those games were very tight, but we still lost.

When the season ended, I was totally, completely, and utterly exhausted. Meanwhile, there were newspaper stories appearing that the players may have stopped listening to me, that maybe they needed a change. On the day we played Game Four of the Chicago series, there was a story in the *Akron Beacon Journal* that this could be my final game as coach of the Cavs, and the next season, don't be surprised if I was coaching the Atlanta Hawks or some other NBA team. This was news to me. But it turned out during the playoffs that the Hawks had asked permission from the Cavs to talk to me after our season was over. I still had a year left on my contract, and I wasn't even aware the Hawks were interested in me.

There was a lot of frustration, a lot of soul-searching after we were swept by the Bulls. Down deep, all of us knew the problem: They had Michael Jordan, and we didn't. This was the fourth time in my seven years with the Cavs that we had been eliminated by Jordan's Bulls in the playoffs. You can look back now and know that Jordan was the greatest ever to play the game, a player who won titles in six of his last seven seasons. But when you're in the middle of it, when you're trying to beat him, and when he breaks your heart over and over and over—it's hard to accept, especially if you're a competitor.

I remember telling one reporter, "If they want to blame someone [for us losing to the Bulls], fine, blame me. I'm the coach. In the end, the responsibility is mine."

And that's true, the coach is responsible for the bottom line. But I also know that the average guy having my health problems would have sat out at least half the season, just collected the paycheck. Was I at my best during that year? Of course not. I just didn't have the energy. But is that why we lost to the Bulls? No way. I was hearing from a couple of other reporters that the front office was disenchanted with me, that they were wondering if the players had tuned me out, if I was losing my drive to win.

I told one reporter, "Someone had to be listening for us to win 54 games."

When the playoffs ended, I was worn down, beat up, and hurt by the whispering about me. I started to think, "I'm a loyal guy. I take a job and I see it through. I'm trying to help this team, and they don't appreciate it. I about died last summer, I came back too soon, I gave them all I had . . ."

You know the thoughts that go through your head when you know you did the best job you could under trying circumstances, but your bosses don't understand what you had to endure.

"Why should I care about these people?" I asked myself. "I know there are other teams that would love to have me as coach, so why stay here?"

That was the first time it ever crossed my mind to leave the Cavs—a few days after the 1993 playoffs. We were supposed to have a postseason meeting to evaluate the players and what we needed to do for next year. I called the front office and said, "I'm not coming in. I need to take some time off."

I'm not sure they understood, but I didn't care. I was exhausted from the season, concerned about the rumors that the front office was unhappy with me. The last thing I needed to do was to sit down and do a verbal autopsy of the season. Mentally, I couldn't handle it. Marilyn and I went to Rhode Island to visit some friends, Ralph and Vi Pari. I had lived with them part of the time I was in college, and they became a second family to me. Ralph is a person to whom I've always turned for advice, so I told him of my concern about the Cavs, how I felt that they were taking me for granted after seven years. Ralph said, "You make your decision. If you want to leave, leave. Life's not worth it."

I hadn't decided anything that weekend. I did have a year left on my contract. I heard that other teams had asked the Cavs for permission to talk to me, because there were rumors that I wouldn't be back as Cleveland's coach.

It wasn't until we came back to Cleveland that I told Marilyn, "I'm going to resign."

She asked why, and I told her that I wasn't healthy last season, and the front office didn't seem to care. I told her that I didn't like some of the comments—or no-comments—made about me and my situation to the reporters. I just felt it was time to move on.

I called Wayne Embry to inform him, but Wayne was out of town. So I decided just to get it over with, and I called Gordon Gund.

"Gordon, I think it's best I resign," I said.

"Are you sure?" he asked. I don't know if he was faking it, but Gordon sounded genuinely surprised.

"You guys are probably right," I said.

"What do you mean?" he asked.

"The players probably need to hear a new voice," I said, referring to the rumors that I'd heard.

"Are you sure we can't work this out?" he asked.

"Gordon," I said, "I respect you, but I want out. It will be best for you, for the team, for me, for everybody."

We talked a while longer, then Gordon said that was fine. A press release was drawn up, and my time with the Cavs was over.

In announcing my resignation, I told the press that it was a good idea for the players to hear a new voice, that coaching seven years in one place is a long time. I thought it was best to follow the party line, and I expressed no regrets about my years in Cleveland. But one question has always nagged at me: Would we have won a title if we'd kept Ron Harper?

Craig Ehlo was a wonderful player for me. I took him with me when I went to Atlanta, and Ehlo played more games for me than any other player. But Craig Ehlo is a role player, best coming off the bench. Nothing was going to change that, but he was my starting shooting guard. We signed other shooting guards—John Battle and Gerald Wilkins—but they obviously weren't the kind of talents needed to challenge Jordan. Ron Harper knew the game, he was capable of scoring 20 points, and he'd get some rebounds and steals; he demanded that Jordan defend him, or he'd put up some very big numbers. A key in trying to neutralize a player such as Jordan is to make him use some energy on defense. You need a player who can score on him, or he'll rest on defense and destroy you on offense. Ehlo averaged 11 points for me in his four years as a starter in Cleveland, mostly on long-range jumpers. He wasn't a player who ran around picks and made his man work on defense: That's not a knock on Ehlo, just a realistic view of his game.

Maybe no one was capable of beating Jordan, but I would have loved to have tried it with that original Cavs group of Price, Harper, Williams, Daugherty, and Nance with Ehlo as my sixth man.

But Harper remained a sensitive topic with the front office and Cavs fans, and I didn't want to bring that up again. So I just said, "The team needs a new voice."

Yes, there are times when that's true, when things get stale. But I don't think that was the case with the Cavs and me. I had an off year, just as a player can. I had a year where I battled injuries and illness, just like a player. But the front office rarely understands that a coach can go through the same things as a player. A smart front office will say, "Our coach wasn't himself, but he had some tough things to deal with. Let's tell him that we believe in him, and see what we can do to help him."

The Utah Jazz did that a number of years ago when there were rumors that the players had tuned out Jerry Sloan. In 1993 and 1995, the Jazz were knocked out of the playoffs in the first round. But the Jazz stuck with Sloan, who had been the head coach for seven years. In 1996, he took Utah to the Western Conference Finals; in 1997 and 1998, they went to the NBA Finals.

It's always easier to fire the coach after a disappointing year. Seldom is a front office criticized for that. It looks as if they are doing *something*, which most fans and writers think is a better idea than saying, "This coach is our guy, and we're sticking with him."

After I resigned, Marilyn was nervous. I had walked out on the last year of a contract worth $650,000. I don't know if the Cavs would have fired me, but if I had waited and they did, then I would have been paid that money.

By resigning, I forfeited that money. But I wasn't fired, I wasn't forced out. I made the decision to leave on my own, and that still meant I needed a coaching job.

In the summer of 1993, there were twenty-seven NBA teams, meaning there were only twenty-seven of these head coaching positions in the world. I had just walked away from one, so there were only twenty-six left. It's hard to become an NBA coach, because there are so few openings each year, and I know that was running through Marilyn's mind. Not that she had any doubt about my ability: Marilyn will tell you that I'm the greatest coach in NBA history. You don't even need to ask. She is my wife, my best friend, my biggest fan. Some people thought I had a job lined up when I resigned from the Cavs, but that wasn't the case. I was just confident that I could find another job, a fresh start, and that it would work out.

My agent, Lonnie Cooper, was in contact with several teams. In the summer of 1991, the Knicks were interested in talking to me. I was still under contract to the Cavs, but I suppose I could have pushed for them to allow me to interview. Even though I'm from Brooklyn and the Knicks were intriguing, my wife and I just didn't want to live in New York. We don't like life at that fast a pace, even though the money would have been incredible. My family is important to me. We go hand-in-hand. It's not just me who has to be happy where I work, they have to be comfortable, too. And by the summer of 1993, Pat Riley was in place as the Knicks coach, so New York was out.

The three teams that emerged were Atlanta, Indiana, and the Los Angeles Clippers. I first talked to the Hawks, and I was interested in them. Marilyn and I liked Atlanta as a city. The Hawks were a decent team the year before, a 43–39 record. Nothing special. They had been swept in the first round of the playoffs by the Bulls, and hadn't been past the first round since 1988. But they had some talent to work with.

The Hawks wanted me to sign a three-year contract, but I told them that I also wanted to talk to Indiana and the Clippers.

"Promise me one thing," said Pete Babcock, the Hawks general manager.

"What's that?" I asked.

"When you go to the Clippers, make sure you talk to the owner [Donald Sterling]," he said. "Don't decide anything until you talk to him."

I promised Babcock that I'd do just that.

The Clippers started as the Buffalo Braves back in 1970, moved to San Diego in 1978, then settled in Los Angeles in 1984. No team has been more futile, made more bad trades, lost more games, and been in such complete disrepair as the L.A. Clippers.

So why even talk to them?

My family and I do like Los Angeles. One of my daughters was attending UCLA. Larry Brown had just left after coaching the Clippers to a 41–41 record, so there was some talent there, including Ron Harper and Danny Manning. The situation wasn't hopeless, as is usually the state of affairs with the Clippers. I also liked Elgin Baylor, the long-time general manager. My talks with Elgin went very well, until I asked him about Stanley Roberts, the Clippers' young center who had just had Achilles surgery.

"What are you doing about his rehab?" I asked. "Who's checking on him?"

No one in the front office had a clue. I asked about some other players with injuries, and received the same nonanswers.

"You really need to follow up on guys in the summer to make sure they're working out and following their rehab programs," I said.

This seemed like an entirely new concept to them, which raised a red flag in my mind.

Next, I met with Donald Sterling, the real-estate tycoon who owns the team. He seemed a little distant, not locked in to our interview. I'd ask him if he planned to sign this player or trade that guy, and he'd just look at me and say, "Ooh, everybody on this team loves each other."

The guy had no grasp of what was going on with his own team.

We talked some more, then he had to leave. I really needed him to talk to my agent, but Sterling was taking the next day off. Baylor said he didn't even know where Sterling could be reached, or where he was going. If the general manager couldn't find the owner, if management doesn't communicate better than that, it's no wonder the Clippers have been such a mess for so long. I called my agent and said, "Lonnie, I'm outta here. This is no place for me."

My next stop was Indiana, which was the best of the three teams. I liked general manager Donnie Walsh a lot, and then I let Lonnie Cooper take over. Both Atlanta and Indiana offered three-year contracts, so it was great to be wanted by two very solid organizations. Marilyn liked Atlanta as a city best, and then the Hawks upped their offer to five years at $1.5 million annually—and that clinched the deal. I know that one of the members of the Hawks board—Mike Gearon—was surprised when I agreed to coach the

Hawks. He thought I was just using them as a bargaining tool with other teams, because I had interviewed first with Atlanta, then went to the Clippers and Pacers.

The Hawks had some talent—Dominique Wilkins, Kevin Willis, Stacey Augmon, Mookie Blaylock, and they traded for Danny Manning in the middle of the 1993–94 season, my first as the team's coach. We started the season at 1–4, and I had to convince the guys that I wanted the ball to move, and I wanted them to defend. To do that, I had to bench some people to get the point across. In one of our first games, I sat Dominique for nearly all of the second half of the game because he needed to become more team-oriented. Dominique was thirty-four years old and not the explosive scorer that he had been early in his career. We ended up trading Dominique at midseason to the Clippers for Danny Manning.

We had a very nice season, winning 57 games, to tie a franchise record for the most victories in a season. The Hawks had been in existence since 1950, when they were called the Tri-City Black Hawks and were coached by a young Red Auerbach, so those 57 victories were a very special accomplishment. I was my old self again. My health was back. My energy returned. I had a good group of guys willing to work together, and we made it to the second round of the playoffs—the first time since 1988 that it had happened in Atlanta. And that 1993–94 season was special for me because I broke Red Auerbach's record of 938 career coaching victories. For the first time in my career, I was voted the NBA's Coach of the Year. It also put me in position to become the coach of the 1996 U.S. Olympic team.

CHAPTER EIGHTEEN

T HERE WAS A TIME IN THIS COUNTRY when many people thought a black man couldn't coach a professional sports team. He could play the game; he could win every individual honor available to an athlete; he could lead his team to a championship with his sheer drive, skill, and athleticism. But he couldn't coach. He didn't have the mental ability to do it, or the character—or maybe, both.

When I broke into the NBA in 1960, there were no black head coaches in any of the big three professional sports—basketball, baseball, and football. Yes, there were black players, and blacks were starting to dominate in every sport. But some people had an ugly explanation for that, too:

Black players were great athletes. They succeeded because they could run faster, jump higher, and were physically stronger than white athletes. It was genetic, a gift from God.

Of course, no one said this outright.

They talked about the black star being "a wonderful athlete." The white star was "savvy, a smart player, an overachiever."

Those were the code words: "great athlete" for blacks, "smart and savvy" for whites. Blacks didn't think, they just played the game, did what came naturally. Whites could only play the game by thinking.

This was not only insulting, it was racist. We couldn't win in the court of public opinion. If a black athlete was better than a white athlete, well, what's the big deal? Blacks are physically superior, right?

If a white athlete prevailed, it was because he "outsmarted" or "outhustled" the black athlete.

In other words, whites had more character than black athletes.

That always galled me, and I've spent a lifetime in professional sports defying that stereotype. When I played, people spoke and wrote about me as if I were a white athlete.

I was "the coach on the floor."

I was "the heady point guard."

I was "an intelligent player."

I was thrilled with those compliments. I just wished the people writing and saying those things didn't believe I was such an exception. If they could watch the game with unbiased eyes, they'd see that a lot of black players played smart. And they'd also see some white players who were pretty good athletes and didn't always squeeze the last drop out of their talent. The truth was, some of them didn't have the aptitude to do so.

One of my hopes for sports is that people can learn to judge each other as people, not by race or stereotypes. This goes back to my days at Providence, when some professors didn't think an athlete, especially a black athlete, could also be a serious student, and it carried over into the pro game, where blacks supposedly couldn't play point guard because they lacked a deep enough understanding of the game. Black quarterbacks fought that same stigma in the NFL for too many years.

Lord knows, no one thought a black person could ever coach a team.

That's why being named head coach of the 1996 Olympic team meant so much to me. A black man was not merely going to represent the United States of America, he was going to lead a group of those representatives onto the world stage.

It wasn't long after the 1992 Olympics that I began hearing I'd be the head coach of the 1996 team. I loved my Olympic experience in 1992, and I wanted the rumors to be true. I wanted the job, but I didn't say much about it because I was afraid it wouldn't happen, even though I felt I was very qualified. Between the 1992 and 1996 Olympics, I'd passed Red Auerbach's NBA record of 938 coaching victories. I'd started to receive a fair amount of national publicity, and a lot of people were writing that I had been underappreciated all these years. I was the logical pick. I had been on the 1992 coaching staff, so I was very familiar with taking NBA stars and adapting them to the international style of play, which has slightly different rules than our pro game. I also was known and respected by the players. If ever I was going to be the head coach of the Olympic team, 1996 was the year.

And when it happened, I was very pleased. I knew the moment would be special, but when I was alone and had a chance to think about it, I was surprised at how emotional I became. I was talking about it with some friends, and I got a little choked up. I started to think of where I came from, of all the things that had to happen for me to reach that point, of the odds against a kid who played only a half-year of high-school basketball going on to have a longer career as a player and coach than anyone in NBA history.

Now, I was the head coach of the 1996 Olympic basketball team.

I was proud because I knew I had earned it. They wanted a good coach, an experienced coach, a winning coach, and I was all of those. That's what made this so meaningful to me.

But after I was named the head coach, I had one profoundly felt wish—that my father could have been there to see it. This has happened to me on a few occasions in my life. I wanted my father there, to see what his son had become and to hear what he thought of it. The great thing was that my mother was still alive. She always told me two things: that I'm always accountable for what I do and say . . . and that I should let honesty and integrity define my character. I don't care if that sounds corny. Being accountable, being honest, being a man of integrity—that's how I've tried to live my life, and, in some ways, I viewed the Olympic coaching job as a reward for all that.

Then, I got scared.

Suddenly, I understood how Chuck Daly felt in 1992. I didn't want to lose. I didn't want to become the first coach to lose in the Olympics with NBA players. And I sure didn't want the first coach to lose to be a black coach.

Any reasonably intelligent person knows that the 1988 Olympic team didn't lose because John Thompson was the coach. It was simply a matter of the rest of the world's pros catching up to our college kids; there was nothing John Thompson could have done about that. But he was the first black head coach in U.S. Olympic basketball history, and the first to legitimately lose the gold medal (the Russians had won in a controversial final in 1972). His race obviously had nothing to do with it, yet I know there were whispers . . .

I didn't want to leave any room for whispers.

Deep inside, I knew no one in the world could beat us. I knew this without even being sure of the composition of the team. I had too much respect for the character and competitiveness of the top NBA players to believe that they'd lose in the Olympics. But what if something happened . . .

That always runs through a coach's mind, especially when your team is an overwhelming favorite. What if you have a night where no one can make a shot? Those nights happen to the best players and best teams. In the playoffs, that's not the end: It's just one bad game. But in the Olympics, one bad game in the medal round and you're done.

I didn't dwell on this. I don't think I ever talked about it. But once in a while, the thought, the fear—it was there. What if we lose?

I also knew that this was going to be a tougher job than coaching the 1992 team. Part of it was that some of the older stars weren't taking part. Magic and Larry Bird had retired. I talked to Michael Jordan, and he said, "Coach, if I thought you really needed me, I'd play. You know that I'd love to play for you. But you already have so many good players to pick from, I think it's good to let some of the younger guys have a chance."

I know he'd have played if I pressed the issue, but Michael was right. There were a lot of other guys who'd love to be on the Olympic team. Michael had been in the Olympics as a college player in 1984 and as a pro in 1992, so he had done his part.

No matter what happened, I realized our team was destined to be compared to the 1992 team, and I knew that wasn't fair. 1992 was the first time we used pros in the Olympics. With Michael, Magic, and Larry, we had three of the five best players in NBA history. That was a team for the ages. Some of those guys were already legends. It was in Spain, where the European fans were in total awe of the Dream Team; the 1996 Olympics would be in Atlanta, where the fans still loved us and we were mobbed wherever we went, but American fans are more used to seeing NBA stars than the fans in Europe.

And our team didn't have Magic, Larry, or Michael.

We had great talent, but we didn't have players who were considered giants of the game. I'm not criticizing the roster. I was blessed to have a team with John Stockton, Karl Malone, Scottie Pippen, David Robinson, Charles Barkley, Gary Payton, Reggie Miller, Mitch Richmond, Shaquille O'Neal, Penny Hardaway, Grant Hill, and Hakeem Olajuwon.

That's not exactly a bad team.

But we were a different team, and I immediately stressed that to the players. We would find our own identity. We would not compare ourselves to the 1992 team, even though people would ask us about that. I stressed that I'd try to play everyone some quality minutes, and I planned to use a lot of different lineups.

We were also facing a bigger challenge than the 1992 team. We were together for a shorter time, only a month. After taking just the bronze medal in the 1988 Olympics, our team had to qualify for the 1992 Olympics by winning the Tournament of the Americas, which gave us some additional time to play together. The rest of the world had continued to improve; more and more foreign players were competing in the NBA, then returning to play for their countries in the summer. But I did have four players who had been on the 1992 team—Stockton, Pippen, Malone, and Barkley. They were a great help to me, just because they had already had the Olympic experience.

I have to say that the Olympic Committee could not have been better to me. I was allowed to pick my own assistants, which was nice: In the past, the committee sometimes wanted their own people as assistants. I asked for Bobby Cremins, Jerry Sloan, and Clem Haskins. There was some debate on the committee, then Wayne

Embry spoke up for me and said, "I think the coach should have people he wants. He knows who he needs to help him win."

I always appreciated that. To see Wayne go to bat for me like that really meant a lot. I thought I'd left the Cavs on good terms, but sometimes there are hard feelings anyway. The committee is a collection of people from the college and pro ranks—mostly former coaches and current executives. Receiving all that support and friendship made me put even more pressure on myself to make sure everything went right. I didn't want to let these people down.

Then we played our first exhibition game. It was against a bunch of college stars called the Select Team. This probably would have been our Olympic team if the pros weren't taking part. Anyway, this was my first game as Olympic head coach, and we came out of the dressing room totally flat. I mean, we couldn't make a shot, we didn't play with much intensity, nothing.

At halftime, we were down by 17 points.

Really, this wasn't much different from that first scrimmage the 1992 team had against some college stars, with one major exception: that scrimmage was played behind closed doors, in front of no one but the players and coaches, while this was on TV in front of a sellout crowd in Detroit. The whole country was watching, and probably wondering just what the deal was with us. I kept telling myself, "We're not gonna lose to a bunch of college kids," but we sure were playing like it.

At halftime, I really jumped on the guys. During practices, we had talked about defense being our calling card, our identity, and we had some spirited practices. The guys worked hard. They were very serious about the Olympic team. They knew that we were carrying the legacy of 1992, that we were the team that represented the best of U.S. basketball.

And we were being embarrassed.

In the second half, I started Olajuwon, Barkley, Pippen, Richmond, and Payton. We pressured the ball, to play a fierce trapping defense, forcing turnovers and creating some easy baskets. The game began to turn in our favor, and I'm telling you, I was relieved. Malone and Robinson played well off the bench, and we won—which was the best thing I could say about it.

We were criticized in the media for our lackluster effort. I knew that was coming, and I was sure it wouldn't happen again. The players didn't like what happened any more than I did. People then said we'd never compare to the 1992 team. I knew that was coming, too: The second-guessing was sure to start, even from some of the members of the Olympic Committee who had voted for me to coach the team. I could still see the doubt in the eyes of some of the people. They'd deny it now, but I knew they wondered if I could do the job. I sensed it. I felt it. No one had to say a word, it was just there, hanging over the room.

If they wanted to compare us to the 1992 team, or compare me to Chuck Daly, there was nothing we could do—but we were a different team. All I could do was stress that over and over, hoping people got the message. But that still didn't make me feel much better after that first game. Later that night, I called my wife, and even Marilyn told me how lousy we played. The one good thing was I knew the players were also hearing it, and they weren't going to like it any more than I did. In retrospect, that game was the best wake-up call we could have had.

Some people think it's hard to coach a Dream Team because of all the egos involved. They're shocked when I tell them that was never a problem.

When we first came together, I told the players that this was a special opportunity, a once-in-a-lifetime thing for most of them. They would be representing their country. We were going to play as a team. No one should worry about individual statistics. We had one—and only one—goal, to win the gold medal.

This wasn't news to the players. They knew it. They understood it. They supported each other. In some ways, it was a pure form of basketball because no one's contract was at stake. No one was going to have to negotiate based upon how many points he scored in the Olympics. There was no reason to become obsessive about playing time. So they had every reason to be very team-oriented, to be willing to sit and watch if the guy playing ahead of them was having a good day. I know that you can't do this for a whole year in an NBA setting, but this wasn't for a whole year.

"Look, this will go by fast," I told the players. "So if we all put the team first, we'll be glad we did at the end. You are special people and this is a special situation. That's why you're here. So let's stay together."

I knew these were men of great pride, and I wasn't going to bury anyone on the bench. They all wanted their moment in the Olympics, and I understood that. I made sure that each guy started at least one game. I never used the same starting lineup twice. The guys bought into it. They wanted to win the gold medal as much as I did, and they certainly didn't want to be on the first Dream Team to lose in the Olympics. Both Reggie Miller and Shaquille O'Neal had gone into the summer as free agents and were negotiating contracts during the practice period, but they didn't seem distracted; they really concentrated and made me proud to coach them.

I was very impressed with Miller. Even though I had coached against Reggie and had a lot of respect for him, I was surprised that he was such a pleasure to have on my team. He showed up in great shape with tremendous enthusiasm. I knew he was a super shooter, but he worked very hard for me on defense. He is very competitive; he's one of those guys you really don't fully appreciate until he's on your team, because he just burns with desire to win.

I always knew that Richmond was an incredible shooter, but I never realized what a good defensive player he was until I coached him, and he responded to our challenge to defend. Hakeem has great, great footwork. Stockton and Malone run the pick-and-roll as well as any two players I've ever seen. I had heard stories that Payton wouldn't always work hard in practice, that he was difficult to coach, but he was great with me. David Robinson is rapped for being soft, which is unfair. That's why I was happy to see him win an NBA title, because he's just such a good person.

Shaquille O'Neal gets criticized a lot, but I've seen a lot of growth in him as he's been in the league. There was some discussion about Shaq not playing in the Olympics, or being unhappy because he had an endorsement deal with Pepsi while Coke was one of the big Olympic sponsors. But Shaq worked that out, and I never worried about that being a problem.

Some of the players kidded Shaq about an All-Star game

where I was coaching and he was on the team. I was watching Shaq shoot around, and I told him that he should work on a drop-step move to the basket. I showed him a few things.

"You're so strong," I said, "even if they foul you on this move, you'll still score."

He was very attentive.

Then Shaq asked, "Coach, did you ever play at this level?"

Scottie Pippen was listening, and he just broke up laughing. He started telling the other guys what Shaq had said.

"Yes," I told Shaq, "I played a little bit."

Now Scottie was really laughing.

The next day, Shaq came in and said he had asked his dad about me.

"He said you were pretty bad, man," said Shaq, which I knew was a sincere compliment. Shaq also had a camera, and he got one of the guys to take a picture of us together, which I thought was a nice touch.

I wasn't shocked that Shaq was unaware of my career. I hadn't played since 1975. Why would players of Shaq's generation know? It would be nice if they had that sense of history, but most don't— and I'm not hung up about that. I liked having Shaq on my team. I'm telling you, I really enjoyed all the guys. Yes, even Charles Barkley. I know he says some really off-the-wall things, but Charles doesn't mean any harm. He plays very hard. He brought some spice to our dressing room, because he'd tease people. He just had so much joy about playing the game, his spirit lifted up the other guys. He also wasn't afraid to challenge the other players to step up the intensity. Charles and I were together on the 1992 team, and I wanted him back in 1996 because I knew that he was a veteran with a strong personality, a real warrior.

One of the areas I discussed with the players was being patient with people and making sure none of us embarrassed ourselves in any way. In the 1994 World Games, some of the NBA players were accused of trash-talking, putting down the opponents, things like that. I told the guys that I didn't expect that to be a problem, but to be extra careful. Everyone was watching us, I mean the whole world. Anything we did reflected not just on us, but on our country.

"We want to show everyone that we're not only the best at what we do, but we want to show everyone that we understand sportsmanship," I said. "We can't do anything that looks like we're showing up the other team."

I had so many good people that I wasn't very worried about that, but I wanted to make sure the players were clear about what was expected from them.

Our biggest challenge happened off the court, when the bomb went off in the downtown Atlanta park. I was back at the hotel, and I felt the building shake. The first thing we did was make sure all the players and their families were accounted for, that none of them were in the park when the pipe bomb blew.

This was another time I realized how much things had changed. When I broke into the NBA, I never imagined a day when the pros would play in the Olympics. That's why I was so upset at being left off the team in 1960: You had one shot at playing in the Olympics and mine was gone. I never imagined that there would be anything like the 1992 Dream Team, where thousands of fans lined up just to see us step off the bus and walk into a building through a police barricade. I never imagined that the whole world would know the names of the top NBA players; I doubt a similar team would have all been recognized at home in 1960.

And I never thought about terrorism.

Even after the 1972 Olympics and the kidnapping and killing of the Israeli athletes, I didn't think something like that would happen—not to us, and not in Atlanta. Granted, the bomb wasn't directed at the athletes, but it could have killed anyone who happened to be walking in that park. And it made you wonder what else would happen, or could happen.

We had tremendous security. The team hotel was sealed off, except for those who had the proper credentials. After the bomb, the coaching staff spent a lot of time reassuring the players that things were under control.

Some guys were like Charles Barkley, who didn't care.

"No SOB terrorist is gonna intimidate me," he said. "I came here to play the games, period."

Karl Malone was worried about his family. The bombing so upset him that he had a friend fly in from Utah, then escort his family home. Other guys were talking about doing the same thing. I said that was their decision, but I believed everything was going to be fine. We had protection. Our families were protected, so I didn't want this to spoil the Olympics for our players or their families. Charles Barkley was a big help, supporting what I had to say, and after a while everyone calmed down.

A few days later, there was a bomb threat. Supposedly someone had left a suitcase in the lobby of our hotel. They quickly escorted everyone out of ground level, and told everyone else on the upper floors to stay in their rooms. It turned out to be a false alarm; they found a bag, but no bomb. That got everyone a little uptight again. I just thanked God that no one was hurt. We'd already had enough damage after the first bomb in the park. That's the most frightening part of terrorism, how innocent people always suffer. Here were some people in the park during the Olympics, listening to the music, enjoying the atmosphere, and a bomb blows up. Things like that can make you paranoid, but you also can't go through life always worrying about it. If you did, you'd never leave your house.

When I was coaching in Cleveland, I think it was in 1989, we had a game in Detroit. We were on a hot streak, and when we arrived at the hotel, we discovered someone had called in a bomb threat. Then I received a death threat, saying someone would take me out if I coached the team that night. NBA security was called in. They made us ride around for forever on the team bus, I'm not sure why. Some of the players got nervous. A few said they wouldn't coach the game if they were in my shoes. I never thought about doing anything but coaching. I wasn't going to let the bad guys intimidate me, but it was a little unnerving having the extra security around, moving to a different hotel and seeing that some of my players were thinking about it. The temptation is to sort of duck every time you walk into a public place, but you can't live like that. I was just angry that there are people who take delight in calling in threats, in ruining something fans enjoy.

I thought of this when the bombing happened in Atlanta. It

helped me because I had been through something like it before. You can't live your life in fear. You can't sit around going through all the horrible things that can happen, because that will paralyze you—which is exactly what the terrorists want. I was not about to give in to them, and I was proud none of the Olympic athletes from any of the other countries did, either.

As a coach, I had a real challenge that had very little to do with basketball. Because we were the Dream Team, a lot of people wanted to be around us. Famous people.

One day, Bishop Tutu wanted to come to our practice. I admire Bishop Tutu. He is an important international figure, so he came. Former Atlanta mayor Andrew Young wanted to speak to our team. I like Andy Young, so I let him talk to the team. I was impressed at how respectful our players were to our guests. That meant a lot to me.

But it never ended. Bruce Willis and some other show business people wanted to come to practice and meet the players. Other celebrities wanted to get into the dressing room after games. We had to control that, and I know some people were disappointed.

A few people criticized us for not living in the Olympic Village with most of the other athletes. They said we were pampered prima donnas who thought we were too good to be with the rest of the Olympians, which was just ridiculous. Our guys couldn't even walk the street without being mobbed. In 1992, when we went to the Olympic Village to pick up our credentials, we were swarmed—by the other athletes! They wanted our autographs! Pole vaulters, shot-putters, they all wanted to meet our guys. We never would have gotten any rest if we'd stayed in the Olympic Village. If anything, some of our guys felt they were prisoners in the hotel because it was virtually impossible for them to venture outside without having to deal with a never-ending stream of fans. Some said the 1996 Dream Team lacked glamour, but you couldn't prove it by the fans; there was a mob of them waiting everywhere for us, staking out the hotel and even the places we practiced to tune up for the Olympics.

When we practiced at Moody College in Chicago, a guy held up signs about the violence in Nigeria. He wanted Hakeem to do something about it. After a couple of days, Hakeem went over and talked to the guy. He handled it with class, and during our last day of practice, the guy held up a sign saying, WISHING HAKEEM WELL. Our players were smart enough to stay away from political questions. For the most part, athletes aren't very political people, so they often don't want to make their opinion public anyway. But I was glad we didn't get into the middle of any social or political controversies.

By the end of the Olympics, I felt just like Chuck Daly had in 1992: I was relieved it was over, relieved we won, and very proud of how the players held up under the pressure. I was happy that we won my way, by playing all the guys, playing different lineups every game, and we still won big. But with some people, we couldn't win: If we beat a team by only 20 points, then we were flat and just going through the motions; if we won by 40 or 50 points, we were pouring it on. I thought the media criticism we got early in the Olympics was unfair; they kept putting us up against the 1992 team, and there was no way we'd ever win that comparison. Then they said the crowds weren't as responsive. Well, we were drawing close to forty thousand a game and the fans seemed happy to see us—and we were playing in Atlanta, not in Europe where the NBA is more a novelty.

When the Olympics were over, there was some discussion about us not using the NBA players in 2000. That would be a mistake. The players from the rest of the world want to play against our best, especially now that they've seen our guys. And whether we want to admit it or not, basketball worldwide keeps improving. Our college players couldn't win in 1988, and they sure won't win in 2000. It's fine to use college players in the Goodwill Games, the Pan-American Games, and other international competitions like that. But in the Olympics, we have to stay with the pros. We can't turn back the hands of time.

Just because our 1996 team supposedly lacked the glamour of the 1992 Dream Team is no reason to drop the concept. We couldn't recreate the 1992 Dream Team because there will never be another team like that one. It was the first time the greatest NBA pros ever joined together to take on the world, and there was a real curiosity about how that would play out. They set the standard of excitement so high, no one could compare. Our critics missed the main point: We were there to win the gold medal and to represent our country with honor, and we did exactly that.

CHAPTER NINETEEN

I'VE ALWAYS RESPECTED the great Buffalo Bills teams, those same Bills teams that never won a Super Bowl. To many fans and writers, that means they can never be great, never be special: Only champions are great, and everyone else is a loser, or at least falls short. I've never believed that. The true measure of a team is how it answers this question: Did they play as well as they possibly could?

Those Buffalo Bills teams did just that. When they lost in the Super Bowl, they were beaten by teams with better talent, period. The remarkable story wasn't that the Bills lost year after year in the Super Bowl, it's that those players came together each year, sacrificed and overachieved, and made it back to the Super Bowl. They didn't get discouraged, and they won a lot of games they never should have just to put themselves in position to play for a title. With the Bills, the whole was far greater than the sum of the parts.

I believe that was true of most of my teams with the Atlanta Hawks.

But to most fans and writers, the Bills were stuck in a rut. Their rut was losing in the Super Bowl, but it was a rut.

And so were my Hawks.

Our rut was we'd win 50 games in the regular season and be near the top of the Central Division, but in the playoffs we'd lose in the second round. The fact that we lost to a more talented team in the second round—or that we never should have won those 50-some games in the regular season . . . well, none of that mattered.

We were good, but not good enough. We won, but we didn't

win enough—or at least, we didn't win at the right time, in the play-offs. In a sense, we were convicted in the court of public opinion for overachieving during the regular season. I thought about the un-fairness of that after I resigned as coach of the Atlanta Hawks in May of 2000. I looked at my record for my first six years coaching the Hawks: Our typical season was 50–32, advancing to the second round of the playoffs. This is a franchise that had been in Atlanta for twenty-five seasons before I arrived, with only five seasons of at least 50 wins. It hadn't made it out of the first round of the playoffs in the five seasons before I arrived in Atlanta in the summer of 1993.

On paper, those three 50-win seasons in my first six years looked pretty good, especially since there would have been a fourth if the strike hadn't shortened the 1998–99 season. Our team was praised for playing hard, playing smart, and usually winning more games than expected. We had some All-Stars in Steve Smith and Dikembe Mutombo, but no superstars. No great players. No Rook-ies of the Year. In my seven years with the Hawks, the only player to make All-NBA was Mutombo, who was picked to the third team in 1998. With all respect to Mutombo, he is a great rebounder and shot blocker, but never considered a force on offense. He was a 12-point scorer for us, and we worked with him a lot to develop some inside moves to help him at least be a factor when he caught the ball near the basket. But 12 points was all that was reasonable to expect from him.

This isn't meant to denigrate my players, but to praise them. It shows how these guys squeezed out every ounce of their talent and blended together to consistently win those 50 games. Our teams had solid pros such as Grant Long, Mookie Blaylock, Tyrone Corbin, and Craig Ehlo surrounding Smith and Mutombo. But we weren't considered flashy. We were a team that appealed more to the basketball purists than the MTV generation.

Exactly how J. R. Rider was supposed to cure all this, I'll never know.

The fact that Rider ended up in Atlanta tells you all you need to know about the mindset of both the Hawks franchise and the

NBA in general. It shows what happens when a front office sees a team "stuck in a rut," even if that rut is 50 victories and a decent showing in the playoffs. It also reveals how even shrewd men such as Hawks president Stan Kasten and general manager Pete Babcock can become so desperate that they do something they know in their heart of hearts will never work.

That something was the J. R. Rider trade.

But first, you need to understand what Atlanta was like during my first six years with the Hawks. I took over a team that had missed the playoffs and then didn't have a great draft when I arrived, our number-one pick being Florida State's Doug Edwards, who barely made a ripple in the NBA before sinking out of sight. I took the same basic team that had won 43 games, and our record improved to 57–25. With Michael Jordan playing minor league baseball that season, we filled the gap by winning the Central Division. And we did it despite making a major trade at midseason, sending Dominique Wilkins to the L.A. Clippers for Danny Manning. This was an excellent deal for us, because Dominque was nearing the end of his career. His mentality was always to score first, and he still had the ability to put the ball in the basket, but Manning's unselfishness and passing skills fit well into our game plan.

When you make a trade of that magnitude at midseason, it often leads to a month where you lose some games that you normally wouldn't because the players are adjusting to someone new in the lineup. Basketball is not like baseball or some other sports. In baseball, if you trade for another guy, you just put him on the mound or in the lineup, and he does his job pitching or hitting. He's part of a team concept, but only as far as his individual skills help the team win. The new player doesn't have to "blend in," other than to be accepted by his teammates in the dressing room. But in basketball, the guy has to fit in all categories. On the court, he has to be able to pass, to defend, to set picks, to help his teammates. He has to understand your offensive and defensive schemes, which may be much different from the schemes used with his old team. In baseball, you don't have to alter your swing or change how you throw your slider after a trade; you just do what you do best. But in basketball, a player traded to a new team may be called upon to shoot more—or less. To defend harder, to rebound more, to dribble less. It all depends on his teammates and his new coach's game plan. That's why so many teams have a dip after making a trade during the middle of the NBA season. When you acquire a guy who is going to make a major impact on your team, you need about a week of solid practices to get everyone on the same page, to familiarize the new player with your playbook and the guys on his new team—but you never have that time, because you're usually playing three to four times a week. You rarely have two practices in a row during the meat part of the season, so you try to work things out from game to game, and sometimes you lose.

But those 1993–94 Hawks were such a receptive team, and Manning's dedication to team play was so obvious, that we were able to keep winning right after the trade. Amazingly, we won five in a row right after the deal. I compare this to what happened when I was in Cleveland and we traded Kevin Johnson, Mark West, and Tyrone Corbin to Phoenix for Larry Nance and Mike Sanders: We lost 9 of 11 before retooling and finishing the season strong. Very few writers and fans understood how well our players adjusted to the Manning deal, and how rare it was that it happened so fast.

When I came to the Hawks, I was told that Kevin Willis was selfish, that Stacey Augmon was moody, and that Mookie Blaylock didn't have the maturity to be a good point guard. I talked with all of those players in training camp, and the message I got was very different: What they wanted most was a sense of direction for the team, a belief that the coaches knew what they were doing—and that the coaches were determined to help them become better players. They were hungry for leadership. They quickly bought into my philosophy, starting with the fact that we had to win at home. Yes, the crowds at the Omni were not always as big or as loud as we'd like, but there still were some rabid fans. Besides, this was our home court; we shouldn't let teams just come in and beat us. The season before I arrived, the Hawks were 25–16 at the Omni; our home record jumped to 36–5 in my first season.

When the playoffs came, we beat Miami in a tough 5-game series, then lost to Indiana in six games. Indiana had a great player in

Reggie Miller, who averaged 23 points in the playoffs that season. Danny Manning averaged 20 for us, but no one else scored more than 13 per game in the playoffs. In the regular season, we won 10 more games than Indiana, but the Pacers had better talent than us. They were coming together and getting healthy at just the right time, and they beat us.

The reason I'm discussing in depth what happened in that first season with Atlanta is that it set the tone for everything that was to come later. In a way, it led to the destructive Rider deal, and to my leaving the Hawks. Here's why: In my first year, we were 57–25 and went to the second round of the playoffs. Suddenly, the bar was set, and was really set too high. The second round of the playoffs wouldn't be good enough. It's nice to win all the regular-season games, but what about the playoffs? I heard that over and over. Furthermore, there is a sports culture that is unique to Atlanta. This is not Portland or Seattle or even Cleveland, which proved it would embrace pro basketball when the product was worth watching. We had some excellent fans in Atlanta, but not enough of them. Those who have spent most of their lives in Atlanta say there are two seasons: college football and spring football. That's stretching it, but not by much. The state is ruled by the University of Georgia football team. The Bulldogs are more popular than the NFL's Atlanta Falcons, Major League Baseball's Atlanta Braves, and certainly more than the Hawks. In fact, if most Atlanta sports fans had to rate the teams in order of interest, it would be: 1: Georgia football; 2: the Falcons; 3: the Braves; 4: the Hawks. That's despite the Braves being the best team in the National League in the 1990s. When we played the Lakers, many of the fans wore jerseys with the names of Kobe Bryant or Shaquille O'Neal on the back. When we played the Knicks, a lot of transplanted New Yorkers came to the games and cheered for them. Naturally, Michael Jordan and the Bulls brought in huge crowds, and most of them backed the Bulls. Our fan loyalty wasn't very deep, except for the truly hardcore.

In my first season, our attendance went from an average of 11,981 per game to 13,335. You would have thought that the 57 wins would have meant an even bigger jump in the attendance the following year, but we slipped back to an average of 12,312 as our record dropped to 42–40. Part of the reason was that we lost Manning to Phoenix via free agency, and that meant our top scorer was gone and we had no one to replace him. Early in the season, we knew we had to find some offense, so we traded Kevin Willis and a first-round draft pick to Miami for Grant Long and Steve Smith. This would turn out to be an excellent deal, but this time we couldn't stave off the downturn that follows a big trade during the season, dropping 5 of 7 after the deal. Smith is a six-foot-eight guard from Michigan State. His boyhood hero was Magic Johnson, and then he went to Magic's university. He came to Atlanta wanting to be like Magic, the big guard who handles the ball and can score, too. But there is only one Magic Johnson. When I looked at Steve Smith's game, I felt his greatest asset matched our biggest need—he could really shoot the basketball. I spent most of Steve's first season convincing him that he was a shooting guard, and a shooting guard was supposed to do just that—shoot! We had a good point guard in Mookie Blaylock. But we were desperate for scoring, and Steve needed to develop that shooter's mentality. I didn't care if he missed five shots in a row, I wanted him to take that sixth shot—assuming he was open. Never have I worked harder on developing a scorer's mentality in a player than I did with Smith, and he became a 20-point scorer for us. But it took time. I loved Steve Smith's attitude. He was a great guy off the court, very active in charity events. He was an excellent teammate. He was always on time. He supported me in all ways. He was the heart of our teams in the late 1990s, those Hawks teams that went 56–26, 50–32, and 31–19 in the strike season. He combined with Mookie Blaylock to give us one of the better backcourts in the NBA. But for me, the greatest satisfaction came from seeing Steve mature as a player and a person. He was one of my favorite people to coach.

The problem was that we couldn't get enough talent around Steve Smith to move beyond that "rut" of winning 50 games and losing in the second round of the playoffs. We won too many games to draft high. Here's a list of our first-rounders during my first six years with the Hawks: Doug Edwards, Alan Henderson, Priest Lauderdale, Ed Gray, and Rashown McLeod. Only Henderson became a starter. Some people tried to say that I don't develop young talent when they saw how the draft choices failed, but that was ridiculous; the team we had in Cleveland proved otherwise, as did our championship team in Seattle. Look at what happened to Edwards, Lauderdale, and Gray after they left the Hawks—nothing. McLeod may become a decent player: He was our first pick in 1998 and was hurt for part of that season with a hamstring injury. Henderson definitely bloomed with us.

We were in that frustrating NBA cycle: We won too many games to draft high, and the only way to really make another step forward was with high lottery picks. And we were unable to attract a major free agent other than Mutombo. While we obtained Chris Laettner in a trade, he blew out his Achilles in his second year with us, then moved on to Detroit as a free agent. Laettner was a good player, but not a true star.

For those reasons, I'm really proud of how our teams played in 1997–98 and 1998–99, especially when you consider that we never had a true home court. Atlanta was building a new arena for us and was doing it on the site of the old Omni. That meant they had to tear the Omni down, so for two years we played some home games at the Georgia Dome and others at Alexander Memorial Coliseum, which is the home of the Georgia Tech basketball team. The Georgia Dome was too big, while Alexander Memorial Coliseum was more like a fieldhouse, a true college facility where many of the seats didn't even have chairbacks, just benches. It's hard to expect people to pay NBA prices for that kind of seat, and even worse, parking was a problem. For two years, we were like nomads, yet we had records of 50–32 and 31–19, and were 41–21 on our "home courts."

But we couldn't get past the second round of the playoffs.

The problem is that talent is the overriding factor in the playoffs. A coach can have a much more dramatic impact on a team over the course of a six-month season. A coach can keep the players' spirits up, keep them interested and motivated; he can juggle lineups when slumps and injuries come, and he can develop players over the course of the season. He can upset teams with superior talent by convincing his players to really pay attention to details, while the more talented team may just be in cruise control.

But that all changes in the playoffs. Every team, every player, gives a maximum effort every minute on the court. Teams are scouted so well that there are few surprises. Plays break down because the opponent anticipates where the passes and picks will come from, and the defense stiffens. That's why the great individual talent, the player who can create his own shot, is so important in the playoffs. Jordan, Bird, Magic, the great Detroit guards . . . they all could do that. They had the ability to make plays, to beat double-teaming defenses, to score critical points. Latrell Sprewell has had more than his share of problems, but when he was traded to New York, he made the most of his second chance, and he was the reason the Knicks beat us in the second round of the 1999 playoffs. He could use his God-given ability to get off a shot even when the defenses were keyed to stopping him. He also had Allan Houston, a great outside shooter, to work with him and to carry some of the scoring load. We had Steve Smith, a Houston-like shooter, but we had no athlete to match Sprewell. Sprewell helped the Knicks go all the way to the 1999 Finals.

The fact that we had a better regular season record than New York, or that we had the best defensive team in the NBA, none of that mattered come playoff time. In my mind, it was amazing we beat Detroit with Grant Hill in the first round, before we even faced New York. I was playing Steve Smith close to forty-six minutes a game in that Detroit series just to counteract Hill, and he had no legs left by the time we reached the Knicks. We also were without LaPhonso Ellis and Alan Henderson in the playoffs. The season before, Henderson had been selected as the NBA's Most Improved Player, and a coach always takes a lot of pride when his player wins that award: It shows that the coaches also were doing something right. So playing without Ellis and Henderson, both injured, meant we had no realistic chance against the Knicks. I know we were swept by New York in the second round, but we had nothing left. Our team had played as well as it could in 1998–99.

At the end of the season, I could tell that team president Stan Kasten was very frustrated. We all were, but he seemed to be even more sensitive to the media criticism we received for being "stuck" in the second round, for not having the kind of player who was charismatic, a player who captured the interest of the fans. Our new building would be ready, and the media were demanding that we didn't put "the same old Hawks" into it. Not getting past the second round of the playoffs was like a bone in all of our throats. It was always there, even when we tried to pretend otherwise. As a coach, the hard part was that the regular season hardly seemed to matter. There was virtually no criticism of how we played the first 82 games. Over and over, we heard that the team overachieved. But then we supposedly "underachieved" in the playoffs. That just didn't seem right.

Which brings us to J. R. Rider.

We were having our off-season meetings about what could take us to "the next level," to be able to seriously compete for a championship. In general, I agreed with the assessment by the front office that we had to change our roster in order to make that next step. We wanted to get more athletic, play a more uptempo game that would interest the fans. We also agreed that athleticism would help us in the postseason, because we needed a player to be able to create a shot as the twenty-four-second clock was ticking down.

That's when J. R. Rider's name was first mentioned.

When Pete Babcock said Portland was offering him around, I remember swallowing hard at the very mention of his name. I didn't know about all of his "problems," I just knew he had a lot of "problems." I am not afraid of a "problem player." As I mentioned before, Willis and Augmon supposedly had "problems" before I arrived in Atlanta, and they were great with me. You just had to communicate with them, gain their respect.

But I knew that Rider was a different story. I knew he had been suspended a couple of times in his career, and that he was late—a lot.

"He's a great offensive talent," said Kasten. "The kind of player we don't have."

This was very true. Rider was a career 18-point scorer. A bullish six-foot-five, 220-pound guard, he could score a lot from the low post, taking opposing guards near the basket, catching a pass, and simply jumping over them or bolting around them to score. He also was a decent outside shooter; his career mark of 36 percent from

3-point range was very acceptable. The coach in me saw that I could take a raw talent such as Rider and really develop his game.

But did Rider want to be coached?

And why was Portland so anxious to get rid of him?

He was twenty-eight years old and had been in the league for six years, so he was no longer a kid. He would be coming to Atlanta already having five suspensions and three arrests on his record. Could he change?

Other coaches had told me that Rider could destroy the morale of a team. He had been suspended for two games for marijuana possession, suspended for three games for spitting on a fan, suspended for a game for missing a practice, benched several times for being late, and fined continually. He also accused some people in Portland of "being racist" when he was booed while playing poorly at home. These were just some of his "problems" in his last two years with Portland. There were others, and I wasn't even aware of all of these when we discussed the trade.

Not that it would have mattered much. Our front office wanted to make the move. They wanted to shake things up, create interest in the team, and, they hoped, create a more exciting image for the Hawks as we prepared to move into the new building.

"Rider is on the last year of his contract," said Babcock. "With free agency coming, it's in his best interest to behave and play the best he can—if for no other reason than it would be worth a lot of money to him."

"This could be a very big risk," I said.

When I heard that Steve Smith was to be in the deal, my heart just sank. Steve usually was the first one at practice, the last to leave. He could be very emotional, but all you had to do was take him out of the game, rest him for a moment, and he'd calm down and be ready to go. He had a tremendous burning desire to win.

"We're worried about Steve's contract and his knees," said Babcock. "He's thirty years old. We worry that his body will begin to break down."

There was some reason for concern, because Steve did have knee troubles for much of his career. He missed a few games every year because of his knees. As for the concern about his contract, I was somewhat amused by that: Who gave him the contract in the first place? The Hawks did. Now they thought the contract was too expensive. The Hawks aren't the only team to do this, you hear it a lot: A team gives a player a contract, then complains that the guy is being "overpaid." Well, they're the ones who decided to pay him that much.

Anyway, there was an economic argument to be made for the trade: Smith made almost twice as much as Rider. Smith would be signed for several more years, his salary increasing. Rider was to be a free agent at the end of the year.

"If the trade doesn't work out, we can just say goodbye to Rider and then use his money on our salary cap to sign a free agent," explained Babock.

In theory, all of this was true.

But if Rider blew up—and there was a good chance of that happening—we were trading Smith for a free agent to be signed later, whomever that would be. And what were the odds of that free agent being the same caliber player as Smith?

"This is still a big risk," I repeated. "A huge risk."

I was told Rider was the most talented player available. I was told we also could get Jimmy Jackson in the deal, and Jackson was a solid pro, a 15-point scorer who could play small forward and shooting guard.

"Rider is not a stupid guy," I was told. "He'll see the light at the end of the tunnel, and he'll play well because it's in his own self-interest. He could be great for us."

I remember one coach telling me, "If you can ever hit the right switch with this guy, you'll have a helluva player. But believe me, he's a handful."

The deal was hanging in the air during the summer, because NBA rules dictated that it couldn't be announced until August 1. I had a lot of anxious moments thinking about it. I was uncomfortable breaking up our team, especially for Rider.

"Stan really wants to make the deal," Babcock told me more than once.

Stan was Stan Kasten, team president. He was Babcock's boss

and my boss. I reluctantly went along with the trade because I could tell it was going to happen anyway. So, we took the risk and made the trade, and in the end we all regretted it. The best thing for me to do was to start thinking how I could motivate Rider and make him a better player. After the trade was announced, we had trouble reaching Rider. He then told some writers that he wasn't happy with the trade, that he didn't think we had a very good team. He said he wanted to stay in Portland, despite all the "problems" he'd had the previous season. He seemed to have little knowledge of, and even less respect for, the Hawks. He acted as if we were 19–31 instead of 31–19.

Portland was 35–15 that strike season and went to the Western Conference Finals in Rider's last season there. He averaged a career-low 14 points and shot a career low 41 percent. The Blazers were weary of all his off-the-court troubles. Would he show up, or not? To them, the deal for Smith was a steal. They saw Smith as a scorer of the same caliber as Rider, only Smith was a magnificent human being, a leader in the dressing room. Rider was still a kid continually testing the boundaries of authority, driving his coaches and team-mates to distraction in the process.

Rider eventually made his first visit to Atlanta, and we had an excellent meeting.

"J.R., this is a great opportunity for you," I said. "It's a time for you to establish yourself with a new team in a new city. I don't care what you did before, I'm just going to judge you on how you do starting today."

Rider said he appreciated that.

"You can be an integral part of this team," I said. "We need a scorer, a player of your talent. You can lead us. This can be the turning point of your career."

He seemed receptive to that.

"Now, everyone is accountable," I said. "We have team rules. We expect everyone to be on time, and to follow the rules. The rules apply to everyone."

"I'm anxious to get going," he said. "Maybe this will be a good thing for me."

He seemed to really mean it. He was upbeat. He listened,

looked me in the eye. After the meeting, I thought, "He's reasonably intelligent, he pays attention. He generally agreed with what I had to say—hey, maybe this will work."

Then training camp came, and he wasn't there.

He said he had problems getting a flight from his home on the West Coast to Atlanta. And when he finally did get to Atlanta, he said he wouldn't get on a small plane to Chattanooga, Tennessee, which was where we held our training camp. He said, "I ain't gettin' on no cropduster."

So there were warning signs even before his first practice. When he finally did get to camp, I went to his room.

"J.R., let's lay the cards on the table," I said. "Let's understand what this is all about. This can be a *great* situation for you. It can be good for us, too, but great for you. You're a free agent at the end of the year. There is a lot of money on the line. All you have to do is play well and you can pick where you want to play next year. You can control your own destiny."

He said he understood that. Again, he listened, he looked me in the eye.

"The important thing is that you're finally here," I said. "Let's focus on basketball. Let's get off to a good start."

"You're right," he said. "There were some things on my mind, but I'm OK now. I'm ready to get going."

Rider was not in good shape when he came to camp, but he really did work hard. I was impressed with how he caught on to what we were trying to do on offense and defense. He had a good understanding of how the game should be played. Initially, I was pleased with him. But I was concerned about our team. We had not only traded Steve Smith, we also dealt Mookie Blaylock to Golden State for Bimbo Coles and a number-one pick, which turned out to be rookie Jason Terry. Suddenly, my starting backcourt was gone, and I had to work Rider and Coles into our team concept, along with having Terry become acclimated to the NBA. Since we didn't re-sign veteran forwards Tyrone Corbin and Grant Long, we were without four of our top seven scorers from the year before. The reason we passed on Long and Corbin was the front office wanted our team to get younger, to create more time for rookies and other kids to play. At the end of most exhibition seasons, I usually have a pretty good idea of what kind of team we'd put on the court, how I could use certain players, and how things would fit in. By the end of the first 15 regular-season games, I usually have a real handle on things.

That never happened with the 1999–2000 Hawks.

We started by losing, and I've never had a team make that many turnovers, or at least what coaches call unforced turnovers. That means passes to nowhere, a guy dribbling the ball off his foot, just careless, silly mistakes. Rider wasn't happy, and he began to try to win games himself. He'd get the ball on offense, and it would just stop. By that I mean he'd catch a pass, then hold the ball, trying to figure out how to beat his defender one-on-one. He often could do that, but it cut the heart out of our offense. The key to any offense is movement, players moving and the ball moving. But when your teammate is a guy who just catches and ball and holds it, trying to set up his own shot, it kills your morale, your motivation for trying to move and get open. When a guy gets the ball and holds it, the result is either a shot or a turnover.

More than once I tried to explain this to Rider. I showed him on video how he was stopping our offense, destroying the flow. I said I understood he could get a shot any time he wanted, but it wasn't always a good shot. And he could get better, easier shots, in the flow of our offense.

J.R. answered that he didn't know if the players were good enough to pass him the ball when he needed it. Nor did he think they were good enough to make shots. Basically, he believed he was the best player on the team, and his forcing shots still gave us the best chance to win. We talked about this often, and his opinion never changed. He just didn't respect or trust his teammates, and they sensed it.

When we had a team with Smith, Blaylock, Corbin, Long, Henderson, Mutombo, and Ellis—those guys trusted each other. They passed the ball. They believed in the system. They helped each other on offense and defense.

But four of those players were gone. That bond was broken and we never could get it back. When a team is losing and the best player appears to be selfish, then the other players fall into the same bad habits. They may not always be forcing shots just to get their own points; they may think it's up to them to make something happen, to help turn the season around. But the result is the same, the team is fractured. As a coach, you talk ball movement. You talk unselfishness. You talk about spacing on the floor, so the players aren't standing next to each other. You talk about giving everyone room to operate. You talk about covering up for each other on defense. You walk through the concepts on the practice floor. You show it to them over and over with video. You teach and you teach and you teach. But if your best player doesn't see it, or just refuses to see it, and plays his own way—then it just won't happen.

That was the case with Rider.

Then he started showing up late for practices and games. Sometimes it was five minutes, ten minutes, three minutes. I'd fine him. I'd tell him that it was a sign of disrespect to be late, both to his coaches and his teammates. He'd say he'd try to do better, and for a week or two, he'd be on time. Then, he'd be late again.

I told Pete Babcock, "This is it, we have to suspend him. What's going on is not good for the team. It's going to affect my credibility as a coach. Every team I've coached, the players know that I don't stand for stuff like this. We can't have it."

Babcock agreed, called Rider in, and suspended him for two games. That made him angry. His attitude was, "Hey, I pay the fines for being late, what's the big deal? I mean, you can't really suspend me for being ten minutes late?"

When Rider calmed down, I met with him a few days later. I said, "What are you trying to accomplish? Do you want to be a great player? Here is a real chance for you. I'm not just saying this to blow smoke up your butt and get you back on the court, I mean it. My job is to coach whether you're on the team or not. But you're in a situation where you can turn things around. Look, if you don't like me or don't like it here, you can get out at the end of the season. But only if you play well will this work. Any shooting guard can flourish in my system. Look at how well Steve Smith played, how much he scored. I'm smart enough to understand the game and take advantage of your talent."

"Coach," he said, "I'm going to try this. I can do it. I really want to. I just get so emotional . . ."

"If things are bothering you, you need to talk to someone," I said. "You can't just hold it in. Come talk to me. I'm a good listener. Whatever you say will be between you and me, and I mean that."

He said he'd come talk.

"J.R.," I said, "this is not about who is the best player. It's about being on time, being here every day, not just showing up for the games. Everybody has to be accountable. I told you that from the first day."

He said he understood.

But he never did, never saw how his actions affected his team-mates. His thinking was, "I play hard when the games come, that's all I need to do."

J.R. is like some players of his generation. They really have trouble connecting themselves to something other than what they think is in their own best interest. Many of them have been "free agents" dating back to high school, when they were recruited to play not just by colleges but by other high-school coaches and sum-mer-league coaches. Some of these kids are recruited each year by different summer-league teams, and this starts as early as when they're twelve years old. They also are surrounded by hangers-on who tell them how great they are, and how they really don't need to listen to the coach, that they're above the rules. I'm not a counselor, but I really tried to work with J.R. I learned that his family meant something to him. I saw his moods, his insecurities, and heard about his broken home in Oakland. He was a great athlete, but was ineli-gible to play basketball in his senior year of high school because of grade problems, according to a *Sports Illustrated* story. He didn't graduate, but he later earned his GED while at Allen Community College in Kansas. After a year at Allen, he transferred to Antelope Valley College. Then he spent the next two years at Nevada–Las Vegas. That makes three colleges in four years. The Hawks were his third pro team in seven years. In a sense, Rider probably felt like a hired gun, a player brought in to score, knowing that he probably won't stick around for long. Minnesota Timberwolves general manager Kevin McHale dealt with Rider in his early NBA years;

McHale told *Sports Illustrated:* "It got to a point where every couple of weeks, it was another incident. We just couldn't depend on him. It's like having a friend who's always late to pick you up. You still want him to be a friend, but after a while, you stop asking him for a ride."

That exactly how it was with us.

I had conversation after conversation with him. I explained the reasons why we did the things we did on offense and defense, and how it would only work if he would try to fit into the system.

"Great players make their teammates better," I'd say. "Like when you're double-teamed, make the quick pass to the open guy. Don't just hold the ball. You don't always have to make a great pass."

Sometimes, Rider sort of agreed.

Other times, he said, "These guys aren't giving me enough space to operate." He wanted us to just clear out a side of the floor, give him the ball, and watch him shoot. I explained that wasn't a good way for any team to play. He said it was our only chance to win, because he was the only player we had who could really score.

One game, he did nothing but pass the ball—as if to prove his point that he was the key to the offense. I mean, he hardly shot at all. He passed up wide-open shots. It was ridiculous. The next game, he was back to shooting whenever he could.

Meanwhile, he was late and late and late some more.

And we fined him and fined him and fined him some more.

"J.R., aren't you tired of paying all this money?" I asked. "Wouldn't you rather just keep it for yourself, or give it to your family or charity?"

Most of the time, he'd just shrug when I mentioned that he had been fined something like $200,000.

Other times, I'd remind him about his contract situation, how he was a free agent and other teams were watching how he acted this season.

Again, he sort of shrugged it off. He didn't seem very worried about it. He was making $4.5 million and just assumed there always will be another team to take him and pay him, regardless of his tardiness and other problems.

This tore our team apart. The other players resented Rider's selfishness, both on and off the court. We didn't have enough veteran players to bring pressure on him and to create the kind of order we had on the court in the past. The front office was just as frustrated with Rider as the rest of us, but nothing we did could reach Rider.

Toward the end of the season, there was a game we lost. Afterward, the rest of the team went into the dressing room, but J.R. just sat on the floor. After I talked to the team, I went out to meet the media. Then J.R. came in and went ballistic. He ripped the players, calling them a bunch of losers, cussing everyone out. We realized he was getting out of control.

Pete Babcock had a meeting with Rider and said we planned to suspended him for three games.

"You just want my money," Rider said, meaning the three-game suspension would cost him $180,000.

"It's not about money, it's about your behavior," Babcock said.

"No, you want my money," he said.

Babcock explained what Rider had done wrong, the lateness and other problems.

"You just want my money," he insisted.

"OK," said Babcock. "We'll give you a choice. You can take the suspension, or we'll put you on waivers and let you go."

Rider said, go ahead, cut him.

With 18 games left, the Hawks waived J. R. Rider. He was not picked up by another team, at least partly because we released him too late for him to be eligible for the playoffs with a new team. I was sad to see it end that way. I had tried everything. I listened to his problems. I gave him fatherly advice. I spoke to him like a coach. I gave him more latitude than any player I've ever coached, hoping my patience would pay off. I suspended him. I fined him. In his last few games, I even jerked him from the starting lineup. Nothing worked. I've never had a player of his talent whom I couldn't reach in some way. Part of me wishes that I'd had him as a rookie; maybe I could have shaped him. The other part says that he's had some good coaches, and no one seemed able to help him. I don't think he's an awful guy; he's just not interested in playing by anyone's rules but his own.

☐

This was my toughest year in the NBA. We finished with a 28–54 record, my worst record in twenty-seven seasons. I played a lot of our young guys, trying to develop the talent for the future once it became obvious we weren't going to make the playoffs.

Rumors about me leaving the Hawks started at the All-Star break. That made no sense, at least the part about me resigning, which appeared in the Atlanta newspaper and on some talk shows. I had two more years at $5 million annually on my contract; I was not about to resign and walk away from that money. I also wanted to coach the Hawks again next season, to start over with the young players I'd been working with. I had no indication that I was in any trouble with the front office until the final few weeks of the season. Yes, I had been hearing from some coaching friends and scouts that the Hawks were going to fire me, but nothing seemed different when I dealt with the front office.

With a couple of days left in the season, my agent, Lonnie Cooper, met with Stan Kasten. He came away with the impression that Stan wanted to change coaches. Stan was talking about doing something to spark interest in the new building, to bring in more fans after such a bad year. I was disappointed when I heard that from Lonnie, because a lot of the moves made by the front office were why we'd had such a long, dreadful season.

Before the last game of the season, I saw Pete Babcock. He was nervous, really fidgety. His color was pasty white. He just didn't look good. We went into my office, and Pete said, "I don't know what's going to happen, but I really enjoyed working with you . . ."

It sounded as if he was giving me a coaching eulogy, and that really bothered me. We still had a game to go, and he was giving me the kiss of death.

I told him that I had a pretty good idea what was going to happen, since Lonnie Cooper had met with Stan Kasten. Pete acted as if he didn't know anything about the meeting.

"Fine," I said. "As soon as the season is over, let's meet with Stan and get this resolved."

A few days later, we did.

I sat there with Lonnie Cooper. Stan had Pete with him.

I opened by saying, "Listen, I'm a grownup. Based on what you told Lonnie . . . I don't want to be in a place where I'm not wanted, OK? If you want to do something, then pay me to resign."

They immediately agreed to that, saying they'd honor the last two years of my contract. They asked me to attend the press conference announcing my resignation, but I thought they should handle it and I'd just issue a statement.

I watched the press conference on TV. I thought Stan did his part well. I was annoyed when Pete said, "People asked me if Lenny was tired or burned out, but that wasn't the case."

Why even say that? No one asked Pete, he just brought it up. Later, he said he was against the Rider deal, that Stan and I wanted to pull the trigger. That just wasn't true, and Pete knew it. That's why I went on ESPN to clear the record about all that, and let everyone know that I still intended to coach. I'm sixty-two, in great health, and I love the game. I'd like a chance to develop one more team, and I'm proud of what I did in Atlanta.

The Rider trade was a big gamble that blew up. The front office said it took responsibility for it. But what happened? Rider was cut, and I had to resign. They kept their jobs.

"When you're a coach, you become a lightning rod for what happens in an organization," Pete Babcock said at the press conference. "It doesn't mean it's fair or right, but it's the reality of the situation."

But should it be?

Why can't an established coach be given a chance to bounce back after a crazy season like that one? When mistakes are made, it's always easier to fire the coach—"even if it's not fair or right," to quote Pete Babcock. The coach can't fire the general manager. It's funny how basketball people always say, "A coach is only as good as his players." Then, when they fail to get the coach the right kind of players, they still fire him. Is that really the best way to run a team?

After leaving Atlanta, I still wanted to coach.

For a while, not much happened; I talked to a couple of teams, but it didn't seem to be a good fit. After what happened with the Hawks and Rider, I didn't want to coach just any team. I wanted a chance to win, and I wanted to coach in a city where my family would be comfortable.

I didn't even think about Toronto.

The Raptors had just won forty-five games and made the playoffs for the first time in their history. I wasn't aware of all the problems between Coach Butch Carter and the front office, so I was a bit surprised when Carter was let go—and delighted when Toronto called. At this point, I had just told Marilyn that I probably wouldn't be coaching in the 2000–2001 season. It would have been the first time since 1960 that I wouldn't be involved in an NBA training camp, at least in some capacity. I had done some TV work during the NBA playoffs for Fox, and they wanted me back for the season. I had enjoyed it more than I expected to, so I thought I'd start the season as a broadcaster and see if any good coaching opportunities came along—not just any coaching opportunity, but a good one.

I knew I wanted to coach again. Not for the money; I had $10 million left on my contract from the Hawks. And not for any sort of records; I already had won more games than any other coach in NBA history. I just like the coaching, even after all the heartache with J.R. Rider. I was going to turn sixty-three just before the start of the season, but I've never felt old—and being around young people energizes me.

Which brings me to Vince Carter.

When Toronto General Manager Glen Grunwald called, one of the first things that crossed my mind was the chance to coach Vince Carter. I'm not one to say he's the next Michael Jordan; I know how unfair it is to put that label on any player, because I saw up close the greatness of Michael as he kept shattering our dreams in the playoffs. There is only one Michael Jordan, just like there is only one Bill Russell, Oscar Robertson, Larry Bird, and Magic Johnson. These are the players who define their generations of NBA basketball.

But Vince Carter . . .

Vince Carter . . .

His name ran through my mind, and I thought of all the outstanding players I've coached: Dennis Johnson, Gus Williams, Mark Price, Ron Harper, Brad Daugherty, Jack Sikma, and Dominique

Wilkins. None of them had the pure basketball gifts and skills of Vince Carter. And making it better, Carter seemed like a good person the few times I'd talked to him.

A chance to coach Vince Carter . . .

Understand, there was more to the Toronto job that I liked. I was very impressed with the new arena and the enthusiasm of the fans when my Hawks played there. Toronto may be a hockey city, but a lot of people really care about basketball. And I liked the international flavor of the city, the friendliness of the people. Ownership seemed top-notch, and Glen Grunwald sounded like a man whom I'd want to be my general manager. Making it even better, when Kevin Willis heard I was a candidate for the job, he called and almost begged me to take it. He said the team had a lot of talent, and all they needed was a veteran coach to really become something special. I thought about a front court of Antonio Davis, Charles Oakley, and Willis. I knew all those players, and I had coached Willis in Atlanta. Three veteran big men who understood the game and would bring some real professionalism to their jobs: Who wouldn't want to coach them?

And there was Vince Carter . . .

He averaged nearly 26 points, 6 rebounds, and 4 assists. He shot 47 percent from the field, 79 percent at the free throw line.

In this era, he's a true superstar, especially because he is so athletically blessed. He is fluid, and the game comes naturally to him; he can run and jump and has a good sense of what's happening on the floor. And he's only twenty-three; this would be just his third pro season.

A chance to work with a young player like that . . .

It's more than just an upgrade from J.R. Rider, it's a coach's dream. You take a player like Carter, surround him with a bunch of hard-working veterans who can set the tone in practice and games, and any coach has a chance to succeed—especially a coach such as myself who has been in the league for a while.

After the initial phone call just to see if the job appealed to me, Glen Grunwald came to Seattle for a more extensive conversation. The more we talked, the more excited I became. Then I went to Toronto, met with the team owners, and I realized that I was being handed a unique opportunity, that Toronto was a wonderful job in a great city. The Raptors clearly wanted me to coach, and they proved it by offering a five-year contract. They didn't dwell on my last year in Atlanta; they understood that a lot of things happened that were out of my control. Rather, they considered my forty years in the NBA, and they thought I could bring stability and experience to a team that is just starting to learn how to win.

At the press conference announcing my hiring, Grunwald said, "Lenny has been dealing with twenty-year-olds for twenty-seven years now as coach. Times have changed a bit. The language changes a little, but as long as you bring in players who have good character and work ethics, they will respond to the professionalism and respect that Lenny talked about. . . . For the job, we had two lists—Lenny Wilkens and all the other candidates. In my wildest dreams, I wouldn't have thought we could get a coach of Lenny's qualities and character. Sometimes, the obvious choice is the right choice."

I appreciated that. It showed the front office really wanted me, which is critical for a coach. And the long-term contract demonstrated a commitment to me. Glen's comments also told me the front office understands that a coach can't fix everything, that character is important. That's part of why I really liked working for Wayne Embry in Cleveland: He made a point of bringing in good people for me to coach, not just taking a guy because he has talent. You win with players who have character *and* talent.

Players like Vince Carter.

In the *Toronto Star*, Chris Young wrote, "Have the Raptors turned the corner? It sure looks that way. In any NBA city, the coming of Lenny Wilkens would be special. . . . In this city, under these circumstances, it's nothing more than extraordinary . . . just the mention of his name connotes respect and rehabilitation and a life spent in basketball."

That was the typical media response to my hiring, and I was really excited by that. I felt the same way about the endorsements I got from players such as Oakley, Willis, Carter, and Dell Curry. I wanted to go straight from that press conference to training camp.

I love the competition. I love close games. I love being in the huddle in the final seconds, needing to draw up a play so that we can score the winning basket. I'm a guy who wakes up and says, "Good morning, God!"—not, "Good God, it's morning." I'm an optimistic person by nature. One of my best attributes is that I'm consistent; I don't say one thing and then do something else. I believe respect is a two-way street, and if you want it, you have to give it. I look at Toronto, and I'm energized. It's an organization that cares about the little things. I'll always appreciate how they sent Marilyn flowers after I was hired. I like how they went out and signed Mark Jackson, another solid veteran, to be our point guard. As a coach, that tells you the front office wants to win as much as you do. And after forty years in the NBA, believe me, I still want to win.

CHAPTER TWENTY

T HEY USED TO DO THESE SEGMENTS called "Red On Roundball" on NBA telecasts, in which legendary Boston Celtics coach Red Auerbach would explain some of the fine points of the game on TV. Red Auerbach didn't just coach the Boston Celtics, it seemed as if he invented professional basketball. He puffed gloriously on that victory cigar. He coached great teams and did nothing but win championships.

As for me, I had dreams while I was in high school and college, but none of them were about playing pro basketball. They certainly weren't about being the first NBA coach to win more games than Red Auerbach, the first NBA coach to win 1,000 games, or to coach more NBA games than anyone else. It would have been enough to imagine a black man coaching a professional team at all, if the thought had ever occurred to me.

Red Auerbach was like a basketball god when I played at Providence College. He went on to win 938 games and nine titles in twenty years of coaching. To pro coaches, the Number 938 was magic, untouchable. I never even thought about reaching that total. I remember what I went through just to win 500 games, 600 games, then 700 games. That 700th game came in Minnesota while I was coaching the Cavs. We were on a four-game losing streak, and Minnesota was an expansion team, really struggling. They must have had four good shots at the basket in the final thirty seconds, and two of those shots went in and out. We were hanging on to an 85–84 lead, and I can still see the ball bouncing all over the rim, before

Larry Nance soared and came down with the rebound as the buzzer blared. Winning that 700th game was agony. It seemed to take weeks to happen. When it was over, someone asked me about Red Auerbach's record. I smiled and didn't say much, but inside I was thinking, "If all the rest of the games are like the last two weeks, they'll bury me before I get to 750."

But it was around this point—somewhere in the early 1990s—that I began to be asked about beating Red's record, about scaling that seemingly insurmountable mountain of 938 victories. The more I heard about it, the more I wanted it. He was the Godfather of NBA coaching because of his use of scouting, strategy, and other innovations. Red was consistently ahead of the curve. Even the coaches who hated him—and there were more than a few—admired his accomplishments. Yes, all of us would have loved to coach Bill Russell. As much as any man, Bill Russell changed the course of pro basketball with his defense, shot-blocking ability, mental toughness, and intelligence. He just shut down the middle. He allowed his teammates to take off on the fast break because they knew Russell would get the rebound, then throw an outlet pass. Russell's general lack of offense was partly a product of his willingness not to focus on scoring, and it was more of an asset than a problem for the Celtics, who had more than enough guys capable of putting the ball in the basket. It meant more shots for Sam Jones, Tom Heinsohn, Bob Cousy, Bill Sharman, K.C. Jones, Frank Ramsey, and John Havlicek and all their other great players. And the Celtics had great, great players. One of their teams had six Hall of Famers.

That's why I wanted the record, why it was so special to me.

Yes, I coached longer than Red Auerbach to win those 938 games, but I didn't have anywhere near the players that Red had. I say this not to compare myself with Red. That's impossible. We come from two different eras, coaching much different teams in totally different circumstances. For example, much of the time when Red coached the Celtics, there were only eight teams in the NBA. That meant you could win a title and still have the number-eight and number-sixteen and number-twenty-four pick in the drafts—all three would be considered first-rounders today. Now, the NBA champion won't draft until the twenty-ninth pick because there are twenty-nine teams. That's a huge difference.

Auerbach was way ahead of most NBA teams in terms of scouting. He did more of it himself and had more contacts than most coaches in the 1950s and 1960s, so he was more likely to make shrewd draft picks. Today, you can have the best scouting in the world, but if you don't draft until the number-twenty-ninth pick year after year, you just aren't going to get many good players. If you draft number-eight every year—as the Celtics often did in the Russell Era—you'll still find some excellent players. But give Red credit for drafting the right players, then convincing them to fit into the Celtics and play unselfishly. Red had a way of coaxing the most out of his players, especially from veterans he'd sign when they were at the end of their careers. Everyone in the NBA would say that a guy was finished, and suddenly Red would bring him to Boston, and players such as Clyde Lovellette, Wayne Embry, or Gene Conley would play an important role off the bench.

That's why I wanted the record as I got closer and closer to it. There was no coach whom I admired more than Red Auerbach, no coach whose name I'd rather be associated with than Red Auerbach. I was amazed that I had been able to survive the NBA storm to win as many games as Red, especially since I never had a player the caliber of Russell or some of his other stars.

I want you to take this the right way, to understand it is not meant as a putdown of anyone. But guess who played the most games for Red Auerbach?

Bob Cousy.

And who played the most games for me?

Craig Ehlo.

That's why it's impossible to compare Red and myself. We coached different teams in different eras with an entirely different caliber of players. The fact is that Red had far more athletes like Cousy on his roster, while more of my players were like Ehlo— hard-working role players. It's also why I was upset when one columnist wrote that my winning more games than Auerbach was simply nothing more than a matter of longevity, that I was able to stand on the sidelines for a long time without offending anyone.

That my teams were seldom bad, but seldom great; they were just OK. Of course, my wife and friends were outraged when they heard that from more than one place. Marilyn told one reporter, "My husband doesn't get the credit he deserves because he's not a self-promoter. He's not a tyrant. He's not a big windbag. He doesn't kick chairs and run all over the court. Those guys get all the publicity."

There is a lot of truth to that.

A lot of people don't understand the nature of coaching in the NBA. The measure of any coach is not his final victory total; it's how his players performed compared to their talent. Did the team improve from the year before? Did the players improve? Was the team healthy or crushed by injuries? There are so many factors.

The reason Red remains a legendary coach is that yes, he had great players, but they also attained greatness playing together. They did it year after year after year. He won titles in each of his last eight seasons, an amazing accomplishment no matter how star-studded the roster. Red had those guys ready to play in big games. He fought off complacency. This was before free agency and big contracts, so players were married to their original teams and usually on one-year deals, making it easier to keep a team together and playing hard. But give Red credit for motivating his players and keeping them striving for excellence as well as any coach has ever done. But it also must be said that Red's career looked much like mine before Bill Russell came to the Celtics in 1956–57. For the first ten years of his coaching career, Red was with three different teams. He won two division titles, but never an NBA championship. Did that make him a lousy coach? Not at all. Red was still a great coach. He got the most out of the talent he had, won a lot of games, but the talent wasn't championship caliber. He didn't have a Bill Russell. Only once in those ten years without Russell did Red even lead a team to the NBA Finals—and he lost.

It's remarkable to look at Red's career and realize what it says about coaching: In his first ten years without Russell, he won no titles. In his next ten years with Russell, he won nine titles.

Great players make great coaches. Of course, lousy coaches can mess up great players, something that many people in the media don't realize. That's why I thought K.C. Jones never received his due when he coached the Larry Bird Celtics. Yes, he had Bird, Kevin McHale, Dennis Johnson, and Robert Parish. But he also had to keep them interested, keep them together. But K.C.'s personality is much like mine—unassuming. We give credit to our players, because we're former players and realize the real impact they have on the game. But it also must be said that our players respect us for that approach, for not hogging the headlines or trying to set ourselves up as geniuses. I've had a lot of good players in my career, and that's why I've won as many games as I have. But to last as many years as I have in the NBA and to win as many games as I have without any players named Russell, Bird, Magic, Jordan, Chamberlain, or Abdul-Jabbar is something that makes me very proud.

My career has been much different from Red's because I coached with five different teams (including Seattle twice). None of them were in major media markets, none of them had what you'd call "franchise players." I'm proud of the fact that when I came to new jobs in Cleveland, Atlanta, and Seattle (both times), my teams either set or tied franchise records for the most victories in a season. That's an indication that the team improved while I was there, which is the real job of any coach.

But our society is tilting more and more each year to a "champion or nothing" mentality. The thinking is that if you don't win a title, then you failed. That's ridiculous. In any given NBA season, only three or four teams are capable of winning a title. Very few NBA people will admit it, but they know it in their hearts. The league has always been dominated by superstars, starting with the George Mikan Era in Minnesota back in the early 1950s. There are only brief windows of opportunity for a team to win a championship without a truly great player. That happened for us in Seattle in 1979, the year before Magic and Bird came into the league; when they did, the power centers became Los Angeles and Boston, and the rest of us were not going to beat them, period. But a lot of teams that don't win a title play entertaining basketball. They are worthy of their fans' attention. Talk to the Cavs fans during our best years of the late 1980s and early 1990s, and they'll still tell you how much they enjoyed those teams, and how they wished they could see Larry Nance, Brad Daugherty, John Williams, Mark Price, Ron

Harper, and Craig Ehlo play one more time. Sure, it was frustrating not to be able to get past Michael Jordan, but that didn't make us failures. Smart fans and media members understand that, even though I've won only one NBA title. I don't think the teams I've coached were good enough to win any more than that one title, and a lot of those teams played far better than most people expected.

Passing a legend is never easy.

I tied Red's record on December 29, 1994, when my Atlanta Hawks beat San Antonio, 127–121. One more victory, that's all we needed.

The next night we played in Cleveland, where it would have been nice to set the record. This was my second year in Atlanta, and the Cavs had been my team for seven years. The Hawks management packed several caps with the number 939 to bring with us, along with a victory cake.

We lost by two points.

The next night, we played at home against Portland. The caps and cake came with us from Cleveland back to Atlanta.

And we lost again.

Then we went to New York, as did the caps and the cake. So much for the third time being a charm.

We lost yet again.

On the flight home, we all just ate the cake before it turned stale.

I knew what was happening. The players were feeling the pressure. It's not like they knew me that well—it was only my second year with the Hawks—but they wanted to win the game, to get the record out of the way. They were tired of being asked about me, about what the record meant, about Red Auerbach. To them, the record meant nothing. They hadn't been with me for those twenty-two years of coaching. To them, Red Auerbach was just a faint name out of basketball's distant past. He quit coaching before most of my players were born. To them, this was just a distraction. And I wanted just to get our team past all this.

Finally, on January 6, 1995, we beat Washington, 112–90, at the Omni in Atlanta. With thirty seconds in the game, I lit up a victory cigar in honor of Red Auerbach. I don't smoke, and I nearly choked to death. But I wanted to pay tribute to Red in some way, and the cigar came to mind. On that night, with the fans standing and cheering and the balloons falling from the ceiling, I remember first the feeling of relief—I was glad it was over. Now we could get back to playing regular games. And then, this enormous sense of satisfaction: No matter what anyone could say, I had become the winningest coach in NBA history, and had done it against enormous odds. There were strange questions running through my mind that night. One was, "What would my father think if he were alive?" Another was, "How does a kid who never even dreamed of playing in the NBA end up as the league's winningest coach?" The only answer I could come up with was that God had a hand on my shoulder, that he was leading me through this life, sending people to help and support me, like Marilyn and Father Mannion. I also remembered something Father Mannion said to me when I was praying for something and it seemed God wasn't listening. He told me, "What makes you think it's going to be easy? God's busy. You think you're the only one he has to worry about?" It was not only a great line, but a great lesson in patience. God has always been there, and He's always gotten to me right in time—His time.

To me, the record was about perseverance.

I see many coaches who are burned out, who not only lose their players and their jobs, but lose their families.

Johnny Kerr once said that coaching nearly drove him insane, "Because I couldn't deal with there being five guys on the court running around with my paycheck." And that's true. You can't play the game for them. Sometimes, you know you've prepared them well, the practices were good, they paid attention in the film sessions—and they walk on the court and act as if they never heard a word. It's like they don't even remember where they're supposed to stand. But usually, if you have good people on your team and you do a good job in getting them ready for a game, they give you a solid effort. But there are nights . . . I mean, if you dwell on those games where your team just seemed to have one massive head cramp, you'll want to blow your own brains out. I refuse to do that. The blessing of having played in the NBA as long as I did is that I understand there are some nights when the guys just aren't with it. Red Auerbach himself could come back and coach, it wouldn't matter. The team just hits a stretch in the schedule where everyone is tired, both mentally and physically, and all you can do is hope the other team is as fatigued as you are, and maybe you can slow down the game and win it ugly.

In the NBA, some things are out of my control as a coach. I never forget that. Every coach will agree, but a lot don't believe it. They think they can put their fingers on everything, that they can dictate what happens on the court. They're so consumed with their teams, their personality and sense of self-worth is tied up in how their team practiced that day. If the team has a lousy workout, some coaches start to doubt themselves. Again, they'd never admit it, but I know how coaches think, how tempting it is to make your team the center of your universe—your entire universe. I've never done that. I'm a sore loser, but I refuse to take it out on my family. I hate it when my players are injured, but I don't blame the player. He didn't want to get hurt. But I know some coaches who barely speak to injured players, acting as if the player intentionally got hurt just to mess up his team.

I never forget that the NBA is a business. If my team doesn't play well, I am accountable. There is a possibility that I could be fired. But I don't spend every minute thinking about that, or looking over my shoulder and wondering what the front office is saying about me. It's easy for a coach to become paranoid, but the fact is that if they are going to fire you, they'll fire you. It doesn't matter if you worry or act paranoid, or if you just do your job. In fact, if you're paranoid about being fired, you probably will get fired, because you won't be doing your job the right way. You'll be distracted, uncertain, hesitant to make the moves you should. The players will immediately sense this, and you'll lose them. They'll say, "If this guy doesn't believe in what he's doing, why should we?" In the modern NBA, every coach has a good contract, most making well over $1 million a year, and nearly every coach has a multiyear contract. So if they fire you, they still have to pay you—and probably have to pay you several million dollars. That means your family will be taken care of, regardless of what happens. That should give a coach the confidence to make the moves he thinks best and not worry about pleasing everyone all the time. But some coaches start to think, "Man, this is a great job. I'm making more money than I ever dreamed. I can't mess this up." Then they become timid and defensive. They're coaching just to protect themselves and to keep their jobs instead of coaching boldly, doing what they know in their hearts is best for the team—even if it means some people will second-guess them.

I also know that not everyone will like me, or my approach to coaching. I do admit that I get tired of being called "laid-back . . . a players' coach," and it being a negative, as if I don't have enough fire to motivate my team. But Larry Bird is even more "laid-back" than I am, and he was considered an excellent coach. Or how about John Wooden? How emotional was he when he was winning all those national titles at UCLA? Even Phil Jackson is not a screamer, and he's considered a genius. Show me the difference between the way those men coached their teams and the way I coach. Sometimes I ask myself, is there something hidden here? Is it a black/white thing? Is it that I'm not a motormouth when some media members first interview me? I wish some people in the media wouldn't approach me with preconceived notions, because perception isn't always reality. To me, being a real "players' coach" is a compliment, because it means you understand the players, can relate to them and communicate with them. It also helps to have been a good player in the league. When Larry Bird first spoke to the Indiana Pacers, he had instant respect. The players knew who he was, and knew of the championships he helped Boston win. I think I receive that same kind of respect from the players, because they know I've been through the same things they're experiencing now.

You can't yell at players all the time. Any boss who constantly yells turns off the people who work for him. They just stop listening. But I'm amused when people say I never yell. I can show you pictures of me screaming at officials, or getting on my players. The key is to pick your spots. I get tired of reading that I'm "stoic," that all I do is "stand there, arms folded across my chest." Sure, there are times in the game when I stand there, arms folded, and just watch the game. It makes no sense to bellow at the officials every minute—they'll just tune you out. But if you only go to them when you have a legitimate complaint, they'll listen. Hey, officials are human. I believe I get better treatment for my team by not attacking them all the time, because when I do question them, I know they say to themselves, "Maybe we should see if Lenny has a point." Officials have told me exactly that. So have players. When I rip into them, they know there's a reason behind it; I'm not doing it just to make a lot of noise and vent frustration.

Here is something else that's always in the back of my mind: I know that if I'm fired, my family will still love me. God will still be there for me. As a person, nothing has changed. The Lord will not judge me based on what kind of record I had with a certain team, or if I was ever fired. I know that God has always been with me. I don't scream about my faith, but my faith is strong. It is central to who I am.

So is my marriage.

To me, the vows of marriage are sacred. When you promised to love and obey for better or worse, that meant something. Those weren't just words to be uttered, then forgotten. We not only made those promises to each other, we made them to God. That meant we had to work at our marriage. Marilyn brought a rule into our house that we never go to bed angry at each other. And guess what? In any marriage, there are times when you'll disagree, when you can't help but argue. But that's no reason to blow up a marriage. Marilyn's idea that we immediately talk out a problem was tough for me, especially at first. I always like to keep things inside. But Marilyn believes if you suppress things for too long, you let them stew inside you—and everything gets worse. But I admit, I had to learn to talk things out. At times, I had to force myself to do it, but it has worked for our marriage. We always remind each other that we love each other before we go to bed, no matter what happened that day.

I respect my wife for the kind of person she is, and how she takes care of our home. I'm always proud to bring people to our house because they can see that the people who live there care about each other. When our kids were little, they were well-behaved when company was around. Marilyn has learned how to handle herself with all kinds of people. She has matured from the quiet young woman who hated to talk to a stranger into a woman who will very quickly let you know what is on her mind. She said she had to learn to be more outgoing, to speak up to anyone, because I was gone so much with basketball. She is the one who often had to deal with the repairmen, with our kids' teachers, with all the duties that come with taking care of a house. She doesn't agree with everything I say, and believe me, she'll tell me about it. But I love that, I really do. Because I know that she loves and respects me. She supports my career. She is a great mother to our kids. So if she disagrees with something I want to do, it's because she has the best interests of our family at heart. And then we talk it out. It's great to have a wife who has her own mind, because I don't have to be over-protective of her. Anyone who has ever met Marilyn knows she can take care of herself.

My family has been supportive of everything I've done. Everything. They've backed me. The fact that God is in our house has helped us to raise our children, especially because I'm in the public eye. My wife has often had to run our family because I'm on the road with basketball. But Marilyn really understands me and what my family needs from me. She knows that I grew up on the streets, that part of me is tough and macho, even though I don't talk like it. She'll come up to me and say, "You need to hug your son." Just like that, "You need to hug your son." I'd go and hug young Randy, and I could tell that she was right, not only did my son need a hug, I needed to hug him. She knew that my family wasn't very emotional, there wasn't much hugging. She brought that into our house, and it's made me a better person, a better father. Marilyn made me notice that when our daughter Leesha was little she would watch me very intently when I came home from a road trip. So I learned to make it a point to go right to Leesha, pick her up, and tell her how much I love her and how special she is to me. Our daughter Jamee would be the first to greet me when I got home from a road trip. She'd say things like, "Dad was away, playing with his friends, now he's home." At least that was the scouting report about me being an NBA coach when she was three years old.

Making everything more difficult for Marilyn is that I'm a

sports celebrity. We'll be out in public, and people will want to talk to me, to get an autograph—and they'll act as if Marilyn isn't even there. I've seen fans just push her right out of the way. I've learned that I have to look out for Marilyn first, to make sure that she's right there with me, that everyone knows she's my wife and she's important. The wives all hear stories about the temptations on the road, but if you have a solid marriage, you don't put yourself in those situations. You call home—a lot. I have friends in virtually every major city in America, and I get together with them for dinner out, or I go to their homes for a visit. Friends watch out for each other and their families.

I look at our three children and I can see how blessed I was to have Marilyn for a wife. I know that God's hand was on me when she came into my life, because she not only has been such a terrific wife, but she's a super mother.

Early in our marriage, Marilyn worked in the accounting department of the telephone company. When she became pregnant with our first child, we talked about her getting a sitter and going back to work. But then I thought about it and said, "Hey, I'd rather have you at home with the baby. There are so many crazy things going on in the world." Marilyn gave up a career to be a full-time mother for our children, which is the most important thing she could have done. Children need parents around, especially at an early age. I look at my daughter Leesha, who decided to stop working—she was in charge of a doctor's office for several years—when she had her daughter, Ashley. She had long talks with Marilyn before the decision was made, and she decided to stay home just as Marilyn did with our children.

When Leesha was little, she never enjoyed my being in the public eye. She was very proud of me, but she didn't want to be known as the daughter of a celebrity. She wanted to have her own identity, and I can understand that. It's tough on the children of celebrities, and it's really not surprising that some of them get in trouble. Dad is away a lot, and when he's home, he's often too preoccupied to really pay attention to them. Some people befriend the children just because they want to get close to the celebrity dad. The children grow up in an affluent home, and people sometimes treat them differently because of their fathers. The kids often feel under extra pressure, especially if they try to be athletes.

My son, Randy, attended a private high school in Seattle. He went out for basketball and made the team, but the coach wouldn't start him. I was sure Randy was good enough to start. So were a couple of area high-school coaches. Naturally, Marilyn was livid about the coach not starting Randy. I sensed the coach didn't play him that much because Randy was my son and he wanted to show that he wouldn't be intimidated by that. It had to be very frustrating for Randy.

But that's when I really began to realize Randy was an outstanding young man. I offered to help him transfer to another school. A local coach virtually guaranteed Randy would start for him, but Randy said, "No, I want to stay here."

He stuck it out. He played on the soccer team and had a wonderful career. He got excellent grades, and I now realize how sticking it out at that school helped him grow as a person. He attended Santa Clara, where the basketball coach wanted him to walk-on to the team. Randy said it was more fun just to play basketball in the dorm league, which was probably true. None of us can fully appreciate what it must be like to be a young player and have to deal with the pressure of being the son of a basketball star. In college, Randy just concentrated on his studies and went on to earn a master's degree in psychology. He also is great with computers and now works in that field.

Our third child, Jamee, attended UCLA, where she majored in art history. After graduating, she returned to Seattle and attended the Seattle Art Institute and earned a degree in computer graphics and animation. She is a bright, determined young woman who works in computer graphics for Boeing.

If there is one key to parenting, it's knowing who the friends of your children are. We always wanted our children to bring their friends to our home, to have them stay overnight, stay for the weekend. I still know all of Randy's best friends, because they'd come over on Friday night, and then I'd cook them breakfast on Saturday morning. Pancakes, french toast, bacon, sausage. Then we'd sit around and talk about everything: sports, politics, school, you name it. If you're able to make kids feel comfortable and show that you're really interested in what they have to say, they will open up to you. But I also had a rule: After that breakfast, I assigned all of the kids a chore before they could go play. One swept the driveway. Another cleaned the dog pen. Someone might rake leaves or help me clean up the kitchen. I'd find things for them to do. I just thought that having them get a little taste of work was good.

One time, Leesha brought a boy to our house. I was in the den, and I could see he was a little nervous when he was introduced. He had on a Sonics baseball cap. After we said hello, Leesha took him to the recreation room with some other friends to listen to music. I went to check on them, and I noticed the kid still had his cap on.

I said, "When you go into someone's house, it's only polite to take off your cap."

He sort of looked at me, but didn't touch his cap.

I said, "In my house, you *will* take your cap off."

He quickly took it off.

Of course, Leesha was mortified. I don't remember that kid coming over again. But most of our kids had wonderful friends. The man Leesha married is named Craig Lipp, and he works for United Parcel Service and has also started his own landscaping business. They have two children—Ashlee and Nicholle. Leesha will watch a game on TV where I'm coaching and tell her daughters, "Look, there's Grandpa on TV."

I admit, I get a kick out of hearing that.

I've spent so much time talking about my family because I'm proud of them. I'm proud of Marilyn, for being such a great wife and mother. I'm proud of all my children because they're just nice people, good people, respectful people. I really like being a grandpa. At the end of every season, I spend a week just with my family. I don't call anyone on the phone. I don't want to go anywhere. I just want to reconnect with them. When the kids were younger, we'd take a family trip right after the season—just us, no distractions. And right before training camp, we'd take another trip.

People want to know how I've survived this long in the NBA, and I point to my faith and my family. I love basketball and there is nothing I'd rather do than coach, but basketball or beating Red Auerbach's record isn't everything to me—and that's healthy.

When I was younger, I'd worry that I wouldn't live very long. Because my father died young and I was never sure exactly why he died, in the back of my mind it made me wonder if that would happen to me. But later, when I had a better idea of the circumstances of his death, I realized I could have a long life, and I've had an amazing life. But I sometimes wish my father could've seen it. I wonder what he'd think of my family, of his daughter-in-law, of our children. I wish he had lived. I wish he had been around to go to for advice. I'd like to hear what he'd learned about life. I wish he could have had the kinds of talks with me that I've had with my kids. Down deep, all of us want the approval of our fathers. That means more than any award, any amount of money. I stare at that picture of my father and I see a man who wanted to raise his children the right way, a man who set out to support his family. He's a man whom I barely remember, a man who died when I was five years old, but a man who still means a lot to me today. I'd like to think I learned all the things he'd have wanted me to know. When I stare hard at that picture, I see myself.

About the Authors

Lenny Wilkens has been part of the NBA scene since 1960. He has coached more games and won more games than anyone in League history. He is a member of the Basketball Hall of Fame as a player and as a coach; only John Wooten also has that distinction. Wilkens has coached in Seattle, Portland, Cleveland, and Atlanta, and is the new coach of the Toronto Raptors. Wilkens is the father of three children and lives with his wife, Marilyn, in Seattle.

Terry Pluto is the author of nineteen books. He has twice been nominated for a Pulitzer Prize. A sports columnist for the *Akron Beacon Journal,* Pluto has been the Ohio Sportswriter of the Year five times, and twice he has been named the nation's top sports columnist for medium-sized papers by the Associated Press. He and his wife, Roberta, live in Akron, Ohio.